Governance and Business Models for Sustainable Capitalism

Governance and Business Models for Sustainable Capitalism touches upon many of the central themes of today's debate on business and society. In particular, it brings attention to a recurrent tension between efficiency, innovation, and productivity on the one hand, and fairness, equity, and sustainability on the other.

The book argues that we need radical rethinking of business models and economic governance, beyond the classical doctrine, which sees social and ecological responsibility as lying with public-policy regulation of purely profit-seeking firms. In spite of the popular CSR agenda, business – as we know it today – is both too transient and too limited in its motivation to carry the regulatory burden. We need to adopt a much wider concept of 'partnered governance', where advanced states and pioneering companies work together to raise the social and environmental bar. The book suggests that civil engagements based on moral rather than formal rights, and amplified through the media, may provide a healthy challenge both to autocratic planning and to solely profit-centered commercialization. The book also proposes a triple cycle theory of innovation for sustainability: a novel framing of the efficacy of green and prosocial entrepreneurship as intertwined with political visions and supportive institutions. In addition, the book offers reflections on the ways in which further digital robotizaton may enable transition to an 'Agora Economy' where productive efficiency is combined with expanded civic freedoms.

Aimed primarily at researchers, academics, and students in the fields of political economy, business and society, corporate governance, business ethics, corporate social responsibility, and sustainability, the book will additionally be of value to practitioners, supplying them with information regarding the challenges associated with the shaping of sustainable or 'civilized' market capitalism for a better world.

Atle Midttun is Professor in the Department of Law and Governance at BI Norwegian Business School, Norway. He has until recently been co-director of two of the School's research centres: the Centre for Energy and the Centre for Corporate Responsibility. His teaching and research interests include economic regulation, innovation, energy and sustainability, corporate governance, and CSR.

Routledge Studies in Management, Organizations, and Society

This series presents innovative work grounded in new realities, addressing issues crucial to an understanding of the contemporary world. This is the world of organized societies, where boundaries between formal and informal, public and private, local and global organizations have been displaced or have vanished, along with other 19th century dichotomies and oppositions. Management, apart from becoming a specialized profession for a growing number of people, is an everyday activity for most members of modern societies.

Similarly, at the level of enquiry, culture and technology, and literature and economics, can no longer be conceived as isolated intellectual fields; conventional canons and established mainstreams are contested. *Management, Organizations, and Society* addresses these contemporary dynamics of transformation in a manner that transcends disciplinary boundaries, with books that will appeal to researchers, students, and practitioners alike.

Governance and Business Models for Sustainable Capitalism

Atle Midttun

Routledge
Taylor & Francis Group

NEW YORK AND LONDON

First published 2022
by Routledge
605 Third Avenue, New York, NY 10158

and by Routledge
4 Park Square, Milton Park, Abingdon, Oxon, OX14 4RN

Routledge is an imprint of the Taylor & Francis Group, an
informa business

Library of Congress Cataloguing-in-Publication Data
Names: Midttun, Atle, 1952- author.
Title: Governance and business models for sustainable capitalism /
Atle Midttun.
Description: New York, NY : Routledge, 2022. |
Series: Routledge studies in management, organizations and
society | Includes bibliographical references and index.
Identifiers: LCCN 2021032598 | ISBN 9781138210592 (hbk) |
ISBN 9780367770440 (pbk) | ISBN 9781315454931 (ebk)
Subjects: LCSH: Capitalism. | Sustainability. | Social responsibility
of business.
Classification: LCC HB501 .M6347 2022 | DDC 330.12/2–dc23
LC record available at https://lccn.loc.gov/2021032598

ISBN: 978-1-138-21059-2 (hbk)
ISBN: 978-0-367-77044-0 (pbk)
ISBN: 978-1-315-45493-1 (ebk)

DOI: 10.4324/9781315454931

Typeset in Sabon
by MPS Limited, Dehradun

Contents

SECTION III
Governance Approaches   87

Figures

Tables

Preface

In the 21st century, Western capitalism is meandering from the era of industrial mass production towards an epoch of digital de-centralization and flexible specialization. While the unprecedented productivity growth and increasing distributive fairness between the 1950s and the 1980s laid the ground for a dream of 'Middleclassia' for all, the digital era has unleashed new commercial and social dynamics.

How are our governance and business models grasping the opportunities and dealing with the new challenges? Are we capable of securing human welfare in the competitive dynamics of transformation? And how is this all playing out under globalization, where multinational corporations are orchestrating production systems across the world? These are some of the questions that have motivated me to write this book.

My perspective is Western, and occasionally Nordic, and I am well aware of the limitations of my approach. I am convinced, however, that having played a leading role in the 19th and 20th centuries – and still representing capitalist societies at their most advanced level – Western modernity, with its peculiar modes of governance and economy, needs a re-appraisal, even if these models are now complemented – or challenged – by alternative economic models from the East and South.

The book draws on dialogues with colleagues and friends over a number of years, that are too numerous to list. I wish to thank my 'better half', Nina Witoszek, for her invaluable constructive critique and suggestions. This book draws extensively on our previous research work together and our ongoing dialogue on the question: "can capitalism be civilized?" I owe a debt of gratitude to my language editor, Mathew Little, who has patiently borne my capricious twists and turns of the manuscript and made sure that the text is hopefully digestible to the English reader.

Thanks also goes to the Research Council of Norway for financing several projects upon which this book draws, the latest being 'Responsible research and innovation in Norway' – AFINO.

Introduction

Capitalism's Resilience in the Face of Crises

As this book is published, capitalism has experienced one of its greatest challenges, with the Covid-19 pandemic leading to a dramatic economic downturn across the world. The corona crisis came a little more than a decade after the financial crisis when the global market economy temporarily broke down. Many radical thinkers (Naomi Klein in Solis 2020, Slavo Žižek in Koshy 2020) have called for radical systemic transformations, such as abolishing free markets, restructuring the global economy, and remaking existing political systems.

Interestingly, in the case of the financial crisis, capitalism survived, and – with minor adjustments – even emerged rejuvenated from the ordeal. What could have been a triumph for many of its adversaries instead became a successful capitalist bounce-back, demonstrating the system's extraordinary resilience. And with mass vaccination, we have seen similar developments emerging in the keel-water of the Covid crisis.

However, to cash in on capitalism's resilience as an argument for its eternal robustness, would be misguided. The financial crisis was only arrested by a massive public rescue operation that re-set the economy and eventually led to new growth. This exercise is being repeated at an even larger scale to meet the repercussions of the Covid-19 pandemic. Even so-called 'liberal' economies like the US and UK have retained massive public economies alongside private capitalism.

In spite of capitalism's survival through the crises, the hardships of transition and the increased inequality that has become a signature of many Western economies point to unresolved tensions between capitalism's creative productivity on the one side, and fairness and social inclusion on the other. In the midst of these tensions and the legitimacy problems they raise, there is the mounting climate challenge – resulting from modern societies' incessant fossil-powered growth.

DOI: 10.4324/9781315454931-101

Governance for Civilizing Capitalism?

What type of governance can align capitalism's dynamic creativity with social inclusion and ecological sustainability, without stifling its productivity? Or in other words: What is the *governance formula* for a 'civilized capitalism'? This question has been with us ever since the potent marriage of the market economy and industrial technology fostered the Industrial Revolution. The 20th century came up with three basic governance designs. Firstly, liberalism: markets can largely govern themselves, with minimal political interference. Secondly, socialism: a planned economy should take over, and relegate markets to a marginal role. And thirdly, the welfare state: regulated, but competitive markets topped by a redistributive and public service providing state. The book argues that while all three governance alternatives remain on the table, they must be redesigned for the 21st century, where technology, the economy, as well as governance theory, are all undergoing a major transformation. This book, therefore, explores the ways of civilizing capitalism in the 21st century, while taking a more pragmatic approach, where a broad span of governance solutions – across ideological divides – are considered.

Contrary to proponents of strong neoliberalism, this book contends that capitalism can, and indeed must, be 'civilized' and made more humane and ecologically sustainable in spite of the inherent contradictions that this rebooting may imply. As the experiences of the 20th century have taught us, crude capitalism is not viable in the long run and leads to conflict, disruption, and growing inequality and injustice. Similarly – contrary to proponents of strong socialism who remain adamant that 'civilizing capitalism' is a contradiction is terms – this book contends that to fulfil the dream of general welfare, we need the creative productivity of a capitalist market economy. Finally, contrary to proponents of the classical welfare state who argue that the welfare-capitalist order can continue in its current form, the main contention of this study is that it needs basic revision in the 21st century if it is to maintain its vitality.

The book argues for a position that can be described as *polycentric, partnered governance*. This form of governance moves beyond ideological agendas and focuses on a pragmatic reassessment of how, in the 21st century, various governance approaches and business models can be made to work together to curb the predatory nature of capitalism – without hindering its creative potential.

Deregulation and Asymmetric Globalization

A central hallmark of economic governance in the late 20th century and the early 21st is the turn toward neoliberal deregulation and marketization and a simultaneous downplaying of the role of the interventionist state. As chapter 6 points out, deregulation soon became a stepping-stone to market globalization, as businesses developed global supply chains across continents. Regulation, however, remained largely national or regional, limited by the territorial jurisdictions of the regulatory nation-state, supplemented by some regional extensions such as the European Union. The result was what I call here an *asymmetric globalization*, marked by a territorial expansion of the market-economy without similar enlargement of regulatory governance. The neoliberal premise for abandoning the interventionist state rested on recourse to a regulatory authority that could supervise a privatized and market-driven economy. While this premise could be fulfilled at the national level, the failure to scale-up regulation at the global level created a regulatory void. Asymmetric globalization therefore represents a major hurdle for 21st-century economic governance and marks an important premise for the exploration of the governance models that are critically discussed in this book. These governance models include the following components and strategies.

Business Regulating Itself: Corporate Social Responsibility

A radical 'liberalist' answer to the question of filling the regulatory void under globalized markets is to delegate governance to business itself to be incorporated into its business model. Given its orientation towards Corporate Social Responsibility (CSR) there should be a potential for business self-governance, especially if a business case can be made for it enhancing value creation. The argument is that business-endogenous in-centives will ensure that social and environmental responsibility is motivated by the latter's consequences for the financial bottom line. Too good to be true, one might argue, as businesses increasingly orchestrates supply chains across the globe, enrolling developing countries with weak economic, social and environmental regulation into the maelstrom of the global economy. However, active critical engagement from civil society organizations (CSOs) and the media may create pressure on business to live up to expectations especially in the case of vendors of brand-sensitive end-user products. Calls for corporate social and environmental responsibility from investors – especially pension funds – may also provide important incentives for pro-social business behaviour. Chapter 7 examines this contention more closely and points out how CSR may play a complementary role together with other governance initiatives.

Enhancing Corporate Responsibility by Re-Chartering the Firm

Chapter 8 examines the potential of alternatively chartered businesses, anchored in pro-social and pro-ecological governance. Discussion of the business potential for CSR has taken the widely found shareholder corporation – typical of the USA – as a point of departure. However, this is far from a universal solution in advanced OECD economies. State and family ownership, prevalent in many countries, open up for alternative strategic orientations beyond profit-seeking. Other modes of corporate organization have pro-social and sustainability orientations inscribed in their foundation. In the U.S., so-called benefit (B) corporations are chartered to create a material, positive impact on society and the environment. In this way, the managers of (B) corporations are able to break out of the straightjacket of fiduciary duty faced by (C) corporations that prevents them engaging in non-financial missions.

Then there are cooperatives – enterprises owned, controlled, and run by their members to realize their common economic, social, and cultural needs and aspirations. In this construction lies a commitment – far beyond simple revenue extraction – to a specific group of stakeholders that benefit from the cooperative's activity. However, the cooperative business model spans a large spectrum, from fairly idealistic organizations to organizations that resemble a standard shareholding company. In short, while cooperative ownership opens up for extensive corporate social responsibility, the degree to which it is implemented depends on the specific cooperative setup.

Partly overlapping with cooperatives, social enterprises provide further anchors for social and/or ecological orientation of their commercial activity: They engage in a production and/or exchange of goods and/or services, while at the same time pursuing an explicit and primary social aim that benefits society.

Can Civic Governance Civilize Capitalism?

Spurred by the availability of information and communication technology, *monitory democracy* – a term coined by the British-Australian scholar, John Keane (Keane 2013) – has also emerged as a new governance channel for civilizing capitalism (see chapter 9). Both civic engagement and bottom-up mobilization – fortified by digitalization – are effective ways of imprinting fairness and ecological sustainability onto the economic governance agenda.

Monitory democracy has been orchestrated by organizations and movements engaged in critical public scrutiny and monitoring of economic and political decision-makers. It also injects creative vitality and brings new issues into mainstream political and corporate decision-making. Such bottom-up processes may therefore serve to bring important social and environmental concerns onto political and corporate agendas. In this way, civic engagement can play a role in governance innovation at both government and corporate levels.

Furthermore, civic action and monitory democracy have great advantages over parliamentary democracy in the age of globalization. While states can forge hard law within their territorial boundaries, monitory democracy may reach beyond borders, and therefore be instrumental in facilitating social and environmental improvement at the international level.

Chapter 9 discusses the role and potential of civic mobilization in civilizing capitalism, while demonstrating how it may interplay with established political and commercial arenas.

Bringing the State Back In

While the two first decades of the 21st century have been dominated by deregulation and globalization, there have been repeated calls for "bringing the state back in" to the economic governance equation. The work of Evans, Rudemeyer, and Skocpol (Evans et al. 1985) and Mariana Mazzucato (Mazzucato 2013) has emphasized the state's contribution to innovation as well as its capacity to forge collective action.

The argument in this book, explored in chapter 10, is indeed that the state needs to be part of the equation for civilizing capitalism. In fact, the activist state has been there for decades but has been ideologically suppressed by neoliberal thinking. The question is how to re-prioritize it theoretically and improve its strategic contribution.

Even if the state under globalization has limited control, it still can pull unique levers: Firstly, the democratic state can credibly represent the public interest better than other actors. Enterprises operating under private capitalist principles are concerned with trimming their investments to optimize returns. A public interest-driven economy is typically more purpose-driven than attuned to immediate market signals. Sustainable capitalism needs to balance these two perspectives.

Secondly, in well-managed advanced economies the public interest-driven units are typically more financially robust, backed as they are by public budgetary commitments, than private corporations. In a crisis-prone global economy this stability is essential for economic and societal resilience. The private interest-driven economy on its own would – in conditions of crisis – easily end up in a 'race to the bottom'. This combination of private and public economies, which is often seen as incompatible, can in fact be complementary. The complementarity in question is necessary for improving the ability of modern advanced society to meld fairness, environmental sustainability, and innovative productivity.

Governing Transitions

As argued in chapter 11, some major challenges to modern economies appear only solvable through major transitions. These demand broad ambidextrous mobilization of both the public and private economies, as well as extensive civic engagement. The 'green transition' discussed in chapter 5 is obviously a societal shift in this category. I also argue that the development of capitalist economies into fair and inclusive societies as well as tempering the effects of the financial meltdown and the Covid-19 pandemic demands transitional change.

In change at this scale, governance may be seen as a parallel evolution of novel visions, new technologies, and business models, as well as emerging institutional approaches, where multiple societal actors and arenas become involved.

Theoretical and Conceptual Inspirations

In the attempt to forge a governance-centred approach to 'civilizing' capitalism, I have been inspired by several perspectives. They include:

A Broad Socio-Economic Lens

One of the major problems in many studies of the economy and economic governance is their narrow scope. Focused as they are on markets and economic factors, they leave out important ecological, social and institutional aspects. Recognizing the need for a broad socio-economic perspective on governance, where the role of business and the economy in society is centre stage, I have drawn upon the Austro-Hungarian economic sociologist, anthropologist and historian, Karl Polanyi, and the American sociologist Talcott Parsons' work on social systems theory.

Karl Polanyi (2001) saw industrial society as the result of a quest for commercial freedom and competitive markets. The breaking loose of the latter from traditional moral norms and conventions in the late 18th and early 19th centuries, led to a process of *dis-embedding*, i.e. the evolution of markets into an autonomous sphere and their disconnection form broader social concerns. The profit of markets built on exploited labour became paramount, and social and environmental consequences were largely neglected. The challenge, in Polanyi's terms, was to achieve a social re-embedding that would restore the social balance. Early moves from progressive liberals established minimum standards of social decency, but it was not until the post-war growth of the labour movement that ambitious re-embedding took shape under the New Deal and the welfare state.

Parsons' contribution lies in his focus on functional requirements for viable societies (Parsons 1970). Production and the economy was, for him, only one of the functions of society. Integration, or the harmonization and convergence of norms was another, and equally important. In addition institutions were needed to stabilize society as well to forge collective action to meet common goals.

Both the Polanyian and Parsonian perspectives stand in stark contrast to the recent wave of neoliberalism, which has once again disembedded the economy and de-coupled it from society, captured in Margaret Thatcher's famous assertion "There's no such thing as society" (Thatcher 1987).

Balancing Competitive Creativity and Social Integration

However, the broader socio-economic focus should not lead to disregarding the value of markets and competitive dynamics. There is, obviously, a danger that the focus on social integration and re-embedding of the economy puts the creative productivity of capitalism at risk. A project of 'civilizing' or re-embedding capitalism must therefore include balancing competitive creativity and social integration. In this respect, I have found interesting parallels in the work of leading American evolutionary biologists, David Sloan Wilson and Edgar O Wilson, on multilevel selection. Firstly, their analysis points to a balance between competitive rivalry and collaborative behaviour as the condition of human resilience, if not success. The so-called 'third wave' of evolutionary biology shows how collaborative behaviour may carry equal, if not stronger, weight than competition in forging resilience and adaptability (Wilson and Wilson 2007). Secondly, they demonstrate how competition and collaboration can co-exist. Based on the principle of multilevel selection, they indicate how a selection at one level can stem from collaboration, while selection at another level can be competitive, and how this combination can lead to enhanced performance.

Applied to economic governance, I have found multilevel selection to be a helpful heuristic tool for combining the efficiency of market competition with inclusive and collaborative teamwork. In a previous work on *Sustainable Modernity* (Witoszek and Midttun 2018), we have shown how the Nordic welfare states have adopted multilevel selection in practice, by ambidextrously operating in the two seemingly contradictory realms – the competitive and the collaborative – through institutional differentiation. At one level, or in one domain, the Nordics have developed prosocial collaboration, and at another they compete, using their collaborative teamwork as a strategic asset. In this way, at their best the welfare states have succeeded in re-embedding the capitalist market dynamic without destroying it. Although the welfare state needs reform in the 21st century, I argue that the ability to blend collaborative and competitive elements and skilfully manoeuvre between them must continue to be at the core of the successful economic governance, as societies are faced with new challenges in the 21st century.

Polycentric Governance

Widening the lens to include a wider socio-economic perspective (on the political economy) invites a broadening of the concept of governance. This involves moving beyond the effects of single mono-disciplinary governance models which are dominant in political science, sociology, and economic regulation. For this purpose, I have found that Nobel Laureate Elinor Ostrom's concept of polycentric governance (Ostrom 1990) offers useful insights. The term "polycentric" – which Ostrom developed in her work on the sustainable management of common resources – refers to governance with multiple centres of decision-making, each of which operates with some degree of autonomy. More recently political scientists with John Gerard Ruggie as a central proponent, have adopted 'polycentric' to deal with governance where the state by itself cannot do all the heavy lifting required (Ruggie 2014).

As I see it, insights from Ostrom's work on sustainable management of common resources carries important implications also for macro-governance. It takes us beyond formal political governance and leads us into a space where civic engagement and civil society organizations jostle with government institutions as well as business and industrial organizations, in defining the public debate and shaping the public interest agenda. Polycentric governance, therefore, allows more actors to play critical supporting roles, and highlights how multiple forms of governance may be active at the same time.

The oil-spill accidents caused by three shipwrecked oil tankers described in chapter 9 illustrate the polycentric complexity in establishing adequate governance responses. In all three cases strong local municipal and civic engagement under extensive media coverage mobilized massive pressure for government reaction, with a demand for legislation to impose a double hull requirement for oil tankers. Stung by this compelling pressure, unilateral legislation followed, first in the USA and later in the EU, usurping the mandate of the International Maritime Organization to come up with solutions. Throughout this process, oil companies and their shipping agents were pushed into line by a critical public to preserve their brand image and license to operate.

Integrating Governance Across Markets and Politics

Studying the interface between business and politics, I have often been struck by parallel thinking in both domains. One example is Edward Freeman's Stakeholder theory (Freeman 1984), and Paul Sabatier's advocacy coalition theory (Sabatier 1998). Freeman has reformed corporate governance and strategic thinking in the business literature by transcending the conventional stockholder-focused model. He drew attention to the legitimate interests of stakeholders – multiple constituencies impacted by business, such as employees, suppliers, local communities, creditors, and others. Similarly, Sabatier adds complexity to formal public policy analysis by exploring coalitions under which actors with different belief systems interact and compete to dominate the policy subsystem. Sabatier has been interested in people who engage in politics to translate their beliefs – rather than their simple material interests – into action. Freeman has shown how stakeholders bring novel perspectives into the business domain. In a broad economic governance approach, these two perspectives should obviously interface and stimulate each other.

To facilitate governance analysis across politics and markets, I have included chapters on industrial self-governance (CSR) and corporate chartering alongside chapters on state and civic governance. Furthermore, I have attempted to show how they can work together, building on previous work on what I have termed "Partnered Governance" (Midttun 2008). Such synergies are clearly illustrated by the Extractive Industries' Transparency Initiative, described in Chapter 11, which represents a common mobilization for transparent money flows in resource-rich countries. This initiative illustrates how advanced democracies and pioneering companies can work together to raise the social and environmental bar, utilizing their common resources.

Governing Dynamic Transition

As already mentioned, some central challenges to modern economies appear only solvable through major transitions. This calls for transformative governance, which I have found can be interestingly explored in terms of innovation theory and learning curve theory in particular. This theory describes how novel technologies evolve through industrial learning, to gradually morph into commercial, mainstream products through the stages of a *product cycle* (Wene 2008, Wantanabe et al. 2000). When adequately coupled with niche markets, where economic conditions are calibrated to the technology's state of the art, they may drive transitions towards a more sustainable world.

As we have previously argued in *Perspectives on Ecomodernity* (Midttun and Witoszek 2015), the principle of techno-economic innovation can also be transferred to governance. However, the perspective has to be broadened. A holistic governance analysis has to take into account the *product cycle,* a *visionary cycle,* and – as a new societal vision develops and matures – also the *institutional cycle* which codifies and formalizes supportive organizational development. Transition-governance may thus be fruitfully analysed as a parallel evolution of novel visions, new technologies, and business models, as well as emerging institutional approaches, where the interplay between the three cycles is also essential.

This expanded learning curve perspective also suggests that different governance regimes may be appropriate at different stages, and hence suggests polycentric governance played out over time.

Addressing 21st Century Challenges

The book discusses the question of 'civilizing' or 're-embedding' capitalism in the context of the core challenges of the 21st century, such as digitalization, financialization, resilience, and fairness. Responding to them individually is difficult, but doing so across the board is extremely demanding. The overview below signals the scale of the problems and dilemmas:

Digitalization: The accelerated pace of digitalization and robotization has raised concerns about the future of jobs and the distribution of income. The book shows how various governance approaches to digitalization may generate dramatically different welfare outcomes. On the one hand, governance facilitating purely private interest-driven market regulation could squeeze workers into the low-paid, unstable gig economy, or substitute many altogether through artificial intelligence. On the other, governance with a stronger public interest focus could facilitate more of the massive productivity produced by AI, enabling it to be deployed for broader public benefit in an alternative classical Athenian-inspired 'Agora economy'.

I also discuss governance of transparency issues raised by the digital technology, as core network-providers monetize data on people's network communication. Current pro-industry governance allows asymmetric transparency, where full information about citizens' internet-behaviour is concealed within non-transparent company information. Civic and government initiatives are being conceived to establish an alternative and more symmetric governance regime where information about citizens' internet behaviour is matched by information about the digital company's sales of data. In addition to strengthening consumer rights, symmetric transparency would also facilitate fairer taxation.

Financialization: The massive growth facilitated in part by financial investment has created obvious values for society. However, as the book points out, this great success has also raised major governance challenges. Failing governance has not only turned a blind eye to excessive risk-taking, but is also enabling the financial industry to challenge states' fiscal basis. The book discusses limitations in the current governance regimes, and suggests paths towards governance improvement. This includes the question of whether this industry in the USA, – the most advanced

Western economy – is in a position to reverse governance so that finance governs the state. In other words, how can society regain control if the financial industry grown too large to fail and too big to govern?

However, the governance of finance concerns more than the traditional financial institutions. New digital actors have emerged with the potential to not only disrupt conventional financial models, but also undermine traditional financial governance. It is essential, then, that efforts to re-embed the financial system also address governance of the new financial arenas, some of them created by the technology giants looking for new market outlets. This includes bitcoins and other forms of cryptocurrency which are becoming widely used in dark markets for money laundering and drug crime. Compared to the public engagement with the conventional banking sector, the book points to how there is a conspicuous lack of government intervention into what appears to be a crypto-financial black hole.

Crises and resilience: The two crises of the first decades of the 21st century illustrate that re-embedding the economy needs to factor in economic resilience as a major concern. Chapter 10 shows how, in this governance endeavour, the private economy must be massively supported by its public counterpart. Both in the 2008 financial crisis – with the subsequent 'Great Recession'– and the Covid-19 pandemic, followed by an even larger recession, much of the private economy moved into lockdown and a downward spiral involving massive repercussions. Only governance through strong public policy intervention and huge mobilization of the public economy managed to arrest it and gradually return the economy back to some kind of normality.

But resilience is only one of the reasons why the state must be brought back into active governance. In this volume I argue that the state (and city governments), as legitimate custodians of the public interest, and with their unique resources, also have major roles to play in innovation and societal transformation. The need for state engagement to represent the public interest does not necessarily imply public ownership, however. The old ideological debate around public or private ownership – I argue – is long passé as a basis for governance arrangements. Current theory of economic organization allows us to move beyond private versus public ownership and combine public interest focused leadership with private entrepreneurial dynamics.

Fairness: While rapid industrialization has lifted millions out of poverty in some developing countries, modern western economies have experienced severe setbacks in fair distribution. Turning this tide remains a major 21st century governance concern, but as yet, without any clear answer. As I argue in chapter 10 mobilizing governance with a stronger role for the public interest in the economy will have to be part of the solution.

However, public governance *per se* does not guarantee fairness. Certain public policies – to secure resilience under crises – are working in the wrong direction with respect to fairness. For example, the direct impact of quantitative easing (QE)on asset prices, especially equities, has predominantly benefited rich investors who save more than the poor. The book, therefore, contends that, from a fairness and sustainability perspective, it is high time for a QE policy overhaul.

In a broader societal perspective, fairness is ultimately also essential to economic stability and prosperity. In chapter 11 I, therefore, contend that social and ecological embedding of the economy is important, not only for reasons of welfare, but also for the preservation of sound, inclusive, liberal societies.

Sustainability: The challenges provoked by the massive human influence on the biosphere compels the economy of the 21st century to take the question of ecological balances into account. The governance challenges to achieve this are formidable. They imply no less than staging an industrial transition from an extractive fossil-driven and massive resource consuming economy to a circular economy and renewable eco-modernity, which also necessarily entails societal transformation. This daunting governance task, I argue, demands massive mobilization of both the public and private economies, as well as strong civic buy-in.

As an example, the book shows how staging polycentric governance through deployment of green technology through public procurement has been one of the major drivers for industrial change out of the fossil economy. Early deployment of new climate-compatible technologies usually lies beyond the capacity and interest of private investors, and demands public governance intervention. Yet such procurement efforts have had to trigger the competitive rivalry of private firms and their innovation systems to drive the necessary technological and commercial innovation. I also inquire into how sustained civic engagement through active CSOs is an essential part of the governance equation, both as a platform to launch and foster new visions and as a tool to pressure governments and businesses to keep up to speed.

In a final reflection, the book also discusses one more pivotal challenge. While governance in the late 20th and first years of the 21st centuries struggled with neoliberal globalization, the subsequent decades have seen the global economy becoming increasingly marked by a new, **bipolar rivalry between authoritarian and liberal spheres.** As nations with authoritarian political cultures, such as China and Russia, emerged as powerful actors on the international scene, rivalry has become a central feature. This new rivalry is reminiscent of the Cold War between communist and capitalist systems. However, this time both blocs subscribe to capitalism and the feud is primarily political.

Case Studies as a Jumping Board

The analysis that follows is illustrated by examples from Western economies, ranging across a wide spectrum of governance configurations. The cases show how governance coalitions evolve and consolidate, thereby responding to the challenges they set out to tackle. In some cases, civic mobilization triggers regulatory responses culminating in hard law. In others, it leads to an industrial reaction, in particular the development of industrial standards that raise social or ecological performance. In yet other cases, the establishment of new normative frameworks creates expectations that trickle down into multiple initiatives for social and environmental upgrading.

Governance Matters

While solving the global challenges of the 21st century has largely focused on technical answers, governance models matter more than ever. The paradox is that while technological advances combined with capitalism's massive productivity have given us the tools to solve most of the problems we face, our capacity to govern ourselves wisely lags far behind. We should therefore revisit the wisdom of the city council of Siena, which, amid the political turmoil of the 14th century, commissioned Ambrogio Lorenzetti's fresco paintings: allegories of good and bad government (Figures 0.1 and 0.2). This was done to remind the nine magistrates of how much was at stake as they made their decisions.

Figure 0.1 Allegory of Good Government.

Source: Ambrogio Lorenzetti, imprint from Museum of Santa Maria Della Scala, Municipality of Siena, Italy.

Figure 0.2 Allegory of Bad Government.

Source: Ambrogio Lorenzetti, imprint from Museum of Santa Maria Della Scala, Municipality of Siena, Italy.

References

Barber, B. (2014) *If Mayors Ruled the World – Dysfunctional Nations, Rising Cities*. New Haven: Yale University Press.

Evans, P., Rueschemeyer, D. and Skocpol, T. (2010 [1985]) *Bringing the State Back In*. Cambridge: Cambridge University Press.

Keane, J. (2013) Civil Society in the Era of Monitory Democracy. In Lars Trägårdh, Nina Witoszek, Bron Taylor (eds), *Civil Society in the Age of Monitory Democracy* (Studies on Civil Society). New York & Oxford: Berghahn Books.

Koshy, Y. (2020) Review of *Pandemic!* by Slavoj Žižek, *The Guardian*, 23 April.

Mazzucato, M. (2013) *The Entrepreneurial State – Debunking Public vs Private Sector Myths*. New York: Anthem Press.

Midttun, A. (2008) Partnered Governance: Aligning Corporate Responsibility and Public Policy in the Global Economy. *Corporate Governance* 8(4).

Midttun, A. and Witoszek, N. (2015). *Perspectives on Ecomodernity*. Abingdon and New York: Routledge.

Ostrom, E. (1990) *Governing the Commons – The Evolution of Institutions for Collective Action*. Cambridge: Cambridge University Press.

Parsons, T. (1970) *The Social System*. London: Routledge & Kegan Paul.

Polanyi, K. (2001 [1944]) *The Great Transformation: The Political and Economic Origins of Our Time*, 2nd ed. Foreword by Joseph E. Stiglitz; introduction by Fred Block. Boston: Beacon Press.

Ruggie, J.G. (2014) Global governance and "New Governance theory": Lessons from Business and Human Rights. *Global Governance* 20.

Sabatier, P. 1998. The Advocacy Coalition Framework: Revisions and Relevance for Europe. *Journal of European Public Policy*5(1).

Solis, M. (2020) Coronavirus is the perfect disaster for "Disaster Capitalism", interview with Naomi Klein, *Vice*, 13 March.

Thatcher, M. (1987) Interview with *Woman's Own* ("no such thing as society"), Margaret Thatcher Foundation, https://www.margaretthatcher.org/document/106689.

Watanabe, C., Wakabayashi, K. and Miyazawa, T. (2000) Industrial Dynamism and the Creation of a "Virtuous Cycle" between R&D, Market Growth and Price Reduction – The Case of Photovoltaic Power Generation (PV) Development in Japan. *Technovation*20.

Wene, C-O (2008) Energy Technology Learning Through Deployment in Competitive Markets. *The Engineering Economist*53.

Wilson D.S. and Wilson E.O. (2007) Rethinking the Theoretical Foundation of Sociobiology. *The Quarterly Review of Biology* 82(4).

Witoszek, N. and Midttun, A. (2018). Sustainable Modernity and the Architecture of the "Well-being" Society: Interdisciplinary Perspectives. In N. Witoszek and A. Midttun (eds), *Sustainable Modernity – The Nordic Model and Beyond*. Abingdon and New York: Routledge.

Section I
Historical Roots and Past Experience

1 The 'Terrible Beauty' of Early Industrial Capitalism

Early Disembedded Capitalism and the Polanyian Critique

A brief flashback to the early history of modern industrial capitalism in the 19th and early 20th centuries highlights how deeply the dilemma of balancing productivity and fairness is woven into the fabric of capitalist societies. Karl Polanyi, as mentioned in the introduction, revealed how modern capitalist innovation and productivity was unleashed through disembedding the economy from many of its ties to the conventional social order. The modern capitalist economy, he argued, was assigned a separate sphere with specialized institutions and transactions, largely severed from the rest of society. 18th-century capitalism, emboldened by the Industrial Revolution, swept aside the economy's traditional social ties. These were ties that had embedded trade and production in moral norms and regulation, guiding it towards social and ethical, rather than purely commercial, goals. While economic transactions in traditional societies had combined enhancing material livelihood with reinforcing social norms, this was no longer the case under early industrial capitalism.

The results of the West's disembedded capitalist expansion were indeed impressive in macroeconomic terms. The rapid growth of Western economic performance outshone the dominant Asian economies, and was subsequently described with terms like the "European Miracle" and the "Great Divergence" (by Eric Jones (1981) and Samuel Huntington (1996) and Pomeranz (2000) respectively).[1] These euphoric phrases reflect the explosive economic growth in European countries like Britain, France, and Germany starting in the 18th century, but rapidly escalating in the 19th and 20th, which left the major Asiatic economies in its wake (Figure 1.1).

Scholars have proposed a wide variety of explanations for the phenomenal European growth, including colonial expansion, resources, customary traditions, and socio-economics. However, common to most of them is the perception of disembedded capitalism as an important component. Liberalization of markets, the evolution of contractual freedom, and access to incorporation with limited liability, were all seen

DOI: 10.4324/9781315454931-1

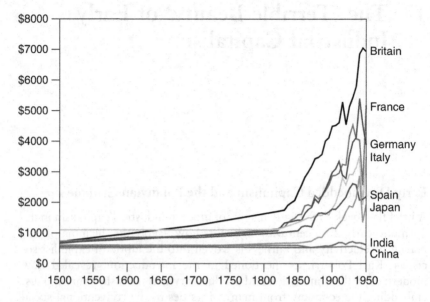

Figure 1.1 Estimates of GDP per Capita.[2]

Source: Angus Maddison & Maddison Project Database.

Note: Maddison Project Database, version 2018. Bolt, Jutta, Robert Inklaar, Herman de Jong and Jan Luiten van Zanden (2018), "Rebasing 'Maddison': new income comparisons and the shape of long-run economic development", https://www.rug.nl/ggdc/historical-development/maddison/releases/maddison-project-database-2018.

as essential factors.[3] As Jared Diamond (1997) has pointed out, the introduction of a system of pricing to match supply and demand gave capitalist markets an advance on medieval markets where prices were set with a view to doing justice, or upholding social conventions. The disembedding of a manufacturing and trading sphere, largely autonomous from political or religious restriction, was thus a central factor behind Western economic growth.

Capitalism's Inherent Contradiction

But underlying capitalism's wonderful productivity was a darker side. The origins of modern industrial capitalism were invariably connected to brutal social transformation, and the discrepancy between economic productivity harvested by the upper classes and social conditions for lower classes was stark.

The mercantilist and industrial capitalism that spurred the European industrial transformation was built on an exploitation of the domestic working class. The appalling human conditions were not only criticized by radicals like Karl Marx, but also by leading establishment intellectuals and writers like Alexis de Tocqueville and Lord Byron.

Lord Byron denounced what he considered to be the plight of the working class, the government's inane policies, and ruthless repression, in the House of Lords on 27 February 1812,

> I have been in some of the most oppressed provinces of Turkey; but never, under the most despotic of infidel governments, did I behold such squalid wretchedness as I have seen since my return, in the very heart of a Christian country (Byron 1812).

Tocqueville, writing about the wonders of industrialization in Manchester in 1835 eloquently observed the terrible beauty of early capitalism (De Tocqueville 1835):

> From this foul drain the greatest stream of human industry flows out to fertilize the whole world. From this filthy sewer pure gold flows. Here humanity attains its most complete development and its most brutish, here civilization works its miracles and civilized man is turned almost into a savage.

In an article in the *New York Daily Tribune* in 1857, Karl Marx echoed Lord Byron's critique of the repressive authorities while adding his disgust with greedy mill-capitalists (Marx 2007):

> The reports of the factory inspectors prove beyond doubt that the infamies of the British factory system are growing with its growth; that the laws enacted for checking the cruel greediness of the mill-lords are a sham and a delusion, being so worded as to baffle their own ostensible end and to disarm the men entrusted with their execution.

The disembedded sphere of commercial profit-seeking with few social limitations on private gain left the emerging working class unprotected. E.P. Thompson, in *The Making of the English Working Class,* writes that life clearly did not improve for the majority of the British people:

> The experience of immiseration came upon them in a hundred different forms; for the field labourer, the loss of his common rights and the vestiges of village democracy; for the artisan, the loss of his craftsman's status; for the weaver, the loss of livelihood and of independence; for the child the loss of work and play in the home; for many groups of workers whose real earning improved, the loss of security, leisure and the deterioration of the urban environment (Thompson (1970) p 445).

Numerous scholars have given similar descriptions: In his *History of Public Health,* George Rosen (2015 p155) likewise argues that for the first generation of workers – from the 1790s to the 1840s – working conditions were very tough, and sometimes tragic. Most labourers worked 10 to 14 hours a day, six days a week, with no paid vacation or holidays. Each industry had safety hazards too; the process of purifying iron, for example, demanded that workers toiled in temperatures as high as 130° Fahrenheit in the coolest part of the ironworks.

Child labour was integral to the first factories, mines, and mills in England. In textile mills, as new power looms and spinning mules took the place of skilled workers, factory owners used cheap, unskilled labour to minimize the cost of production. And child labour was the cheapest of all.

Szreter and Mooney (1998) document that, in almost all British cities, mortality in the 1860s was often worse than in the previous decade. In Liverpool in the 1860s, life expectancy fell to an astonishing 25 years. They also found a marked decline in children's growth profiles from approximately the birth cohort of the 1820s until that of the 1850s. Not until the 1870s and 1880s did urban mortality truly recede and children's normal height recover.[4]

Baten and Komlos (1998) show that the height of English soldiers declined from 1730 to 1850 – a period which captures the first Industrial Revolution. Their point is that industrialization also fostered urbanization, and that town dwellers were at a disadvantage in procuring nutrients because they were farther from the source of food supply, and, unlike the rural population, were not paying farm-gate prices for agricultural products.[5]

The crudeness of early capitalism highlights how governance challenges stalked capitalism and the Industrial Revolution right from the start. The new industrial capitalist class emerged with novel technologies and business models but with little concern for the health, environment, and safety of their workforce. Yet the massive productivity increase that followed the capitalist and Industrial Revolution carried the potential of broad welfare for all, under the right governance conditions. A prerequisite, though, was to find a governance approach that would reembed capitalism under social and environmental decency without undermining its productivity.

Colonialism and Exploitation

The internal social disruption caused by the expanding industrial market economy had an external colonial extension. Colonialism provided the Europeans with a double benefit: Firstly, the colonies enjoyed access to valuable resources that could feed the labourers and the machines of the emerging European industrial economy. Secondly, colonization allowed the colonial powers to stifle competing industrialization in the colonies and use them as potentially captive markets. The result was a massive social disembedding of the colonial economies as they were subordinated to Western powers under a combination of biased commercialization and military occupation.

British colonization, for example, forced open the large Indian market to British goods while restricting Indian exports to Britain. Raw cotton was imported from India to British factories without taxes or tariffs with those same factories manufacturing textiles from Indian cotton and selling them back to the Indian market. India thus served both as an important supplier of raw goods such as cotton to British factories and a large captive market for British manufacturing. The flip side of the colonial stimulus to Britain's Industrial Revolution was thus a parallel deindustrialization of India's impressive textile manufacturing base. While British colonialism in India was the prime example, scholars like Paul Bairoch (1982) argue that European colonialism played a major role in the deindustrialization of other countries in Asia, the Middle East, and Latin America, and also contributed to a sharp economic decline in Africa.

While securing market outlets for European industrial production was important, access to resources was also essential. According to Pomeranz (2000), the most important advantage for Europe was the vast amount of fertile, uncultivated land in the Americas which could be used to grow large quantities of farm products required to sustain European economic growth which allowed labour and land to be freed up in Europe for industrialization. Chen (2012) also suggested that the New World was a necessary factor for industrialization, and trade a supporting factor, causing less developed areas to concentrate on agriculture supporting industrialized regions in Europe.

However, while colonization and foreign resource-extraction may have been important contributing factors, they are not sufficient to explain the European growth advantage in and of themselves. As Rosenberg and Birdzell (1986) have pointed out, colonialism and colonial resources were no guarantee for economic success: imperialist Spain and Portugal did not achieve long-term growth, while imperialist Britain and Holland grew, but had already been strong before they became imperial powers. And they continued to grow after they gave up their empires. Switzerland and the Scandinavian countries, which did grow, were not imperialist countries or only marginally so. Hence, colonialism alone could not explain all of the exceptional European growth. Other factors such as disembedded capitalism with markets, property rights, commercial freedom, and facilitating political governance were needed for exploitative colonialism to bear industrial fruits.

The Misalignment

As argued by Polanyi (Polanyi 2001 [1944]), the social challenges of early industrial capitalism sprang out of a misalignment between the economy and society created by the liberal disembedding of the economy. In a first step, laissez-faire reformers had sought to disembed the economy from traditional social norms and regulations in order to establish what Polanyi called a "market society" governed by market-friendly rules. In a second step, he observed that this created exploitation that provoked a reaction. "Countermovements" then arose to re-embed the economy through the creation of social protection. However, the same forces that disembedded the economy from social decency and provoked a decay in work and living conditions for much of the urban working class, could also if – governed wisely – provide a basis for wider welfare. In the longer run, capitalism could be pushed to generate more inclusive growth.

Beginning in the early 19th century, economic prosperity, albeit very unevenly distributed, rose greatly in the West due to technological improvements such as the railroad, steamboat, steam engine, and the use of coal as a fuel source. In the 20th century, the introduction of electric power and the internal combustion engine unleashed new industrial revolutions that spurred further welfare leaps in Western societies – now spearheaded by former British colony, the USA. A major precondition for evolution towards fairer and more inclusive societies was, however, the mobilization of labour behind the social re-embedding of the economy. On top of the evolution of domestic democracy and fairer distribution of the massive industrial value creation, colonies would also demand independence, free themselves and start their complex journeys towards dignity and prosperity.

Early Battles for Re-Embedding Capitalism

The attempts to re-embed capitalism in a fairer and more inclusive environment did not emerge by themselves, however. They were the fruits of a long uphill battle fought by the growing working class along with enlightened 'priviligencia' allies, many of them, such as Wordsworth, Rousseau, and Schiller, drawing inspiration from the Romantic movement. This was a movement that had criticized environmental degradation, inequality, and brutality of the capitalist industrial system.

Early crude capitalism sparked worker protest and collective engagement for improved work conditions and better livelihoods. In their early stages, the protests were local and focused on immediate demands. Eventually, they evolved into a broader movement that took on political power, as voting rights were gradually extended to the general public in many Western countries in the late 19th and early 20th centuries. The social re-embedding of the expanding capitalist economy was in the making, and evolving towards a new 'formal' embeddedness, anchored in the emerging western democratic nation-states.

The re-embedding of the capitalist economy was carried out by the rise of organized labour and signalled an unprecedented development in the history of European popular protest, a development that would eventually lead to extensive revision of capitalist practice. It involved clawing back social control and forging institutions capable of balancing the crude market dynamics, while moulding the industrial economy into socially sustainable forms. In some cases it even turned capitalist countries into welfare states.

Worker Engagement and Protest

In Britain, the early mover of disembedded capitalism, one of the early worker initiatives was the Luddite movement that emerged during the harsh economic climate of the Napoleonic Wars. Luddites objected primarily to the rising popularity of automated textile equipment, which threatened the jobs and livelihoods of skilled workers as it allowed them to be replaced by cheaper and less-skilled workers. The movement was known for destroying weaving machinery as a form of protest. Machine-breaking was one of the few mechanisms workers could use to increase pressure on employers, undermine lower-paid competing workers and create solidarity among workers. The Luddite movement began in Nottingham and culminated in a region-wide rebellion that lasted from 1811 to 1816. Mill owners took to shooting protesters and eventually the movement was suppressed with military force (Brain, nd).

Eventually, protest merged into a broader trade-union movement. However, trade unions in Britain were subject to often severe repression until they were legalized in 1824. Growing numbers of factory workers joined these associations in their efforts to achieve better wages and working conditions. From 1830 on, attempts were made to set up national general unions, most notably Robert Owen's Grand National Consolidated Trades Union in 1834, which attracted a range of socialists, from Owenites to revolutionaries.

In the later 1830s and 1840s, trade unionism was overshadowed by political activity. Of particular importance was Chartism, which was a working-class movement for political reform in Britain. It took its name from the People's Charter of 1838 and was a national protest movement. Support for the movement was at its highest in 1839, 1842, and 1848, when petitions signed by millions of working people were presented to Parliament. The strategy was to use the scale of support that these petitions and the accompanying mass meetings demonstrated to put pressure on politicians to concede manhood suffrage. The government did not yield to any of the demands, however, and broader suffrage had to wait another two decades.

From an early stage, some members of the middle and upper classes lent their support to worker welfare and improving work conditions by engaging in philanthropy and civil societies. This group included members of the landed gentry, industrialists, merchants, civil servants, members of Parliament, writers, clerics, and pensioned military officers (Himmelfarb 2004). More politically oriented engagement came with the Fabian Society, which at first attempted to permeate the Liberal and Conservative parties with socialist ideas, but later helped to organize the separate Labour Representation Committee, which became the Labour Party in 1906.

In the meantime, the Union movement continued to grow. The strongest unions of the mid-Victorian period were unions of skilled workers such as the Amalgamated Society of Engineers. Trade unionism was quite uncommon amongst semi-skilled and unskilled workers. The union officials avoided militancy, fearing that strikes would threaten the union finances and thereby their salaries. However, an unexpected strike wave broke out in 1889-90, largely instigated by the rank and file. Its success can be explained by the dwindling supply of rural labour, which in turn increased the bargaining power of unskilled workers. In its aftermath, the 'New Unionism', starting in 1889, extended its outreach to bring in as union members the striking unskilled and semi-skilled workers. With broader male suffrage, unionism also translated into parliamentary politics. Unions played a prominent role in the creation of the Labour Representation Committee which formed the basis for today's Labour Party.

Initiatives to re-embed the capitalist market economy in socially sustainable form had thus moved from protest action through broad civic mobilization until they found a focused political expression in the Labour party, leading to a formal anchoring in the emerging democratic nation-state.

Work Legislation[6]

Work legislation became an important pillar of the social re-embedding of laissez-faire capitalism. In this process the emerging labour movement found support and stimulation from liberals and the Anglican Church. To take Britain again as an example: A great milestone in labour legislation was attained with an Act of 1833, which limited the employment of children under 18 years of age, prohibited all night work, and, crucially, provided for inspectors to enforce the law. This legislation was further amended by the 1844 Textile Factory Act, which strengthened the powers of the inspectors and required certified surgeons to examine all workers for physical fitness. Against strong opposition from conservatives and factory owners, but with support from the Anglican

Church and prominent figures like the Earl of Shaftsbury, an addition to the Factory Act was passed in 1847. It restricted the working hours of women and children in British factories to effectively 10 hours per day (Bloy nd).

In 1872 an Act included the first comprehensive code of regulation to govern legal safeguards for health, life, and limb. Any wilful neglect of these safety provisions became strictly punishable. The remit of the law steadily expanded to incorporate more industries, as reformers moved from one pressing issue to another. By the end of the century, a comprehensive set of regulations were emerging in England.

While Britain with its early industrialization became a front-runner in legislative efforts to civilize capitalist practice, other European countries soon followed suit:

In France, the working day was first limited in factories for adults in 1848, to 12. The limit of 12 hours was reduced, as regards works in which women or young workers were employed, in 1900 to 11. A law of 1905 provided for miners a nine hour day and, in 1907, an eight hour day.

In The Netherlands the first law for the regulation of labour in manufacturing industry was passed in 1874, but related only to the employment of children. The basis of all existing regulations was established in a law of May 1889, which applied to most industrial undertakings. Employment of children under 12 was prohibited, and hours were limited for youngsters under 16 and for women of any age. In 1895, the first legislative provision was made for the protection of workers against risk of accident or injury to health.

Regulation of the conditions of labour in industry throughout the German Empire was provided for in the Imperial Industrial Code and the orders of the Federal Council, which were based on the code. By far the most important amendment in social terms was a 1903 law regulating child-labour in industrial establishments. Sunday rest was, in 1891, secured for every class of worker. Annual holidays were also prescribed on church festivals.

In Scandinavia, Norway was an early mover by its factory inspection law of 1892 (Bjørnson 1997), which applied to industrial works, including metal works of all kinds and mining. Women were prohibited from underground employment, protected from dangerous or exhausting work during pregnancy and for six weeks after child birth. Further, work on Sundays and public holidays was prohibited to all workers, adult and youthful, with conditional exceptions under the authority of the inspectors. In Sweden, the Factory Law was amended in a similar direction in January 1901, and in Denmark in July of the same year.

Throughout the second half of the 19th and early 20th centuries legislative action started inculcating renewed social decency into hard, formal law in several European countries. The first steps to rein in crude disembedded laissez-faire capitalism were taken, in a battle to balance it with fairness and social decency that in some countries would mature into full-blown welfare states.

In the United States, railroads and mining were critical sectors in work-life regulation. As Aldrich (2020 nd) has shown, Individual States established railroad regulatory commissions as early as the 1840s. But most of the commissions had few powers and were rarely able to exert much influence on working conditions. Similarly, the first state-mining commission began in Pennsylvania in 1869, and other states soon followed. Yet, most of the early commissions were ineffectual.

Aldrich points out that far more important was the Federal employers' liability law, passed by Congress in 1908. Worker fatalities that had once cost the railroads perhaps $200 now cost $2,000. Two years later in 1910, New York became the first state to pass a workmen's compensation law. If the employer was negligent, the new law automatically compensated all injuries at a fixed rate (Aldrich 2020 nd).

Furthermore, the Adamson Act, passed in 1916, provided workers with an eight-hour day, at the same daily wage they had received previously for a ten-hour day, and required time and a half pay for overtime work.

Political Voice: The Emergence of Labour Parties

With the emerging democracy, the project of re-embedding laissez-faire capitalism was gradually extended to include Parliamentary politics. The British Labour Party grew out of the trade union movement of the late 19th century, and in an early phase it made progress through an informal electoral pact with the Liberals. After the First World War the party made great strides, owing to a number of factors: first, the Liberal Party tore itself apart in a series of factional disputes; second, the 1918 Representation of the People Act extended the electoral franchise to all males aged 21 and above and to women aged 30 and above; and third, in 1918, Labour reconstituted itself as a formally socialist party with a democratic constitution and a national structure. The party's new programme, "Labour and the New Social Order", drafted by Fabian Society leaders Sidney and Beatrice Webb, gave political voice to further embedding, committing Labour to the pursuit of full employment with a minimum wage and a maximum workweek, democratic control and public ownership of industry, progressive taxation, and the expansion of educational and social services. By 1922 Labour had supplanted the Liberal Party as the official opposition to the ruling Conservative Party.

Similar political mobilization took place in other European countries. German elites of the late 19th century considered the very existence of a socialist party a threat to the security and stability of the newly unified Reich, and from 1878 to 1890, the SPD – The Social Democratic Party of Germany – was officially outlawed. Nevertheless, the party attracted growing support and was able to continue to contest elections. By 1912 it was the largest party in the Reichstag ("Imperial Diet"), receiving more than one-third of the national vote for a programme of social re-embedding of the capitalist economy.

However, its vote in favour of war credits in 1914 and Germany's disastrous fate in the First World War led to an internal split, with the centrists under Karl Kautsky forming the Independent Social Democratic Party and the left under Rosa Luxemburg and Karl Liebknecht forming the Spartacus League, which in December 1918 became the Communist Party of Germany (KPD).

In Sweden, the Social Democratic Party (Wikiwand nd) was founded in 1889, as an outgrowth of the strong and well-organized working-class emancipation in the 1880s and 1890s. This was based on popular movements by which peasant and workers' organizations had penetrated state structures early on and paved the way for electoral politics. Since the party held office for a majority of the electoral terms after its founding in 1889 until the early 21st century, the ideology and policies of the Social Democratic Party (SAP) have had a major influence on Swedish politics. As in Germany, a schism occurred in 1917 when the left socialists split from the Social Democrats to form the Swedish Social Democratic Left Party (later the Communist Party of Sweden and now the Left Party).

As with front-runner nations in European industrialization, the rapid industrialization of Russia also resulted in urban overcrowding and terrible conditions for urban industrial workers. Between 1890 and 1910, the population of the capital, Saint Petersburg, swelled from 1,033,600 to 1,905,600, with Moscow experiencing similar growth. Workers had good reasons for discontent: overcrowded housing with often deplorable sanitary conditions, long hours at work; constant risk of injury and death from poor safety and sanitary conditions, harsh discipline, and inadequate wages. This created a new 'proletariat' which, due to being crowded together in the cities, was much more likely to protest and go on strike than the peasantry had been in previous times.

In addition to common problems shared with other industrializing nations, Russia experienced regime-instability, following catastrophic defeats in the war against Germany and the crumbling authority of an unpopular Tsar. The Tsarist regime had limited capacity to counter the revolutionary uprising and regime change to a communist 'dictatorship of the proletariat'. The social causes of the Russian Revolution included not only suffering in the new industrial economy, but also hardship from centuries of oppression of the lower classes by the *ancien regime*.

In the US, powerful industrial leaders used common law to curb un-ionizing and other joint employee activities in the early history of the labour movement. These were seen to be restraints of trade that violated antitrust laws. In addition, the common law doctrines of conspiracy enabled criminal enforcement against joint employee actions and agreements (Brief history of labor organization 2020 nd).

With the antitrust-law exemption in the Clayton Act, the labour movement gained some traction in 1912. However, it was not until the Great Depression and the New Deal that the right of collective bargaining was recognized in the National Labor Relations Act. Subsequent legislation (Taft-Hartley and Landrum-Griffin) added limits to union activities and controls over unions in their internal functions (Brief history of labour organization 2020 nd).

Two Paths

The early 20th century thus saw a fundamental split in the paths taken by the labour movement: 1) reformist, pursuing an agenda of social re-embedding of capitalism by building in regulatory limitations to raw profit-seeking, and by supplementing markets with extensive public planning and public infrastructure management; 2) a revolutionary strategy pursuing an agenda of substituting capitalism with a communist economy, based on planning and public agency and doing away with private ownership and competitive markets.

The reformist social democratic path emerged as a strategy to civilize capitalism not by replacing it with socialism, but imposing social agenda in work life, and by extending basic welfare to the public at large. To achieve this, the state was given a central role in the economy. While important elements of the reformist path emerged with the labour movement in the late 19th and early 20th century, the full contours of the social-democratic alternative to communism didn't materialize until the early post-war period.

Matching ideas about extensive state ownership within the context of a market economy had already been advanced by the Swedish Social-Democratic party that formed a minority government in 1920. It created a "Socialization Committee" that declared support for a mixed economy combining the best of private initiative with social ownership or control and supporting a substantial socialization "of all necessary natural resources, industrial enterprises, credit institutions, transportation and communication routes".

A similar development also occurred in Germany, but only after the Second World War. With the adoption of the Godesberg Programme, the German Social Democrats (SPD) renounced the Marxist revolutionary approach, and substituted it with a democratic, pragmatic, and reformist programme for social development.

As opposed to the reformist patterns that emerged in Britain, Germany, and Scandinavia, the dramatic Bolshevik takeover in Russia in 1918 entailed a communist revolution which empowered the radical replacement of the capitalist market economy with Soviet-based socialism. Socialism was subsequently to be followed by communism, characterized by common ownership of the means of production with free access to the articles of consumption. A core idea of the revolutionary approach to capitalism was to substitute markets and private ownership with planning and public ownership.

The communist path highlights the governance dilemma facing the civilization of capitalism. On the one hand the need to secure a fairer distribution of wealth and improvement of work conditions. On the other the necessity of ensuring productive value creation. The soviet-based communist path failed dramatically in the second task, particularly when it came to consumer products. By comparison, the mixed economy path chosen by the reformist social democrats 'delivered the goods' much more effectively.

Notes

1 This meteoric growth led Samuel P. Huntington to coin the term "the Great Divergence" (Frank 2001), an expression that was subsequently used by Kenneth Pomeranz in his book *The Great Divergence: China, Europe, and the Making of the Modern World Economy* (2000). The same phenomenon was discussed by Eric Jones, whose 1981 book *The European Miracle: Environments, Economies and Geopolitics in the History of Europe and Asia* popularized the alternative term "European Miracle".

2 Purchasing power parity between 1500 and 1950 in 1990 international dollars. Maddison's estimates of GDP per capita at purchasing power parity in 1990 international dollars for selected European and Asian nations between 1500 and 1950, showing the explosive growth of some European nations from the early 19th century.

3 Rosenberg and Birdzell (1986) describe these freedoms as including: 1) individual authorization to form enterprises, with less and less political restriction; 2) authorization of enterprises to acquire goods and hold them for resale al a profit or loss; 3) authorization of enterprises to switch from one line of activity to another that seems more promising; 4) authorization of enterprises to hold property. In addition there was growing immunity from arbitrary seizure or expropriation by the political authorities. All these freedoms have become essential elements of capitalism.

4 The anthropometric evidence provided by Szreter and Mooney indicates that, notwithstanding probable rises in male real wage rates, during the second quarter of the 19th century there was a serious deterioration in the standard of living of the growing proportion of the population recruited into the urban industrial workforce.

5 Town dwellers paid for the costs of transporting food and for the services of middlemen. Furthermore, the rapid growth of population and of urbanization, the greater inequality in the distribution of income, the increase in the variability of income, including a rise in the frequency of unemployment, also accounted for life quality deterioration. Thus, Baten and Komlos argue, "the "early-industrial growth puzzle" turns out to be not such a puzzle after all. There is no real theoretical contradiction in the divergence of the secular trend

in real income and that of physical stature in the early industrial period. It took a long time, indeed, and several technological breakthroughs for these societies to return to their previous nutritional level".
6 Building extensively on https://en.wikipedia.org/wiki/History_of_labour_law

References

Aldrich, M. (2020) History of Workplace Safety in the United States, 1880-1970 https://eh.net/encyclopedia/history-of-workplace-safety-in-the-united-states-1880-1970/. Accessed November 2020, nd.

Bairoch P. (1982) International industrialization Levels from 1750 to 1980. *Journal of European Economic History* 11.

Baten J. and Komlos J. (1998) Height and the Standard of Living. *Journal of Economic History* 58(3).

Bloy, M. (nd) The Factory Question. http://www.historyhome.co.uk/peel/factmine/factory.htm. Accessed October 2020.

Brain J. (nd) *The Luddites*. Historic UK, https://www.historic-uk.com/HistoryUK/HistoryofBritain/The-Luddites/. Accessed October 2020.

Brief History of Labor Organization (2020) https://saylordotorg.github.io/text_government-regulation-and-the-legal-environment-of-business/s22-01-a-brief-history-of-labor-legis.html Accessed November 2020.

Bjørnson, Øyvind (1997) *Arbeiderhistorie (Workers' History)* file:///C:/Users/FGL86008/Downloads/Arbeiderhistorie1997_2.pdf Retrieved November 2020.

Byron, Lord (1812) Speech in the House of Lords on 27 February 1812. https://www.historyofinformation.com/detail.php?id=4654

Dallas, R.C. (1824) *Recollections of the Life of Lord Byron*. London: Charles Knight.

De Tocqueville, A. (1958 [1835]) *Journeys to England and Ireland*. New Haven: Yale University Press.

Diamond, J. (1997) *Guns, Germs and Steel: The Fates of Human Societies*. New York: W.W Norton.

Frank, A (2001), Review of *The Great Divergence*. *Journal of Asian Studies* 60(1).

Himmelfarb, G. (2004) *Five Roads to Modernity*. New York: Alfred Knopf.

Jones, E.L. (1981) *The European Miracle: Environments, Economies, and Geopolitics in the History of Europe and Asia*. Cambridge University Press.

Maddison, A. (2006) *The World Economy: Volume 1: A Millennial Perspective and Volume 2: Historical Statistics*. Paris: Development Centre Studies, OECD Publishing, https://doi.org/10.1787/9789264022621-en. Retrieved October 2020.

Marx, K. (2007) *Dispatches for the New York Tribune: Selected Journalism of Karl Marx*. Penguin Classics.

Polanyi, K. (2001 [1944]) *The Great Transformation – The Political and Economic Origins of Our Time*. Boston: Beacon Press.

Polanyi, K. (2018) *Economy and Society – Selected Writings*. Michele Cangiani and Claus Thomasberger (eds). Cambridge: Polity Press.

Pomeranz, K. (2000) *The Great Divergence: China, Europe and the Making of the Modern World Economy*. Princeton University Press.

Rosen, G. (2015) *A History of Public Health* (revised ed). Baltimore: Johns Hopkins University Press.

Rosenberg, N. and Birdzell, L. (1986) *How The West Grew Rich: The Economic Transformation Of The Industrial World*. New York: Basic Books.

Szreter S., and Mooney G. (1998) Urbanization, Mortality, and the Standard of Living Debate: New Estimates of the Expectation of Life at Birth in Nineteenth-Century British Cities. *The Economic History Review* 51(1).

Thompson E.P. (1970 [1963]) *The Making of the English Working Class* (2nd ed). Pelican Books. Wikiwand (nd) http://www.wikiwand.com/en/Swedish_Social_Democratic_Party. Accessed November 2020.

2 Re-Embedding Capitalism Under Social Democracy

The early attempts to re-embed capitalism within a fairer and more inclusive society came to their full fruition only in the second half of the 20th century. In a number of European countries, the social democratic parties that took up government positions after the Second World War had by then established policy approaches that allowed them to run *mixed economies* that combined free markets with state intervention. Profit-seeking enterprise and the accumulation of capital remained the fundamental driving force in the production of private goods, but it was subjected to strong regulatory oversight. In the parallel public economy, public utilities, agencies, and enterprises were designed to deliver public goods, welfare, and essential services.

This massive re-embedding of the economy could build on sweeping acceptance of state intervention after the Great Depression and the following strong state leadership of the war-economy. From 1945 to 1951, the British Labour government, for example, nationalised the Bank of England, civil aviation, telegraphs, coal, transport, electricity, gas, and iron and steel (Millward 1997). This was facilitated by powerful direct controls by the state over the economy that had already been implemented by the British coalition government during the Second World War.

The rise of Keynesianism provided the social democrats with an analytical tool for re-embedding the capitalist economy in a socially responsible format, without destroying its core dynamic. Keynesian demand-side management was seen as capable of both preventing capitalism's recurrent crises and averting mass unemployment – both core demands for the working class. At the factory level, health, safety, and environmental legislation, and industrial co-determination were adopted as major parts of the social-democratic formula.

At its peak in the 1980s, the social democratic mission to civilise capitalism had managed to upgrade work life and social conditions extensively across much of Western Europe. Across the Atlantic socially progressive Rooseveltian Democratic policy had performed a comparable role. But the strongest 'catchment' for this capitalist re-embedding policy was in the Nordic welfare states.

DOI: 10.4324/9781315454931-2

With high economic productivity, fair income and wealth distribution, and high quality of life, the Nordic welfare states – towards the end of the 20th century – proved that a re-embedded market economy, or 'civilised capitalism', was indeed achievable. Having moved beyond civil and political rights to also guarantee extended social rights, these states provided their citizens with a broad set of public services, including free health care and schooling at all levels.

The Nordic health care systems were all built on the principles of universalism and equity, and provide equal access to largely tax-financed health services, under public ownership (Magnussen et al. 2009). The Nordic school systems, based on the goals of equity and participation and lifelong learning, followed in the same tradition. Students in publicly funded schools are not selected, tracked, or streamed until the age of 16. Higher education and research is regarded as a public good with instruction provided for all qualified students largely free from tuition fees (also at the postgraduate level) with publicly provided loans at subsidised rates for subsistence (Antikainen 2006).

However, the Nordics combine social inclusion and free welfare services with competitive engagement in international markets. At the core of the Nordic success has been their ability to blend collaborative and competitive elements and skillfully manoeuvre between them (Midttun and Witoszek 2019). They have done so by ambidextrously operating in the two seemingly contradictory realms – the competitive and the collaborative – through institutional differentiation, much in the fashion of the management of the contradictory logics of innovation and efficient production in business (O'Reilly and Tushman 2004) and what evolutionary thinkers would term "multilevel selection" (Wilson and Wilson 2007). At one level, or in one domain, the Nordic countries collaborate, and at another level they compete, using their collaborative teamwork as a strategic asset. In this way they have – at their best - succeeded in re-embedding the capitalist market dynamic without destroying it.

While Polanyi tended to assume that modern societies are faced with either neoliberal disembeddedness or post-capitalist re-embedding through collaborative planning, the social democratic parties in Western Europe, and Nordics welfare states in particular, highlight a third alternative – an ambidextrous combination of competition and collaboration. This is an alternative that far superseded the Soviet socialist attempt at taming the brutal forces of disembedded capitalism, delivering productivity on a par with advanced liberal market economies.

Nordic style ambidexterity presupposes high collaborative capacity, though. Strong trade unions and employers' organizations, capable of mobilising support for combined economic and social sustainability, are one important element. But equally, if not more, important are deeply entrenched cultural and religious norms and values (habitus). This broader and shared normative founding tradition – rooted in the ideals of the Nordic Christian Enlightenment – was essential to the Nordic capability to take the re-embedding of the market economy under social sustainability as far as they did (Witoszek 2011).

Re-embedding the economy by blending economic value creation with prosocial engagement permeates Nordic societies in most domains. It characterizes work life, including female participation, resource management – illustrated by the Norwegian petroleum economy – and, of course, the provision of social welfare, health, and education.

The Flexicurity Model

One of the hallmarks of Nordic capitalist management is the *flexicurity model*. It entails re-embedding the economy by establishing coordinated welfare state guarantees, family subsistence, and retraining for redundant employees, while allowing competitive market dynamics to play out in a liberal labour market.

The term 'flexicurity' was first coined by the Danish social democrat prime minister, Poul Nyrup Rasmussen, in the 1990s. As practiced in Denmark – the pioneer of this model – the trade unions accepted short notice for laying off workers in return for an insurance system that ensures the lowest-paid workers are entitled to benefits equal to 90% of their former wage for up to two years. This has enabled a liberal labour market policy where employers can hire and fire at a very short notice, whilst at same time ensuring generous social security arrangements that enable a decent livelihood. A precondition for the generous benefits is the so-called 'active labour market policy', whereby all unemployed individuals are obliged to participate in publicly provided education and training (Østergård 2011).

The ambidextrous combination of a liberal labour market, intended to serve entrepreneurship and productivity in small and medium businesses (Nørgaard 2007) and supportive welfare arrangements to cater for social sustainability, highlights a basic pragmatism that allows the Nordics to maintain support for policies across ideological divides. The whole system is mainly collaboratively financed through income taxes and value-added. In addition, the employees pay a small element through membership fees.

The 'flexicurity' model became widely embraced in the other Nordic economies and in the European Union too. It was also geared up from its traditional function as an employment facilitator, to take on a stronger role in industrial transformation, thereby illustrating how prosocial re-embedding can be combined with innovation.

The Front Industries and Wage Compression Models

Other examples of ambidextrous re-embedding of the market economy in advanced welfare states are 'front' industries' wage bargaining and the wage compression models. By re-embedding work-life and industrial relations through coordinated and solidaristic wage bargaining, the Nordics have been able to achieve a competitive advantage in product and service markets, while at the same time securing a fair distribution of wages (Aukrust 1977).

In the 'front' industries' model, wage negotiations in the internationally exposed sectors – the front industries – have been prioritised, and provide competitive settlements by international wage standards (Aukrust 1977, Moene and Wallerstein, 2006). These settlements have subsequently been used as a guiding norm for wage negotiations in domestic sheltered sectors. Calibration of wages to industrial competitiveness in liberal markets through coordinated negotiations can avoid the difficult tradeoff between employment and inflation that would arise under decentralised negotiation (Bjørnstad and Nymoen 2015). By moderating wage demands to productivity in internationally exposed sectors, industry has retained profitability, while labour has retained high employment. The collective bargaining in centralised unions has limited excessive wage spikes for strategically positioned groups, while contributing to social sustainability by solidaristically lifting wages for weaker groups.

Through wage compression, centralised wage settlements have also aided economic modernization. As Moene and Wallerstein (2006) have pointed out, on the one hand, centralised wage determination has prevented industries with low levels of productivity from staying in business by paying low wages. But it has also moderated wage demands from workers in industries with high levels of productivity. Hence the effect has been to reduce profits in low-productivity firms and raise them in high-productivity firms, stimulating labour and capital to move from low to high productive activities. As a result, the pace of economic development and competitive success in international product and service markets has been increased (Moene and Wallerstein 1997, Agell and Lommerud 1993). Re-embedding the economy for social sustainability could thus become a vehicle for enhanced competitiveness, indicating how the social-democratic model, at its best, might demonstrate the 'competitive advantage of collaboration'.

Female Participation in Production

Re-embedding the Nordic welfare economies has also involved gender equality. And again, broad female inclusion in the productive economy comes with a competitive advantage (Holst 2018, Teigen and Skjeie 2017). A central premise for high levels of female participation in liberal product and service markets has been the expansion of the welfare state to include generous public subsidy of parental leave schemes and extensive child care arrangements. To take Norway as an example, all employees are eligible for parental benefit if they have been gainfully employed. Parents are entitled to a year's salary. Fathers can take three and a half months paid leave. In addition, parents receive child benefit of 970 NOK per month (tax free) (2019 rates), from birth to 18. Similar arrangements exist in the other Nordic countries.

Like the governance arrangements for flexicurity and wage compression, the arrangements for generous maternity and paternity leave aim at combining welfare and productivity. And the collaborative facilitation of female work participation has clearly paid off. According to the OECD, the growth in women's employment alone accounted for the equivalent of about 10–20% of average annual GDP per capita growth over the past 40–50 years in Denmark, Iceland, Norway, and Sweden (OECD 2018). The increased value creation and broadening of the tax base that comes with female participation, has boosted Nordic societies' competitiveness and promoted the high welfare levels that characterize them. Along with Switzerland and New Zealand, the Nordics thus stand out as having the highest female labour market participation among OECD countries.

Norway's Equitable Petroleum Economy

While work life has been the 'iconic' focus for much of the literature on the Nordic model, the re-embedding of the market economy through an ambidextrous combination of competition and collaboration applies to other domains as well, such as the management of natural resources. The governance of Norwegian petroleum resources is an interesting case in point. Through a hybrid governance regime, the country has managed to adroitly handle its extraordinary petro-wealth, building collaborative arrangements to cater for the public interest, while securing competitive participation in international petroleum markets and establishing a leading position in the offshore petroleum industry (Hanish and Nerheim 1992, Ministry of Petroleum and Energy 2019).

Norway's petroleum governance has been fashioned through four core regimes: 1) a regulatory regime – to bring petroleum resources under public control and organise exploration and production efficiently; 2) an industrial regime – to guarantee the build-up of domestic industrial capabilities; 3) a taxation regime – to secure the public revenue from the extraordinary profits into a public pension fund; and 4) a wealth management regime – to safeguard world-class international financial investment of the fund's assets on the public's behalf. Together, these regimes constitute an ambidextrous mix of collaborative and competitive elements that embed one of the most profitable sectors of the economy into a framework for value creation and social sustainability, albeit with some question marks with respect to ecological sustainability, which will be discussed in Chapter 5.

The resources under management are formidable. Around the turn of the millennium, petroleum comprised 15% of GDP, over 40% of exports, and 25% of state income, with nearly a fifth of total investment coming from this sector. Norway shares resource abundance with many other oil-rich countries. However, the societal embedding of the petroleum economy is where the difference lies. A 'mixed economy' approach with a focus on the appropriation of super-profits for public benefit, while governing production and financial management under a competitive market regime, sets Norway apart. As shown in Figure 2.1 countries such as Venezuela, Nigeria, Angola, and to some extent Russia, Iran and Iraq, have failed to use their petroleum endowments to transform into high value-creating economies, while Kuwait, and to some degree, Saudi Arabia, have not had their petroleum wealth trickle down as equitably to the population (Figure 2.1).

Resilience Through Ambidexterity

By pursuing strategies to embed the market economy for social sustainability, whilst leaving room for market dynamics to play out, the Nordics – along with many other welfare states – have managed to combine high productivity with welfare and fair income and wealth distribution. A key factor in this achievement has been their ability to govern their mixed economies, where competition and collaboration productively co-exist within the same socio-economic system. The seemingly contradictory, and – in Kolakowski's (1963) terms – inconsistent "logic" of the ambidextrous mixed economy model provides a broader spectrum of options to deal with the difficult task of achieving both fair

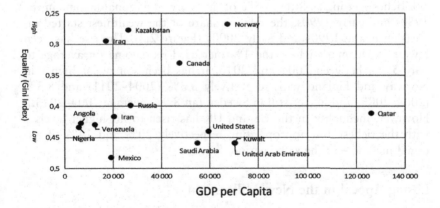

Figure 2.1 GDP per Capita and Equality.

Source: GDP average as provided by World Bank 2017, CIA 1993–2017 and IMF 2017.[1]

distribution and high productivity than those envisioned by either classical liberalism or the traditional socialist planned economy.

The Welfare State Under Pressure

Nevertheless, the welfare state model, which was highly successful in the post-war economy has come under pressure since the turn of the millennium. It had rested on legitimacy of serving a broad working-class, under an industrial economy. The shift towards a service economy and the fragmentation of working-class identity has shaken its industrial base as well as its political legitimacy. This has raised a need for adjusting the welfare state's industrial policy 'toolkit' as well as re-anchoring its political foundations. These challenges illustrate how re-embedding the economy is not a static 'once and for all' affair, but must be re-defined to suit new conditions.

Towards New Inequality

The transformation from class societies to inclusive welfare societies is one of the major achievements of many mature western industrial economies in the second half of the 20th century. With the welfare states leading the way, most Western industrial nations saw massive economic growth and an extensive drop in inequality from the 1950s and into the early 1990s, under a prosocial re-embedding of the economy. However, towards the end of the 20th century, the trend reversed. Even in the Nordics, where the 'golden age' of social-democratic values went further towards equality and lasted longer than elsewhere, the trend towards distributive fairness has gone into retreat. While the Nordics saw the top 1% richest getting as little as 5% of the share of national income in the 1980s and early 1990s, the relative share of the wealthiest started increasing in the 1990s and early 2000s (Figure 2.2). The rise has been lowest in Denmark where the 1% increased its income on average to only 5.9% between 2004 and 2010. It has been somewhat higher in Norway and Finland with respectively 8.3% (2004–2011) and 8.3% (2004–2009) and higher still in Sweden (an 8.9% average 2004–2013.). However, inequality in the US and UK has risen to far higher levels – with the richest 1% appropriating respectively 20% and 14% of national income – in the same period.

Losing Appeal in the New Millennium

The late 20th and early 21st centuries also saw the legitimacy of social democracy – the prime carrier of the welfare state idea – under siege. While it had success in framing capitalism in the 20th century, social democracy as a political movement started to lose appeal. It had

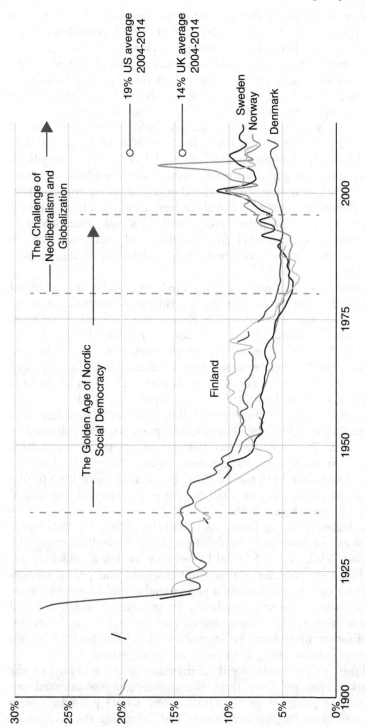

Figure 2.2 Income Inequality, Nordic Welfare States Benchmarked Against US and UK.

Source: World Inequality Database https://wid.world/data/.

succeeded in mobilising political support on the back of the growing working class in the early 20th century, and after the Second World War, successfully reached beyond its traditional working-class base to include public sector employees, urban professionals, and agricultural labourers. However, towards the end of the 20th century these electoral bases were palpably weakening in Europe. As shown by Benedeto et al. (2019) the structural change from the industrial in favour of the service economy had altered the vocational basis of society. Industrial employment fell from over 40% of GDP in the 1960s to under 20% in the new millennium and severely diminished the core social democratic voter-base. Stagnation in the growth of the public sector since the 1990s – another core social-democratic voter-base – also diminished the electoral support for social democratic parties. Then there were challenges from political competitors. Centre-right parties confronted the social-democratic governance formula with market liberalization and monetarist macroeconomic policies, while green movements started squeezing support from the left.

In response, social democracy reinvented itself and took on board several elements from the centre-right and the green movement agendas. Tony Blair and Anthony Giddens in Britain and Gerhard Schröder in Germany championed this reinvention under the labels of the 'Third Way' or the 'New Middle' (neue mitte), which emphasised regulating free markets, supply-side economic management, balanced budgets, and social liberalism and environmentalism (e.g. Giddens 1998). The formula worked for a while and social democrats were back in office in most western European countries for a period. But, as shown by Benedetto et al (2019), starting in 2000, social democratic party support collapsed in many countries. This decline was so dramatic, in fact, that between 2000 and 2017 most social democratic parties secured their lowest levels of electoral support since 1918 for the older democracies, since 1945 for the post-war democracies, or since 1989 for the new democracies of central and eastern Europe (Figure 2.3).

But the decline of Social Democracy, and the setback for distributive fairness, does not necessarily imply abandoning the welfare state. The massive post-WWII wave of Social Democracy has left an indelible impact on European societies. Public infrastructures and public services were built up on a massive scale, and a partial re-embedding of 'crude capitalism' in most countries endures, irrespective of which political party is in power. The social-democratic movement with its institutionalization of welfare arrangements, therefore, lives on – and deeper layers remain – in spite of more recent accretions.

In addition to the institutional momentum of the build-up of the social-market economy over time, the centre-right has adopted important welfare policy elements. Quite a few liberal politicians were supportive of extending workers' rights and improving the position of

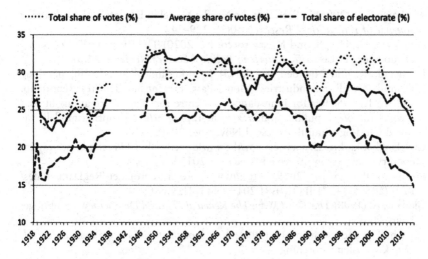

Figure 2.3 Three Measures of the Electoral Performance of Social Democratic Parties.

Source: Benedetto, Hix and Mastrorocco, American Political Science Review 2019.

working families in the early and brutal stages of the Industrial Revolution, and in the 21st century the political landscape, at least in many parts of Western Europe, has moved towards including stronger buffering against poverty and misery than the crude market economy model would entail. Rudimentary social welfare policies have remained in place in Europe, also under centre-right governments. Public expenditure has remained as high, around 45% (European Parliament 2019), as under social democratic leadership, even though many sectors of the economy have undergone radical deregulation.

Note

1 GINI average as provided by World Bank (2006–2015) and the CIA (2006–2014). Departing from calculations made by the World Inequality Database, Kuwait and the United Arab Emirates are estimated to be on the same level as Saudi Arabia, whose level of income inequality we gathered from the World Bank (2013).

References

Agell, J. and Lommerud, K. (1993) Egalitarianism and Growth. *The Scandinavian Journal of Economics* 95(4).

Aukrust, O. (1977) Inflation in the Open Economy: A Norwegian Model. Reprinted from: L.B. Krause and W.S. Sålant (eds), *Worldwide Inflation: Theory and Recent Experience*. Washington, DC: Brookings.

Antikainen, A. (2006) In Search of the Nordic Model in Education. *Scandinavian Journal of Educational Research* 50(3): 229–243.

Benedetto, G., Hix, S. and Mastrorocco, N. (2020) The Rise and Fall of Social Democracy, 1918-2017. *American Political Science Review* 114(3).

Bjørnstad, R. and Nymoen, R. (2015) Frontfagsmodellen i fortid, nåtid og framtid (The Front Industries' Model Past, Present and Future) Report no. 1–2015 from Senter for lønnsdannelse (Centre for Wage Formation) https://www.fafo.no/zoo-publikasjoner/eksterne-rapporter/item/frontfagsmodellen-i-fortid-natid-og-framtid. Accessed November 2020.

CIA Factbook: https://www.cia.gov/the-world-factbook/field/real-gdp-per-capita/country-comparison. Accessed December 2017.

European Parliament (2019) http://www.europarl.europa.eu/RegData/etudes/BRIE/2019/634371/IPOL_BRI(2019)634371EN.pdf

Giddens, A. (1998) *The Third Way: The Renewal of Social Democracy.* Cambridge: Polity Press.

Hanish, T.J. and Nerheim, G. (1992) *Norsk oljehistorie: En gassnasjon blir til,* Norsk petroleumsforening.

Holst, C. (2018) Scandinavian Feminism and Gender Partnership. In Witoszek, Nina and Midttun, Atle (eds), *Sustainable Modernity. The Nordic Model and Beyond.* New York: Routledge.

IMF: World Economic Database: https://www.imf.org/en/Publications/SPROLLs/world-economic-outlook-databases#sort=%40imfdate%20descending. Accessed December 2017.

Kolakowski, L. (1963) In Praise of Inconsistency. *Dissent* Magazine 11(2).

Magnussen, J., Vrangbæk, K. and Saltman, R.B. (2009) Nordic Health Care Systems. Recent Reforms and Current Policy Challenges. In Jon Magnussen, Karsten Vrangbæk and Richard B. Saltman (eds). *European Observatory on Health Systems and Policies Series.* Open University Press.

Midttun, A. and Witoszek, N. (2019) The Competitive Advantage of Collaboration – Throwing New Light on the Nordic Model. *New Political Economy* 25, 2020(6).

Millward, R. (1997) The 1940s Nationalizations in Britain: Means to an End or the Means of Production? *Economic History Review* L(2).

Ministry of Petroleum and Energy (2019) *Norway's Petroleum History.* Available at: https://www.norskpetroleum.no/en/framework/norways-petroleum-history/. Accessed 1 May 2019.

Moene, K.O. and Wallerstein, M. (1997) Pay Inequality. *Journal of Labor Economics* 15(3).

Moene, K.O. and Wallerstein, M. (2006) 'The Scandinavian Model and Economic Development': Special Report. New York, NY: World Bank Institute.

O'Reilly, C.A. and Tushman, M.L. (2004) The Ambidextrous Organization. *Harvard Business Review*, April.

OECD (2018). Is the Last Mile the Longest? Paris: OECD. Available from: https://read.oecd-ilibrary.org/social-issues-migration-health/is-the-last-mile-the-longest-economic-gains-from-gender-equality-in-nordic-countries_97892 64300040-en#page5. Accessed November 2020.

OECD Data: https://data.oecd.org/gdp/gross-domestic-product-gdp.htm. Accessed December 2017.

Østergård, U. (2011) Current Challenges to Nordic Labor Policy: The Danish 'Flexicurity Model'. In A. Midttun and N. Witoszek (eds), 'The Nordic Model: Is It Sustainable and Exportable?' Report. BI Norwegian Business School and University of Oslo.

Nørgaard, A.S. (2007) Parterne og a-kassesystemet – de forbundne spils politi-ske logik. In I.J.H. Pedersen and A. Huulgaard (red.), *Arbejdsløshedsforsikringsloven 1997 -2007 – udvikling og perspektiver*. København: Arbejdsdirektoratet.

Teigen, M. and Skjeie, H. (2017) The Nordic Gender Equality Model. In Oddbjørn P. Knutsen (eds), *The Nordic Models in Political Science. Challenged, but Still Viable?* Bergen: Fagbokforlaget.

Wilson, D.S. and Wilson, E.O. (2007) Rethinking the Theoretical Foundation of Sociobiology. *The Quarterly Review of Biology* 82.

Witoszek, N. (2011) *The Origins of the Regime of Goodness: Remapping the Cultural History of Norway*. Oslo: Norwegian University Press.

World Inequality Database: https://wid.world/wid-world/. Accessed 15 March 2018.

Section II

21st Century Challenges

3 Technological Challenges

Digitalization and Robotization

By the beginning of the 21st century, the accelerated advance of digitalization and robotization prompted fears that humans could be relegated to unstable, poorly paid positions in the gig economy, or supplanted entirely by artificial intelligence. The increased productivity from digitalization would then accrue to financial elites. The network economy, typical of digitalization, has an inbuilt tendency to undermine competition and favour oligopoly, which further stimulates a skewed wealth distribution, allowing the winners to pocket super-fortunes.

By the close of the 20th century, digitization represented, aside from its other ramifications, a new dis-embedding of the economy and the work-life model in advanced welfare states. Under welfare state governance, work-life was oriented towards long-term stable employment, with salaries secured by collective wage bargaining between business and strong trade unions. If necessary, solutions would occasionally be brokered through state intervention.

Humans and Robots

The concern with robotization decimating jobs is reflected in books such as Jeremy Rifkin's 1995 *The End of Work* and Martin and Schuman's *The Global Trap* (1996). However, perhaps the most radical vision of robotic penetration in work life has come from Dr. Hans Moravec at the Carnegie Mellon Robotics Institute. As Moravec sees it, digitalization and artificial intelligence can be described in terms of four generations of universal robots which he expected to take over work-life the first four decades of the 21st century (from an interview with *Wired* magazine in 1995):

> A first generation of universal robots, around 2010, will have enough general competence to do relatively intricate mechanical tasks such as automotive repair, bathroom cleaning, or factory assembly work.

DOI: 10.4324/9781315454931-3

By adding more memory and computing power and enhancing the software, he assumed that by 2020 we would have a second generation that can learn from its own performance. This means that it can learn and adapt.

By 2030, according to Moravec, we should have a third-generation of universal robots that emulate higher-level thought processes such as planning and foresight. He envisages that "it will maintain an internal model not only of its own past actions, but of the outside world". This means that "it can run different simulations of how it plans to tackle a task, see how well each one works out, and compare them with what it has done before. An onlooker will have the sense that it's imagining different solutions to a problem, developing its own ideas".

We will still be designing and programming them to serve and obey us. They'll learn everything they know from us, and their goals and their methods will be imitations of ours. But as they become more competent, efficiency and productivity will keep going up, and the amount of work for humans will keep going down.

By around 2040, Moravec argues, "there will be no job that people can do better than robots". From a purely commercial perspective robots/AI and workers are input factors in the production of goods and services, and – as AI/robotic capabilities increase and costs decrease through technological learning – AI/robots will be preferred to humans and re-place workers over time. According to Moravec's scenarios AI will take over much of human work-life, and represents a fundamental rupture with the basic coupling between production and human work. Without a major re-orientation of economic governance, this would in turn entail driving large parts of the population into unemployment and relegating provision for human livelihood to other sources and domains, such as citizens' wages or basic income. In other words, governance initiatives to re-embed the economy according to wholly new principles are needed.

However, a strong tradition for liberal market-oriented governance in economics argues that, for every job lost to technological improvement, a new one will be created. This contention goes back to Jean-Baptiste Say (1803) who asserted that supply creates its own demand, and that any displaced workers would automatically find work elsewhere once the market had had time to adjust. Say's position was followed up by the influential neoclassical theory that takes full employment as the characteristic long-run equilibrium condition of an economy, thereby dismissing any need for governance intervention (Oana 2015).

In this perspective, technological change is one factor among many, and may disturb the economy's equilibrium, but only temporarily. Like all disturbances, technological change could be seen as setting in motion price adjustments towards a new equilibrium that would again bring about full employment (Woirol 1996). In this perspective, one may see AI as yet another technological revolution, but one that will enable pioneering business sectors to flourish and secure future employment.

Yet, faced with the massive potential of AI, influential economists have retreated from the optimistic market flexibility thesis and voiced concerns about the work-life effects of digitalization, if the latter is left purely to market governance. In an op-ed in *The New York Times* (2013), Nobel Prize winner, Paul Krugman, recognized that in the past the painful problems generated by mechanization were solved thanks to more intensive education. However, the problems generated by artificial intelligence are not solvable in the same way because they affect educated workers as well. Today, he argued, a much darker picture of the effects of technology on labour is emerging. In this picture, highly educated workers are as likely as less-educated workers to find themselves displaced and devalued, and pushing for more education may create as many problems as it answers.

The concern with the limited capacity of the economy, under liberalist governance, to combine AI & robotization with an inclusive work life has been expressed by the MIT researchers, Brynjolfsson and McAfee (2015). A central feature of digital technologies, they point out, is that once algorithms are digitized they can be replicated and delivered to millions of users at almost zero cost. On the one hand, this new context creates a massive bounty for consumers and investors, as more goods, services, and revenue will be created with less work. On the other hand, in a competitive economy under de-regulated governance, this progress will deplete employment dramatically within affected sectors and have large ramifications on the distribution of jobs, income, and wealth.

In the longer run, Brynjolfsson and McAfee, in line with Moravec and Krugman, question whether new job-creation will be sufficient to keep pace with digital rationalization. If left to liberally governed market dynamics, they contend, it is likely to create a massively uneven distribution of wealth and potentially large unemployment. As digital labour becomes more pervasive, capable, and powerful, Brynjolfsson and McAfee argue, companies will be increasingly unwilling to pay people wages that they'll accept and that will allow them to maintain the standard of living to which they've been accustomed. When this happens, they risk remaining unemployed.

As of the early 2020s we have only seen the first rounds of digitalization of work life, and AI capacity is rapidly improving. As Moravec argues, by 2030, we should have in place a third-generation of universal robots that emulate higher-level thought processes such as planning and foresight. By around 2040, Moravec predicted, there will be no jobs that people can do better than robots. As the high-tech visionary Vernor Vinge (1993) has argued, we will soon create intelligence greater than our own. When this happens, human history will have reached a kind of singularity, an intellectual transition where the world will pass far beyond our understanding.

Employment, but Inequality

It still remains an open question to what extent AI & robotization, under permissive liberalist governance, will destroy human jobs beyond replacement. Until the Corona crisis major unemployment had been avoided. OECD statistics show that the labour force participation rate for the economy as a whole has been maintained in OECD countries in the first two decades of the 21st century, in spite of digitalization (OECD nd). While employment has fallen in technically progressive sectors, such drops have been outweighed by positive spillovers to the rest of the economy (Autor and Salomons 2017).

The problem is that many of these positive spillovers have come in service activities with highly divergent income distribution. While this shift of employment has included some high skill-intensive and well-paid jobs, there has been a predominance of low skill-intensive services, many of which are to be found in the so-called 'gig economy'. This is apparently a major factor behind the decline of the global labour share of value, a share that according to many researchers such as Karabarbounis and Neiman (2014), has fallen significantly since the early 1980s. An OECD study of 12 countries indicates that these trends are present in most nations (Figure 3.1) testifying that existing governance for fairness and social inclusion has not been robust enough to keep up with technological options under commercial pressure.

The Gig Economy

The typical organization of the new low-skilled, loosely organized, and digitally mediated economy has been labelled the 'gig economy'. It is driven by the desire for flexibility, while at the same time lowering the cost of labour and shifting risk away from the employer. As such it represents a major challenge to the 20th century welfare state work-life model. As illustrated in Figure 3.2, gig jobs, or 'atypical' work, are usually organized around some form of digital mediation, like a web-based platform; and the combination of online platforms and isolated independent workers, poses fundamental challenges to traditional models for work organization and wage bargaining. These are work conditions that may easily press workers into a 'precariat' – position where labour insecurity and insecure social income, undermine a work-based identity (Standing 2014).

While operating partly under the radar of established work-life governance, gig workers typically face irregular work schedules, driven by

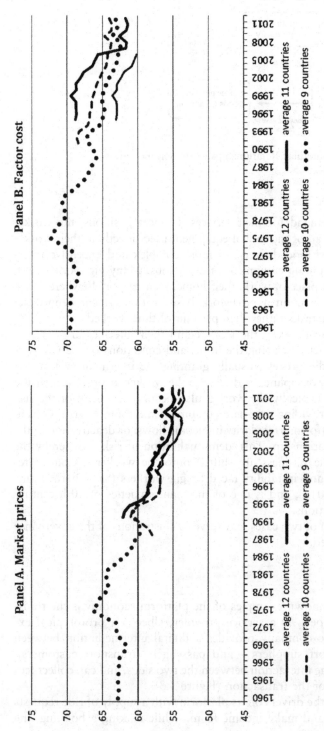

Figure 3.1 The Adjusted Labour Income Share in Selected G20 Countries and Spain Estimated by AMECO.[1]

Source: OECD/ILO (2015), The Labour Share in G20 Economies: https://www.oecd.org/g20/topics/employment-and-social-policy/The-Labour-Share-in-G20-Economies.pdf.

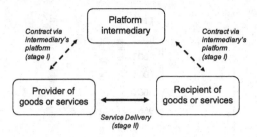

Figure 3.2 The Triangular Relationships of the Gig Economy.

Source: Author.

fluctuations in demand for their services. In most positions, the worker provides some or all of the capital equipment used directly in their work – from a bicycle for food delivery, to more complex and expensive transportation or computing equipment in other jobs. Many gig workers also provide their own place of work: their home, their car, or elsewhere. Most jobs are compensated on a piecework basis, with payment defined according to specific tasks rather than per unit of time worked.

The relationship between the worker and their intermediaries is governed by a contract describing the terms and conditions of the worker's participation in the process, usually granting the intermediary firm the right to supervise, discipline, or discharge the worker or prevent their use of the platform. Typically the worker also bears most or all of the risk associated with providing necessary equipment and tools: interruptions in service by the platform; irregularity in income flows; or deactivation of the service or the relationship. This 'demutualisation of risk' – whereby the major risks of the business are shifted onto the worker – exacerbates the vulnerability and instability faced by gig workers (Slee, 2016; Kaine and Josserand, 2016), and is one of the main anxieties of 20th century work-life expectations.

A brief mention of two cases may serve as illustrations of the governance challenges involved.

Case I: Uber

One of the best-known examples of the platform economy is the transport company Uber. As a service provider, Uber is a prototypical example, where the company provides a digital intermediation between drivers – transport suppliers – and passengers (transport customers). Uber facilitates the interaction between the two sides, and can collect fees from both sides of the transaction (Figure 3.3).

Uber provides the drivers on its platform with a supply of ride requests to accept, fulfil, and make income from. While making a booking, the

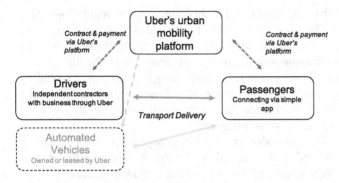

Figure 3.3 Uber's Business Model.

Source: Author.

passenger pays Uber for the ride through the app. Uber then transfers the payment to the partner's account after taking some amount of commission for doing the job of a digital broker. The commission rates may vary from 15% to 30%, depending on the market. By adopting dynamic or surge pricing, Uber is also able to secure a better fit between supply and demand. Put into practice by easy to detect coloured zones on a mobile map-display, drivers are attracted to zones with a surplus of customers and a higher willingness to pay.

Like many platform providers, Uber uses its platform to expand into new related business, such as Uber Eats and Uber Freight with specialized apps. In the first case Uber has tapped into an expanding market for on-demand food delivery, which can be naturally added on as a new opportunity for its large fleet of drivers. In the second, Uber has created an on-demand market for trucks, where it seeks to seamlessly match shippers with carriers (Uber, nd).

Many customers have found Uber's transport solution attractive, and this has boosted the company's expansion in several markets. However, claiming to be a communication platform rather than a taxi service, Uber has expanded by ignoring existing governance rules and conventions. This has prompted protests against ride-hailing company by drivers, run-ins with national authorities, and new laws designed to curb its activities. Stripping away basic work contracts, Uber has taken the ultimate step towards a dis-embedded market economy, reducing work relations to short-term iterations against market demand.

With its radically market-driven business model, the company has aroused confrontation with work-life governance around the world. As reported in *The Guardian* (Henley 2017):

- In Austin, Texas Uber suspended operations in May 2016 after the city's voters rejected a proposal to allow the company to self-regulate its drivers, instead of upholding stricter regulations proposed by the liberal city council that required ride-sharing drivers to pass fingerprint-based security checks. About 10,000 drivers lost their jobs, with some moving to nearby cities where the hailing app was still allowed. But alternatives respecting the new rules, including a not-for-profit ride-sharing service, RideAustin, soon emerged and a year later Uber was allowed back into Austin after the Republican-controlled state legislature intervened.

- In Bulgaria, Uber suspended its activities in September 2015, following mass protests and a threatened strike by Sofia's traditional taxi operators, which accused the service of "unfair trade practices" because its drivers were working without a taxi licence, a professional driver's license or defined legal status.
- In Denmark in April 2017 Uber pulled out of the Danish market, where it had 2,000 drivers and more than 300,000 customers, when fare meters and seat occupancy sensors became mandatory for all vehicles providing a taxi service.
- In Italy, following a complaint and six-day strike by Italy's taxi associations, a Rome court blocked the use of the Uber app in April 2017 on grounds of unfair competition. An appeal court lifted the ban the following month – but only for the company's premium Uber Black service, which uses fully-licensed professional drivers.
- In Hungary, Uber suspended its operations in Budapest in July 2016 when the nationalist government passed legislation making it impossible for it to operate following months of persuasive protests by Hungary's taxi drivers.
- In Canada, Uber threatened to suspend its operation in Quebec if Canadian authorities passed new legislation requiring Uber drivers to undergo a police criminal records check and do the 35 hours of training expected of regular taxi drivers.

These cases illustrate the disruptive nature of Uber. The disruption is technological, as it simplifies the taxi business by connecting customers to drivers through a web application, as well as institutional as Uber claims to be a technology company without responsibility for the drivers who are independent contractors. In December 2019 in San Francisco, the case against an Uber driver who allegedly made sexual comments to a 16-year-old passenger was settled. Uber's attorneys argued that "the partner driver was an independent contractor responsible for his own means and methods" and that Uber is "a technology company, not a transportation company" (*Washington Post* 2019).

The long series of conflicts with cities around the world also bears witness to Uber's confrontational strategy in dealing with regulators, especially under the leadership of its founder, Travis Kalanick, who is supposed to have argued for what he termed "principled confrontation".

Uber's strategy was generally to commence operations in a city, then, if it faced regulatory opposition, to mobilize public support for its service and mount a political campaign, supported by lobbyists, to change regulations towards an ultra-liberal work-life governance regime (Walker 2015; MacMillan 2015).

Case II: Foodora

One of the digital transport companies that has undergone a serious upgrading of its employment policy is Foodora. Like Uber, the company is built around a website and a mobile app where customers can browse restaurants near them, place their order, and pay. The order is then prepared by the restaurant, picked up by one of Foodora's couriers (foodsters), and delivered to the customer.

In 2020, Foodora operated in numerous countries worldwide: Austria, Hong Kong, Taiwan, the Philippines, Bulgaria, and Romania (Foodora.com 2020). Previously the company had also operated in Australia, France, Germany, Italy, and the Netherlands, but exited because of labour conflicts.

The Australian example is a case in point. As with Uber, Foodora's insistence on defining its workers as independent contractors became a bone of contention. A dismissal of one of its workers/contractors/riders led the rider to commence unfair dismissal proceedings in the Fair Work Commission.

Noting that the correct approach to determining whether a person is an employee or an independent contractor required a consideration of both fact and law, Commissioner Cambridge of the Fair Work Commission, declared: (Megan Bowe 2018):

> In this instance, the correct characterisation of the relationship between [the rider and Foodora] is that of employee and employer. The conclusion that must be drawn from the overall picture that has been obtained, was that the [rider] was not carrying on a trade or business of his own, or on his own behalf, instead the [rider] was working in [Foodora's] business as part of that business. The work of the [rider] was integrated into [Foodora's] business and not an independent operation. The [rider] was, despite the attempt to create the existence of an independent contractor arrangement, engaged in work as a delivery rider/driver for Foodora as an employee of Foodora.

According to lawyer Megan Bowe, the Foodora case represents the first instance where the Fair Work Commission has been prepared to assess and determine the nature of the working relationship that exists in the gig economy, having previously declined to do so on two separate occasions involving drivers engaged by Uber. Whether the decision in the

Foodora case has follow on implications for other players in the gig economy including Uber, Deliveroo and/or Taxify remains to be seen, although one might expect to see an increase in claims by aggrieved deliver drivers/riders for underpayment and unfair dismissal. The conflict led to Foodora leaving the Australian market. The case nevertheless illustrates how platform companies are starting to be subsumed under traditional work-life governance

A year and a half later, Foodora was again in conflict over their work-life arrangements, this time in Norway. Workers, supported by trade unions, undertook a five-week-long strike leading to Foodora signing a tariff agreement, including a wage increase and compensation for the cost of clothes and equipment. In line with Nordic traditions of negotiated work-life agreements, the issue was solved through bargaining between the parties and not in court. In the end, both parties expressed satisfaction with the result, whereby Foodora was subsumed under the Norwegian governance tradition. The CEO of Foodora Norway expressed support for the Norwegian work-life model, "This is a unique agreement that makes the bicyclists' everyday even better, and which we as a company can use to develop ourselves" (translated from *Aftenposten* 27 Sept 2019). The head of one of the trade union's central divisions, Fellesforbundet, Jørn Eggum also praised the agreement, which he claimed set a new and important standard for future work-life (Aftenposten 2019).

The gig economy is clearly a step back towards disembedded capitalism, neglecting many of the basic precepts of 20th century work-life governance in advanced welfare states. However, the Foodora case illustrates that, in collaboration with strong trade unions, there is a possibility to re-embed work relations so that they are more in tune with traditional welfare state practices.

The Digital Network Economy

In addition to the work-life issues, the digital economy is also challenging basic market governance. So-called 'network effects' that lead the sector to converge towards 'natural oligopoly' (Economides 1996) sets it at odds with conventional market theory, and established principles of economic regulation.

The tendency toward oligopoly is the result of self-reinforcing growth as more users create incentives for even more users to join. A core driver is the utility a participant derives from complementary goods in the network. A common example is a PC operating system: to be successful an operating system needs both users and vendors of complementary application programs. Likewise, communication platforms like Google, Facebook, Twitter, and the like, steadily increase the offers of available products that attract more customers.

The increasing number of customers, in turn, creates growing attraction to marketers. Since the value for customers and for marketers increases with increasing size, smaller actors will soon lose out. This in turn, gives the IT oligopolist the financial muscle to acquire innovations that further augment the attractiveness of their network, which of course again attracts more customers and so on.[2]

The 'natural oligopoly' that characterizes the (equilibrium) market structure of the digital network economy has radical implications for competition policy. The ability of antitrust authorities to alter market structure in such industries is limited as strong antitrust intervention could generate very significant losses for society. Besides the network effects, the innovative character of digi-tech also speaks against strong regulation. The potential damage that antitrust intervention can produce is larger when it is applied to an industry with rapid technological change, where leaps to new and more efficient technologies are expected while the specific nature of the future winning technology is unknown. Often, it is just plain difficult to predict future winning technologies and therefore very hard to fashion an antitrust remedy with an accurate prediction of its effect on industry structure and competition a few years down the road (Economides 1996). The digital network economy, therefore, represents a conundrum for economic governance.

Digital Surveillance Capitalism

On top of their problematic effect on market competition, business models of the digital network oligopolies have unwelcome implications for individual privacy. Following an early period of digital network expansion – with limited generation of revenue and a major fall in stock prices as the dot-com bubble burst – the network industry finally found its core business model: monetizing data on people's network communication. These data proved to be a highly attractive channel for marketing. Not only could marketers reach billions of consumers with hardly any transaction costs, but one could also personalize special messages to targeted groups. As algorithms were designed to automatize sales of communicating-customer information, a massive new industry was born, estimated to have generated over $333 billion in 2019 (Emarketer nd).

The American sociologist, Shoshana Zuboff, has characterized this development as "surveillance capitalism" a "radically dis-embedded and extractive variant of 'information capitalism'", based on the commodification of "reality" and its transformation into behavioural data for analysis and sales. She argues that hidden mechanisms of extraction, commodification, and control threaten core values such as freedom, democracy, and privacy (Zuboff 2016, 2019). According to Zuboff, surveillance capitalism has been pioneered at Google and later Facebook, in much the same way that mass-production and managerial capitalism were pioneered at Ford and General Motors a century earlier, and has now become the dominant form of information capitalism. Zuboff argues that while industrial capitalism exploited nature, surveillance capitalism exploits human nature. If that is the case, the dis-embedded nature of capitalism has reached its apogee. The governance challenges of surveillance capitalism are evident. Users of digital media, which means most of us engaged in everything from sharing intimate feelings, to seeking health information or shopping, are systematically registered and internet privacy is a luxury for advanced cryptologists. In spite of emerging legislation such as the General Data Protection Regulation (GDPR) in the EU, the options offered on many websites are frequently absurdly complex, and often leaves the visitor with little choice. On the other hand, the revenue streams from selling personal data on internet behaviour are critical to financing the internet-world, the backbone of digital modernity.

Besides the commercial exploitation of private net-behaviour, such data has also been exploited for political purposes. The Cambridge Analytica scandal has become an iconic case. The personal data of millions of Facebook users was harvested without consent by the firm Cambridge Analytica, predominantly to be used for political advertising. Cambridge Analytica sold the data of American voters to political campaigns, providing assistance and analytics to Donald Trump's 2016 presidential campaign in particular.

The Digital Challenge to Governance – Concluding Reflections

Digitalization raises a broad set of challenges, reflecting the technology's deep penetration into society – from work-life to communication and civil rights. The transformative character of digital technology indicates that governance cannot be a simple matter of regulatory intervention, but must involve innovation and learning such that adequate governance solutions emerge over time.

Yet governance may be a cornerstone in determining the direction of technological development and its social consequences – dictating if, for instance, the robotization of work turns out to be a curse or a blessing. Under one type of governance, it may lead to a race to the bottom, where workers are thrust naked into the gig economy, and profits accrue to a few oligopolists. Under another governance regime, however, the huge productivity benefits can be used to give everyone a better life, as this book shows in a later chapter.

The privacy issues related to implicit digital surveillance also demonstrate governance-complexity, where private business and public authorities clearly must work together to exploit the benefits and evade the downsides of digital communication. Besides a striking a balance between commercial interest and privacy issues, wise governance is needed in order to avoid placing our democracy in peril.

Notes

1 The 9 countries are Australia, Canada, Germany, France, Italy, Japan, Spain, the United Kingdom, and the United States. The other series include respectively the Republic of Korea (10 countries), Mexico (11 countries), and Turkey (12 countries).
2 In many ways, the digital network economy turns the conventional economy upside down and breaks with the so-called law of demand which is traditionally considered to hold for almost all goods. This law states that at a higher price consumers will demand a lower quantity of a good, which is in turn derived from the law of diminishing marginal utility; the fact that consumers use economic goods to satisfy their most urgent needs first. However, the existence of network effects implies that, as more units are sold, the willingness to pay for the last unit may be higher. This follows as increased sales of a network good imply an expansion in the sales of complementary goods, whereupon the value of the last unit increases – while creating more interesting opportunities for consumers, and more consumers for marketers.

References

Aftenposten (2019) 27 Sept 2 'Foodora-streiken er avsluttet – ble enige om tariffavtale etter 14 timers mekling' (the Foodora-strike has ended – agreement reached after 14 hours of mediation).
Autor, D. and Salomons, A. (2017) Does Productivity Growth Threaten Employment? Robocalypse Now? European Central Bank. https://www.ecb.europa.eu/pub/conferences/shared/pdf/20170626_ecb_forum/D_Autor_A_Salomons_Does
Bensinger, G. (2019) *Uber: The Ride-Hailing App That Says It Has 'Zero' Drivers. Washington Post.* 14 October.
Bowe, M. (2018) Foodora delivery rider classed as an employee wins unfair dismissal case. Colin Biggers and Paisley Lawyers. https://www.cbp.com.au/insights/insights/2018/november/foodora-delivery-rider-classed-as-an-employee-wins Accessed November 2020.
Brynjolfsson, E. and McAfee, A. (2014) *The Second Machine Age: Work, Progress and Prosperity in a Time of Brilliant Technologies.* New York: W.W. Norton.
Cramer-Flood, E. (2020) Global Ecommerce 2020: Ecommerce Decelerates amid Global Retail Contraction but Remains a Bright Spot. Emarketer.com.
Economides, N. (1996) The Economics of Networks. *International Journal of Industrial Organization* 14, http://neconomides.stern.nyu.edu/networks/Economides_Economics_of_Networks.pdf
Emarketing (nd): 'What's Shaping the Digital Ad Market' https://www.emarketer.com/content/global-digital-ad-spending-2019 Accessed November 2020.
Henley, J. (2017) Uber clashes with regulators around the world. *The Guardian,* 29 Sept. https://www.theguardian.com/business/2017/sep/29/uber-clashes-with-regulators-in-cities-around-the-world Accessed November 2020.
ILO and OECD (2015) The Labour Share in G20 Economies. Report prepared for the G20 Employment Working Group.
Karabarbounis, L. and Neiman, B. (2014) Labour shares, inequality and the *relative* price of capital. Vox EU, https://voxeu.org/article/labour-shares-inequality-and-relative-price-capital

Kaine, S. and Josserand, E. (2016) Workers are taking on more risk in the gig economy. *The Conversation*. 6 July. Available at: https://theconversation.com/workers-are-taking-onmore-risk-in-the-gig-economy-61797 Accessed November 2020.

Krugman, P. (2013) Sympathy for the Luddites. *New York Times*, 14 June. https://www.nytimes.com/2013/06/14/opinion/krugman-sympathy-for-the-luddites.html Accessed November 2020.

Macmillan, D. and Fleisher, L. (2015) 'How Sharp-Elbowed Uber Is Trying to Make Nice' *The Wall Street Journal*. https://web.archive.org/web/2017032 0052630/https://www.wsj.com/articles/hard-driving-uber-gives-compromise-a-try-1422588782 Accessed November 2020.

Martin, H-P and Schumann, H. (1997) *The Global Trap*. London: Zed Books.

Moravec, H. (1995) 'Superhumanism' Interview in *Wired* https://www.wired.com/1 995/10/moravec/ Accessed November 2020.

Oana, S.H. (2015) Classical, Neoclassical and New Classical Theories and Their Impact on Macroeconomic Modelling. *Precedia Economics and Finance* 23.

OECD (2015) 'The Labour Share in G20 Economies' Report prepared for the G20 Employment Working Group Antalya, Turkey, 26–27 February 2015. https://www.oecd.org/g20/topics/employment-and-social-policy/The-Labour-Share-in-G20-Economies.pdf Accessed November 2020.

OECD (nd) Indicators: Labour force participation rate https://data.oecd.org/emp/labour-force-participation-rate.htm#indicator-chart Accessed November 2020.

Pereira, D. (2020) The Uber Business Model. The Business Model Analyst.

Platt, C. (1995) Superhumanism. *Wired*. 10 January.

Rifkin, J. (1995) *The End of Work*. New York: Putnam Publishers.

Say, J-B (1803) *A Treatise on Political Economy*. https://oll.libertyfund.org/titles/say-a-treatise-on-political-economy

Slee T (2017). *What's Yours is Mine – Against the Sharing Economy*. New York and London: OR Books.

Standing, G (2014) *The Precariate: The New Dangerous Class*. London: Bloomsbury.

Uber (nd) Get in the driver's seat and get paid https://uber.com

Vinge, V. (1993) Technological Singularity. *Whole Earth Review*, Winter.

Walker, E. (2015) The Uber-ization of Activism. *The New York Times*. https://web.archive.org/web/20161218022220/http://www.nytimes.com/2015/08/07/opinion/the-uber-ization-of-activism.html Archived from the original on December 18, 2016. Retrieved February 28, 2017.

Woirol, G. (1996) *The Technological Unemployment and Structural Unemployment Debates*. Westport: Greenwood Publishing Group.

Zuboff, S. (2016) The Secrets of Surveillance Capitalism. *Frankfurter Allgemeine Zeitung*. Accessed February 2017.

Zuboff, S. (2019) *The Age of Surveillance Capitalism: The Fight for the Future at the New Frontier of Power*. London: Profile Books.

4 Financial Challenges

By placing markets centre stage and turning stock value performance into an overriding societal purpose, finance is a showcase of Polanyi's idea of dis-embedded capitalism – a showcase that illustrates finance's potential for driving massive growth, but also its speculative risk and exposure to crisis. Given the sector's formidable scale and scope, a major challenge to governance is: Has the financial industry grown too large to fail and too big to govern? Or, even worse, has it achieved governance in reverse, where finance governs the state and society and not the other way around?

Too Large to Fail, Too Big to Govern?

Unleashed by deregulation and globalization, finance has stood out, generating huge growth and aggressive commercialization. In a broad definition of the financial sector,[1] its GDP share in the United States increased from 23% to 31% from 1990 to 2006, hitting a peak before the financial crisis. Other advanced western nations such as the UK, France, and Germany have followed the same pattern. The figures on profits are even more striking. For example, the financial services industry's share of corporate profits in the United States was around 10% in the early 1980s but peaked at 40% in 2007 (Gudmundsson 2008). The finance sector – even in a more moderate definition – surpassed the manufacturing sector in size as early as the late 1980s (Figure 4.1) (Witko 2016).

With its exponential growth in the 21st century, has finance become a 'cuckoo in the nest'? A cuckoo baby that dictates the conditions, consumes the resources, and squeezes others out? And do we have the governance capacity to deal with it? De-regulation has contributed to this development, by slackening restrictive legislation and thereby allowing massive expansion. This has given the financial industry the capacity to move fairly easily across national boundaries and to relocate to countries with attractive (lack of) regulations. The governance challenge is that finance has increased its bargaining power vis-à-vis regulatory authorities, and that global competition sets limits as to how far one

DOI: 10.4324/9781315454931-4

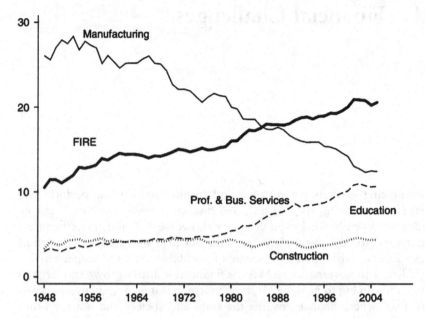

Figure 4.1 Finance as a Share of the Economy.

Source: *Witko, British Journal of Political Science 2016.*

country can go in reining in its financial sector without losing valuable business abroad. As Henderson (2020) remarks: 'In a globalized economy, sovereign states' ability to set their own "rules of the game" is limited by multinational companies' ability to operate across borders'.

With the wisdom of hindsight, after the 2008 financial crisis had hit, Paul Krugman (2009) looked sceptically at the de-regulation of financial markets and the behaviour of financial actors. He noted that the post-Reagan era deregulation of the US financial system had prepared American bankers for "finding sophisticated ways (.....) of hiding risk and fooling investors" (Krugman 2009), p 16 (Quoted from Das 2010). Krugman's statement reflects a general insight pinpointed by another well-known economist, William Baumol, that the economy includes productive, unproductive, and destructive entrepreneurship (Baumol 1990). Allowing the financial sector to exert strong influence over financial governance may therefore not only lead to neglect of societal concerns for pro-sociality, but facilitate non-productive rent-seeking or outright destructive commercial behaviour. As the World Council for Sustainable Development has put it: "Beyond a certain point, 'financialization' fuels inequality and undermines stability, while channelling financial resources into speculation rather than real economy investment and lending" (WBCSD 2020).

A core governance challenge is that finance's dominant position in the economy makes it prone to regulatory capture. According to Johnson and Kwak (2010), before the financial crisis, Wall Street firms largely succeeded in persuading the American political system and regulators to accept the ideology of financial deregulation and the legalization of novel financial instruments. And the trend of lax financial governance was widely followed internationally. Contributions to political campaigns, lobbying, and revolving doors that positioned financial industry leaders in key policy-making and governance roles were some of the means used. The reverse side of the process saw sympathetic senior government officials rewarded with super high-paying Wall Street jobs after their government service. The former International Monetary Fund chief economist, Simon Johnson, went so far as to argue that the increased power and influence of the financial services sector had fundamentally transformed the American polity, endangering representative democracy itself through undue influence on the political system and regulatory capture by the financial oligarchy (Johnson 2009). Under such conditions, re-embedding the economy to serve a balanced combination of societal and commercial interest may seem utopian, not least because of the lack of committed public-interest representation in core governance positions. The governance challenge facing regulatory authorities today is how to reverse this situation. The 'footloose' character of finance makes the threat of exit from unwanted regulation more real than for materially grounded parts of the economy, a fact that strengthens its bargaining power vis-à-vis the state.

The Financial Crisis as a Governance Challenge

The array of problems caused by an over-sized and under-governed financial economy, with biased pro-industrial regulation, became starkly evident when the financial economy collapsed and the world went headlong into crisis in 2008. Under the expansive financial spree facilitated by lax governance in the US, banks had allowed people to take out loans for 100% or more of the value of their new homes. New financial instruments had been developed, supposedly to reduce risk, but in reality obscuring risk exposure. Through innovative financial engineering under lenient public governance, the banks had chopped up the original mortgages and resold them in tranches. The risks were therefore supposedly minimized by the spread of exposure to individual mortgage default, thereby justifying minimalist regulatory intervention. As an extra insurance, credit default swaps were designed to safeguard the investor.

However, although the securitization based on a number of different loans had limited *individual risk* exposure, the products were all exposed to the *general systemic risk* of an over-hyped real estate market. Furthermore, the insurers were undercapitalized, operating in a market unregulated by public authorities (Amadeo 2019). The novel mortgage-backed securities became an attractive product that was sold to investors around the world. Financial institutions in many different countries – including hedge funds, mutual funds, pension funds, corporations, and public enterprises – bought the mortgage-backed securities, apparently with naive confidence in the risk-minimizing and insurance mechanisms and the minimal regulatory oversight. As the housing market started collapsing, however, the market for mortgage-based securities turned into a Black Peter game, where better-informed actors pushed the toxic products onto others who were less informed.

Two major regulatory shortcomings, both facilitated by the strong pro-industry bias, were at the core of this governance failure. The first was a dualist framework that permitted regulatory arbitrage between the regulated sector of depository institutions and the parallel banking system of structured vehicles and investment banking. By governing the first under a relatively strict public interest-oriented regime, the illusion was created that the banking system was subject to sufficient governance. However, by allowing an unregulated 'shadow banking' sector free rein, governance of the financial system as a whole was weakened and became vulnerable.

The second shortcoming was a governance regime that set qualitatively and quantitatively insufficient capital requirements. Under global competitive pressure, public regulators had been pressed to lower standards, resulting in massive costs to society when the system broke down.

The Losses

The losses associated with the financial crisis were huge. The International Monetary Fund (IMF) estimated the loss in GDP, calculated over the first three years of the crisis, as amounting to 23% of GDP in the Euro area and 31% in the US, and the increase in debt as totalling, respectively, 19.9% and 23.6% (Laeven and Valencia 2012).

The crisis affected all the large banking systems, as mortgage-backed securities had been widely sold across international financial networks. But some were worse hit than others. Banks in the euro area, the United Kingdom, and the United States suffered large losses at the height of the crisis, those in Australia, Canada, and Sweden fared better and did not need government capital support. Emerging economy banks were more insulated from the turmoil given their domestic focus, relatively low use of market funding, and generally higher regulatory buffers, the last reflecting in part the lessons of prior financial crises (Bank of International Settlements - BIS 2018).[2]

The financial crisis and the ensuing 'real economy' recession illustrates the dominant influence of finance on the national economy, and the limitations of endogenous market governance. Challenged by the commercial exposure of firms and regulatory competition among nations, such regulation risks spiralling down to a liberalist mimimum. Adding to this, creative product innovation, with hidden systemic risk exposure, tilted this permissive regulatory regime towards disaster.

A long-time advocate for deregulation, the former chair of the Federal Reserve, Alan Greenspan famously admitted to a Congressional committee that he had been "partially wrong" in his hands-off approach towards the banking industry:

> I made a mistake in presuming that the self-interests of organisations, specifically banks and others, were such that they were best capable of protecting their own shareholders and their equity in the firms. (Alan Greenspan, quoted in *The Guardian* 2008)

Greenspan's statement indicates that not only society, but also banks themselves were victims of their own speculative commercial innovation.

Governing Financial Architecture in the Grey Zone

Failing governance has not only allowed excessive risk-taking, but is also enabling the financial industry to challenge states' fiscal basis. As it facilitates commercial transactions across value chains and national borders, global finance holds a key to the information needed to ensure fair taxation. And fair and efficient taxation is essential to modern economies dependent on extensive public infrastructure to provide security, education, industrial regulation as well as health care and social services.

Severe governance deficits are documented in several scandals that reveal that banks are involved in advanced tax planning operations across the grey zone between legal and criminal practice: (UBS 2008; Offshore leaks 2013; Bowers 2014; Caruana Galizia et al. 2015; Panama Papers 2016). The leaks detailed the intermediary role of global financial institutions in setting up shell companies, foundations, and trusts to ease tax avoidance for their clients. These revelations have been corroborated by statistics that record the highly lucrative nature of such practice: In a study of EU banks' foreign affiliates, Bouvatier et al. (2017) found that while tax havens represented 0.8% of their sample in terms of population and 2% in terms of GDP, they accounted for 18% of the turnover and 29% of the profits recorded abroad.

Their over-expansion into tax havens indicates how banks are central facilitators of financial architectures that serve to weaken public institutions by minimizing tax payments by multinationals and rich individuals. Present governance regimes allow these architectures to exploit the legal loopholes of states through complex arrangements which make it possible to avoid paying taxes. As financial flows are increasingly becoming paperless and the economy going digital, complex tax transactions are facilitated and prosocial governance weakened, making fair societal sharing in value creation increasingly difficult.

Tax minimizing and money laundering is traditionally associated with tax havens like Jersey, the Cayman Islands, Bermuda, and the British Virgin Islands, which are open about zero rates of taxation. To counteract the flow of money from their own taxation base, many governments have limited bilateral tax treaties that allow tax planning to take place. The governance challenge is, however, that advanced tax planning often involves complicated arrangements in several steps across various new corporate tax 'havens' until the money finally ends up in a zero tax zone.

In such arrangements new corporate tax havens – featuring respectable nations such as the Netherlands and Ireland who have large networks of bilateral tax treaties – often serve as 'conduits' to traditional tax havens (Boffey 2017). The tax governance problem is that advanced tax minimizing architectures enable corporates to achieve 'effective' tax rates closer to zero, not just in the haven itself but in all countries with which the haven has tax treaties, putting those countries on tax haven lists.

According to modern studies, the Top 10 tax havens include corporate-focused havens like the Netherlands, Singapore, Ireland, and the UK, while Luxembourg, Hong Kong, the Caribbean (the Caymans, Bermuda, and the British Virgin Islands), and Switzerland feature as both major traditional tax havens and major corporate tax havens (Wikipedia 2020). With the lack of internationally coordinated governance, there are strong incentives for corporations and the financial industry to entice governments into a race to the bottom.

At the core of the governance challenge in international corporate taxation is the practice of "Base erosion and profit shifting" (BEPS) where legal financial experts help multinationals 'shift' profits from higher-tax jurisdictions to lower-tax jurisdictions, thus eroding the tax base of the higher-tax jurisdictions (Gumpert et al. 2016).

The problem is that international tax governance lacks efficient control of the core mechanisms made use of in globalized tax minimization such as:

> *Inversion,* where a corporation restructures itself so that the current parent is replaced by a foreign parent, and the original parent company becomes a subsidiary of the foreign parent; thus moving its tax residence to the foreign country.

> *Transfer pricing,* where a multinational adjusts the internal prices at which its affiliates trade with each other across borders, in order to minimise profits in the high-tax countries and maximize them in corporate tax havens.

> *Earnings stripping,* for example, a US parent's subsidiary in a low-tax jurisdiction can lend to its subsidiary in a high-tax jurisdiction,

with the interest deductible as a business expense because the high-tax jurisdiction recognizes the firm as a separate corporation.

The favoured domiciles for the new partners are Ireland, the Netherlands, Switzerland, the United Kingdom, and Canada, which all have relatively low corporate tax rates and a so-called 'territorial tax system', which does not tax foreign source income.

The "Double Irish, Dutch sandwich" method that became highly popular with US firms may serve as an example of the tax-evading ingenuity that undercuts efficient taxation governance. In this arrangement, the US firm transfers its intangible assets to an Irish holding company. The Irish company has a sales subsidiary that sells advertising (the source of Google's revenues) to Europe. However, sandwiched between the Irish holding company and the Irish sales subsidiary is a Dutch subsidiary, which collects royalties from the sales subsidiary and transfers them to the Irish holding company. The Irish holding company claims that the company's management (and thus its tax home) for purposes of determining its corporate income tax, is in Bermuda, which has a zero percent tax rate. The addition of a Dutch sandwich to the double Irish scheme further reduces tax liabilities because Ireland does not levy withholding tax on certain receipts from EU member states. There are also equivalent Luxembourgish and Swiss sandwiches (Wikipedia 2020). Companies such as Amazon, Apple, Facebook, GE, Google, IBM, Microsoft, and Starbucks have all used this scheme.

Weak international governance and the flourishing of tax haven arrangements that it allows is a product of competition between nation-states. While formally they have exclusive legal competence over tax policy, their actual capacity to design their tax systems according to national political preferences has long been eroded by corporate financial maneuvering in the global economy.

Under conditions of an open economy, governance based on national political autonomy to organize a socially fair and efficient taxation system can only be regained if the states do not simply adapt themselves to tax competition individually, but regulate tax competition collectively. However, such common strategies are hard to forge, even at the EU level, not to speak of amongst OECD countries.

In spite of initiatives like the EU's Anti Tax Avoidance Package, the attempts to adopt a "Common Consolidated Corporate Tax Base" (CCCTB), and the OECD's anti-BEPS initiative, effective political governance is lagging behind financial creativity, and corporate taxes have been falling (Figure 4.2).

Again, the diversity of interests across nations with their own specific vested interests prevents collective action to govern the global economy. Even a first step of providing open information on ultimate ownership and money flows has raised major controversies, and acting upon it in

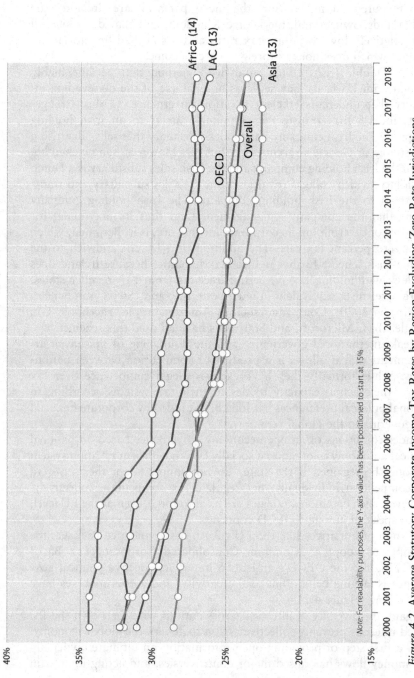

Figure 4.2 Average Statutory Corporate Income Tax Rates by Region Excluding Zero-Rate Jurisdictions.

Source: OECD 2019: Corporate Tax Statistics First Edition: https://www.oecd.org/tax/tax-policy/corporate-tax-statistics-database-first-edition.pdf.

order to devise a fairer system of taxation lies, at best, a long way ahead. De-regulation under asymmetric globalization has ended up without efficient regulatory intervention – the tax evasion schemes are examples of regulatory failure – and leads to underfunding of prosocial and sustainability-oriented investments.

Governing Digital Finance

While the financial crisis and the subsequent recession revealed major regulatory and strategic flaws in the traditional financial sector, the last decade has also seen the emergence of new digital actors with the potential to not only disrupt conventional financial models, but also to undermine traditional financial governance. Effort to re-embed the financial system must therefore also address governance of the new financial arenas, some of them created by the technology giants looking for new market outlets.

Tech giants approach financial services delivery from a number of different 'fintech' starting points. Firms like Microsoft, Apple, and Google are application- and data-centric, entering into financial cloud computing from a technology and data management perspective. In contrast, ecommerce firms like Amazon and Alibaba have a focus on creating a frictionless customer experience, such as using customer data to better manage credit risk and working capital.

While technology companies could allow more people access to financial transactions, their business models raise extensive governance challenges when it comes to privacy, competition, and market-concentration issues. As mentioned in the previous chapter, the massive and non-transparent commercial use of personal information on web platforms such as Google and Facebook raises serious concerns about privacy. If this information becomes widely available in banking, unacceptable discrimination might ensue.

The relationship between the new fintech players and the banking sector is also a point of governance concern. Depending on banks' capability to adapt their business models, fintech innovations could represent a competitive threat to some banks or bank business lines, or conversely, they may provide banks with an opportunity to improve customer experience or significantly lower their fixed costs. The creative development of new financial products in the run-up to the financial crisis indicates that there is a great potential for creative innovation if the strategic interests of technology and financial players could be aligned. However, the complexity that this might unleash could lead to vulnerabilities in the financial system and undercut current present governance arrangements. The IMF warns that "significant disruption to the financial landscape is likely to come from the big tech firms, who will use their enormous customer bases and deep pockets to offer financial products based on big data and artificial intelligence" (Detrixhe 2019).

How to Govern Crypto-Currencies[3]

Moving into currency creation, the fintech industry is not only challenging established banks but regulatory authorities as well. Cryptocurrencies use decentralized control through distributed ledger technology, typically a blockchain, that serves as a public financial transaction database. This is opposed to centralized digital currency and central banking systems, thus contesting role of national banks and their currency monopolies. In contrast to traditional currencies, the system does not require a central authority; it is maintained through distributed consensus. This poses the question of how to govern a monetary system that lacks both corporate governance and public regulatory access.

There are several areas where using cryptocurrencies may be superior to fiat money. According to the European Banking Authority (EBA) (2014), these include micropayments, international payments, and payments in countries with unstable currencies. However, the governance risks, in the eyes of the EBA, are manifold. They include the fact that a virtual/cryptocurrency scheme can be created and then its function changed by anyone, and in the case of decentralized schemes such as Bitcoins, by anyone with a sufficient share of computational power. Other issues are that payer and payee can remain anonymous and that virtual/cryptocurrency schemes do not respect jurisdictional boundaries and may therefore undermine financial sanctions and seizure of assets.

As market participants lack sound corporate governance arrangements, bitcoins and other forms of cryptocurrency are becoming widely used in dark markets for money laundering and drug crime, putting pressure on law enforcement agencies around the world. United Nations investigation has also detected crypto-currencies used by rogue nations to evade international sanctions. For example, the UN has found North Korea engaging in "mining of cryptocurrency both through attacks on exchanges and users and mining of cryptocurrencies, which has become a source of funds for a professional branch of the military". The experts stressed that implementing these increasingly sophisticated attacks "is low risk and high yield", often requiring just a laptop computer and access to the internet.

The Case of Libra

The launch of Libra in 2019, spearheaded by Facebook, represents a major move towards a new private currency with strong crypto-elements and extensive governance challenges. On June 18, 2019, the tech giant announced its intention to offer its users a payment service with its own currency. This attempt marked the first time that a private currency has tried to compete with traditional sovereign currencies (Finance Watch 2019).

With respect to governance, U.S. regulators and politicians expressed concerns about the issue before the mid-2019 announcement. The European Banking Authority has previously evinced a generally critical attitude towards virtual and cryptocurrencies. The EBA recommends that EU legislators consider declaring market participants at the direct interface between conventional and virtual currencies – such as virtual currency exchanges – 'obliged entities' under the EU's Anti Money Laundering Directive. They would thus be subject to its anti-money laundering and counter-terrorist financing requirements.

Governance for Social Embedding of Fintech

Emerging as the ink had barely dried on the last financial crisis – in part due to creative product innovation with a disregard of risk – fintech and cryptocurrencies represent new innovative initiatives that are resistant to governance. That they promise societal benefits – such as allowing better access to banking for people in regions with under-developed banking infrastructure – is hard to dispute. Mobile banking and evolution of digital transfer technology may make it possible to minimize arbitrage and facilitate entrepreneurship in the Global South. On the other hand, sluicing large money streams through non-transparent channels facilitates criminal entrepreneurship, endangers public finances, and exposes regular business to unfair competition.

In addition to the complexity of governing a rapidly innovating field, asymmetric globalization – globalized markets in the context of nationalized/regionalized governance – makes the governance task even harder.

The Corona Crisis as a Financial Challenge

As the corona pandemic hit the economy, its financial impact has become a, if not *the*, major challenge of our time. Just over a decade after the financial crisis, the pandemic reminds again us of the need to build economic resilience into the governance regime.

Initially unleashed in China and neighbouring Asiatic countries, the pandemic then spread to the West, followed by outbreaks, and societal lockdowns in the Americas, and in Africa, and has had massive effects of a truly global nature. The financial effects arise because large parts of the population have cut back on socializing – including travel, eating out, etc. – prompted by lockdowns undertaken by governments, but also by individual attempts to avoid contagion.

The crisis has been aggravated by the fact that, after initial repression of the virus due to the lockdown, many countries experienced second and third waves of Covid-19 as they started opening society to a more normal life. This indicated that severe restrictions on social life, and their economic consequences, were likely to persist until massive vaccination is completed.

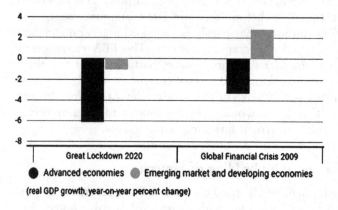

Figure 4.3 Global Crisis.

Source: Gopinath, IMF 2020:'The Great Lockdown: Worst Economic Downturn Since the Great Depression' IMF blog. https://blogs.imf.org/2020/04/14/the-great-lockdown-worst-economic-downturn-since-the-great-depression/.

The Projected Financial Losses Due to Pandemic

The Covid-19 crisis has posed enormous challenges to economic governance. Both the IMF and the OECD published early analyses of the economic impacts with dire predictions. According to an early IMF study in April 2020 (IMF 2020), the advanced economies were likely to experience a massive recession, with contraction of -6.1% in 2020. The Euro area was likely to be harder hit (-7.5%) than the US (-5.9%). In the double-hit scenario where a second wave of infections hit before the end of 2020, world economic output was estimated to plummet 7.6% for 2020, and the unemployment rate in OECD countries would nearly double to 10% with little recovery in jobs by 2021. Furthermore, the Covid-19 crisis has struck both the developed and developing world alike, as opposed to the financial meltdown a decade ago, (Figure 4.3).

The Challenge

In spite of an emerging recovery in the wake of vaccination, the Covid-19 pandemic and its economic aftermath poses immense challenges to economic governance. As numerous sectors of the economy, such as travel and tourism, culture & the arts, and retailing have been spiralling downwards into bankruptcy, there has been a need for massive financial transfers to the unemployed and threatened businesses. The neoliberal formula of privatization and competitive exposure is partly counterproductive under such conditions, and has had to be supplemented with massive public transfers to inject more resilience into the economy. As we will argue in later chapters, this necessitates strong state engagement and ambidexterity across the public and private divide.

Notes

1 Finance, insurance and real estate (FIRE).
2 Report prepared by a Working Group established by the Committee on the Global Financial System. The Group was chaired by Claudia Buch (Deutsche Bundesbank) and B. Gerard Dages (Federal Reserve Bank of New York), January 2018.
3 A cryptocurrency (or crypto currency) is a digital asset designed to work as a medium of exchange that uses strong cryptography to secure financial transactions, control the creation of additional units, and verify the transfer of assets (Wikipedia Cryptocurrency 2020).

References

Amadeo, K. (2019) Causes of the 2008 Global Financial Crisis. *The Balance*. https://www.thebalance.com/what-caused-2008-global-financial-crisis-3306176 Accessed November 2020.

Bank of International Settlements - BIS (2018). CGFS Papers No 60 Structural Changes in Banking after the Crisis.

Baumol, W.J. (1990) Entrepreneurship: Productive, Unproductive, and Destructive. *Journal of Political Economy* 98(5), Part 1.

Boffey, D. (2017) Netherlands and UK are biggest channels for corporate tax avoidance. *The Guardian*, 25 July.

Bouvatier, V., Capelle-Blancard, G. and Delatte, A-L (2017) Banks in Tax Havens: First Evidence Based on Country-by-Country Reporting. European Commission. https://ec.europa.eu/info/sites/info/files/dp_055_en.pdf.

Caruana Galizia, M, Carvajal, R, Cabra Mar, Díaz-Struck, E, Garcia Rey, M, Fitzgibbon, W, Reuter, D, Gallego, C.S, and Boland-Rudder, H (2015). Explore the Swiss Leaks DataInternational consortium of Investigative Journalists 8 February. https://www.icij.org/investigations/swiss-leaks/explore-swiss-leaks-data/.

Bowers, S. Luxembourg tax files: how tiny state rubber-stamped tax avoidance on an industrial scale. https://www.theguardian.com/business/2014/nov/05/-sp-luxembourg-tax-files-tax-avoidance-industrial-scale.

Clark, A. and Treanor, J. (2008) Greenspan – I was wrong about the economy. Sort of. *The Guardian*. 24 October.

Das, D. (2010) *Financial Globalization – Growth, Integration, Innovation and Crisis*. London: Palgrave Macmillan.

Detrixhe, J. (2019) The IMF is worried that big tech could make the financial system less stable. *Quartz*. 10 June.

European Banking Authority (2014) EBA opinion on 'virtual currencies', European Banking Authority, 4 July. https://eba.europa.eu/sites/default/documents/files/documents/10180/657547/81409b94–4222-45d7-ba3b-7deb5863ab57/EBA-Op-2014-08%20Opinion%20on%20Virtual%20Currencies.pdf?retry=1 Accessed November 2020.

Finance Watch (2019) Libra: Heads I win – tails you lose: Ten reasons why Facebook's Libra is a bad idea. https://www.finance-watch.org/wp-content/uploads/2019/07/Libra-Paper_Finance-Watch_EN.pdf.

Gopinath, G. (2020) The Great Lockdown: Worst Economic Downturn Since the Great Depression IMF blog. https://blogs.imf.org/2020/04/14/the-great-lockdown-worst-economic-downturn-since-the-great-depression/ Accessed October 2020.

Gudmundsson, M. (2008). How might the current financial crisis shape financial sector regulation and structure? Address to the Financial Technology Conference, Boston, 23 September 2008. https://www.bis.org/speeches/sp081119.htm.

Gumpert, A., Hines, J. and Schnitzer, M. (2016) Multinational Firms and Tax Havens. *The Review of Economics and Statistics* 98(4). https://repository.law.umich.edu/cgi/viewcontent.cgi?article=2831&context=articles.

Henderson, R. (2020) *Reimagining Capitalism in a World of Fire*. New York: Hachette Book Group.

International Consortium of Investigative Journalists (2013) *ICIJ Releases Offshore Leaks Database Revealing Names Behind Secret Companies, Trusts*. Washington: ICIJ.

International Consortium of Investigative Journalists (2014) *Explore the Documents: Luxembourg Leaks Database*. Washington: ICIJ.

International Consortium of Investigative Journalists (2015) *Swiss Leaks: Murky Cash Sheltered by Bank Secrecy*. Washington: ICIJ.

International Consortium of Investigative Journalists (2016) *The Panama Papers: Exposing the Rogue Offshore Finance Industry*. Washington: ICIJ.

IMF - International Monetary Fund (2020) *World Economic Outlook*: 'The Great Lockdown'. https://www.imf.org/en/Publications/WEO/Issues/2020/04/14/weo-april-2020 Accessed October 2020..

Johnson, S. (2009) The Quiet Coup. *The Atlantic Monthly*, May. https://www.theatlantic.com/author/simon-johnson/ Accessed November 2020.

Johnson, S. and Kwak, J. (2010) *13 Bankers: The Wall Street Takeover and the Next Financial Meltdown*. New York: Pantheon Books.

Krugman, P. (2009).Revenge of the Glut, Opinion New York Times 1 March. New York.

Laeven, L. and Valencia, F. (2012) Systemic Banking Crises Database: An Update: IMF Working Paper, Research Department, WP/12/163. https://www.imf.org/external/pubs/ft/wp/2012/wp12163.pdf.

OECD (2019) Corporate Tax Statistics First Edition. https://www.oecd.org/tax/tax-policy/corporate-tax-statistics-database-first-edition.pdf.

WBCSD (2020) *Reinventing Capitalism: A Transformation Agenda*. World Business Council for Sustainable Development Visions 2050 issue brief 32. https://docs.wbcsd.org/2020/11/WBCSD_Reinventing_Capitalism_Vision_2050_Issue_Brief.pdf.

Witko, C. (2016) The Politics of Financialization in the United States, 1949–2005. *British Journal of Political Science* 46(2).

Wikipedia: Tax havens (2020) https://en.wikipedia.org/wiki/Tax_haven Accessed October 2020.

Wikipedia Cryptocurrency (2020) https://en.wikipedia.org/wiki/Cryptocurrency Accessed October 2020.

5 Ecological Challenges

The Climate Challenge in the Age of the Anthropocene

The impact of the massive human population enjoying industrial modernity, with the enormous resource demands and emissions that that entails, has led to a redefinition of our time as the era of the 'Anthropocene'. The Anthropocene depicts Earth's most recent geologic time period as human-influenced, or anthropogenic, based on overwhelming global evidence that atmospheric, geologic, hydrologic, biospheric, and other earth system processes are now being altered by humans (Encyclopedia of the Earth, 2020).[1]

The knowledge that human activity now rivals geological forces in influencing the trajectory of the Earth System has challenging implications for governance of the economy, as it must factor in ecological sustainability in addition to striking a balanced solution between social and economic concerns. Thus re-embedding is transformed from a dilemma into a trilemma.

The governance regimes of the 20th century industrial societies prioritised sealing a social compromise with dynamic but disruptive market forces, and as a result, saw the material wealth of humankind explode beyond all previous imagining. GDP per capita increased 10-fold in Western Europe and 'Western Offshoots" (Figure 5.1) as the population left behind the realm of necessity and entered the realm of freedom in which production was no longer made up largely of the necessities of survival, but of conveniences and luxuries (DeLong 2000).

This huge growth in material consumption has been reinforced by accompanying population growth, and together they have started transforming our planet's ecological boundaries. Following dramatic population rises in the early 20th century, there was a widespread belief in the 1960s and '70s that population growth was reaching unsustainable proportions. *The Population Bomb*, a best-selling book written by Stanford University Professor Paul R. Ehrlich and his wife, Anne Ehrlich, in 1968, was symptomatic of this outlook. It predicted worldwide famine in the 1970s and '80s due to overpopulation, as well as other major societal upheavals, and advocated immediate action to limit population growth. The challenges were seen as twofold: 1) Food production would not be sufficient to feed

DOI: 10.4324/9781315454931-5

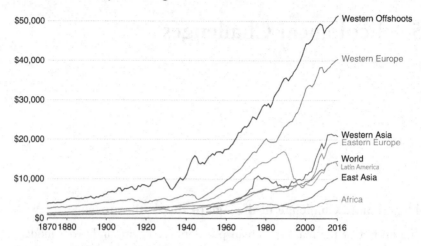

Figure 5.1 GDP per Capita.[2]

Source: Out World in Data, building on the (Maddison Project Database/2018).

https://ourworldindata.org/economic-growth.

https://www.rug.nl/ggdc/historicaldevelopment/maddison/releases/maddison-project-database-2 018?lang=en.

the rising population; and 2) the growing population was placing escalating strains on all aspects of the natural world. Following these concerns, strong governance initiatives were taken in China, which initiated its one-child policy in 1979. The Indian government also introduced strong family planning initiatives with sterilization in return for economic incentives (Dragger, *New York Times* 2011).

However, since its peak in the mid-1960s, population growth has come down rapidly from an annual growth rate of 2.1% to one of around 1% in 2020. For the last half-century, therefore, we have lived in a world in which the population growth rate has been declining, while the population itself is still growing as result of previous expansion. The UN projects that this decline will continue in the coming decades, but that the global population will grow to around 11 billion by the end of this century.

Although we are on the way to a new balance, the more than 6-fold increase of the world population over the last century has already amplified humanity's impact on the natural environment. To provide space, food, and resources for a large global population in a way that is sustainable into the distant future is without question one of the most serious governance challenges of the 21st century, not least because of expectations for economic catchup by the billions of inhabitants in low- and middle-income countries. Of particular concern is the remaining strong population growth in Africa, which is predicted to approach Asia in population size by the end of the century. In many places in Africa, the population is already is under great duress and staging massive migration.[3]

Pressing the Planetary Boundaries

The huge growth in population, combined with increasing welfare expectations has led to a rising recognition among natural scientists that the pressure exerted by humanity on eco-systems increases the risk of generating large-scale abrupt or irreversible environmental changes. Changes that could turn the Earth system into states detrimental or catastrophic for human development (Rockström et al. 2009; Steffen et al. 2018).

As a diagnostic tool for measuring the world's ecosystem balance, the group has developed a planetary boundary model with a focus on nine processes that regulate the stability and resilience of the Earth system. The framework proposes precautionary quantitative planetary boundaries within which humanity can continue to develop and thrive, also referred to as a 'safe operating space'.

The nine processes include (1) climate change; (2) change in biosphere integrity; (3) stratospheric ozone depletion; (4) ocean acidification; (5) biogeochemical flows — interference with phosphorus (P) and nitrogen (N) cycles; (6) land system change; (7) freshwater use; (8) atmospheric aerosol loading; and (9) introduction of novel entities such as new substances or modified life forms (Figure 5.2).

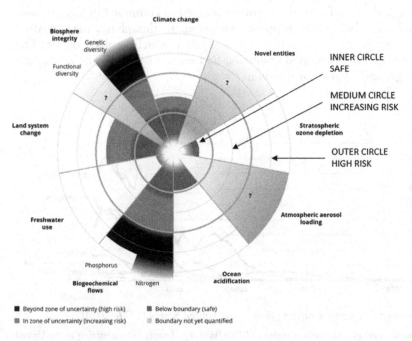

Figure 5.2 The Planetary Boundary Model.

Source: European Environmental Agency (2019)*The European environment — state and outlook 2020.* Luxembourg: Publications Office of the European Union: https://www.eea.europa.eu/soer/2020urceEuropean Environmental Agency (2019).

Against this background, the group has estimated that humanity already has overshot the limits that define a safe operating space for four planetary boundaries, namely those for biosphere integrity, climate change, land system change, and biogeochemical flows (Steffen et al. (2018).

The Fossil Legacy

The overshoot of planetary boundaries necessitates a major revision of current governance regimes which must oversee a green transition in industrial societies. One of the serious obstacles, however, is these societies' deep carbon dependence. Since its takeoff in the 19th century, industrial capitalism has been closely coupled to fossil fuels. As illustrated in Figure 5.3 for the U.S., the largest capitalist economy, the industrial economy has been dominantly fuelled by fossil energy since its emergence.

The challenge of steering the economy out of fossil dependency is formidable, as fossil fuel is deeply embedded in layers of industrial history. For over a century, governance has been oriented towards securing a steady fossil energy supply. During the Industrial Revolution demand for coal soared thanks to its use in iron production and as fuel for the rapidly proliferating steam engine. The second industrial revolution exchanged steam for the combustion engine but continued to rely on fossil fuel, this time in the form of petroleum. In this phase, the industrial centre shifted from Europe to the USA which, unlike the leading European industrialised countries, had some of the world's largest underground petroleum reservoirs.

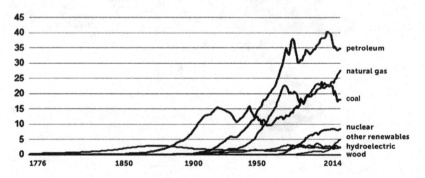

Figure 5.3 Energy Consumption in the United States (1776–2014).

Source: Energy Information Agency (2020) 'History of energy consumption in the United States' https://www.eia.gov/todayinenergy/detail.php?id=10.

After the wells were built to secure a steady supply of oil, the internal combustion engine became the main successor to the steam engine. In turn, the manufacture of automobiles became the largest industry of the 20th century, with the USA as the leading producer. However, while petroleum expanded rapidly in the first half of the 20th century, it did not put the coal industry out of business. Instead, electricity provided a transition for coal from steam to power generation. Thus the market for coal continued to grow throughout the 20th, and well into the current, century.

In the 19th century, natural gas also emerged, used almost exclusively as a source of light. But once effective pipelines began to be built in the 20th century, gas penetrated new markets, including home heating and cooking, appliances such as water heaters and ovens, manufacturing and processing plants, and electricity-generating boilers. In 2020, natural gas supplied more than one-half of the energy consumed by residential and commercial customers, and about 41% of the energy used by the U.S. industry (APA 2020).

In this way, the leading industrial market economies of the 20th century were overwhelmingly fossil-fuel driven, backed up by governance to ensure a reliable supply of fossil energy. The enormous challenge of forging climate-induced green transition can be seen in the fact that despite growth in renewables outpacing the increase in all other forms of energy since 2010, the share of fossil fuels in global primary energy demand still exceeded 80% in 2018 (Table 5.1).

Table 5.1 World Primary Energy Demand by Fuel (Mtoe)

	2000	*2018*
Coal	2317	3821
Oil	3665	4501
Natural Gas	2083	3273
Nuclear	675	709
Renewables	659	1391
Hydro	225	361
Mod. Bioen.	374	737
Other	60	293
Solid Biomass	638	620
Total	10037	14315
Fossil Fuel share	80%	81%

Source: IEA World Energy Outlook 2019, based on table 1.1. Other includes wind, solar, PV, geothermal, concentrating solar power, and marine. Solid biomass includes its traditional use in three-stone fires and in improved cookstoves.

Advancing green development through strong governance initiatives may, even if successful, only provide a coating on top of entrenched layers of pro-fossil governance. The regression to even stronger fossil energy dependence over the last decades apparently underwrites John Gray's pessimistic conclusion that "there is no Green energy mix that can sustain industrialization in a world of high and rising human numbers" (Gray 2009). Furthermore, It is still the case that fossil subsidies massively outweigh support for green energy (Taylor 2020).

With major sectors of the economy directly dependent on fossil energy, transforming the world's market economy into a model of ecological sustainability is a massive governance challenge. It means largely exiting fossil fuels while developing alternative substitutes. Some of the revenue that would then need to be replaced would be revenue from oil & gas exploration and production ($3.3 trillion); revenue from (largely petroleum fuelled) car manufacturing and sales ($2.9 trillion, and $3.1 trillion) as well as income from auto parts manufacturing: ($2.2 trillion) (IBIS 2020). Other important sectors of the global 142 trillion dollar economy are dependent on energy supply. Given the massive investments in fossil fuel that have already been made, transition out of fossil fuels also implies large stranded assets, as a significant amount of oil, gas, and coal reserves would need to be left untouched in the ground.

The projected scenarios by the International Energy Agency for fossil fuel dependency and carbon emissions indicate the challenge of the carbon lock-in, and the difficulty of forging policies for transition (Figure 5.4). As of 2020, the actual energy transition policies when

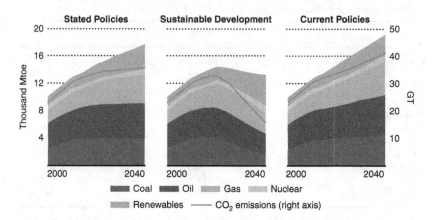

Figure 5.4 World Primary Energy Demand by Fuel and Related CO_2 Emissions by Scenario.

Source: World Enery Outlook 2019, figure 1.1, World Energy Outlook. Mtoe = million tonnes of oil equivalent; Gt = gigatonnes. Other includes wind, solar PV, geothermal, concentrating solar power, and marine.

summed up across the world imply an extensive *increase* in coal, oil, and gas consumption as well as in CO_2 emissions. Thus the 'stated policies' will continue both fossil and CO_2 growth. The sustainable development scenario that is needed to reach the Paris Agreement goals is far ahead of policy commitments.

The Covid pandemic, and subsequent massive economic downturn, have set a downward trend for carbon emissions. However, as with the financial crisis, this is likely to be temporary unless strong governance initiatives are able to re-set the economy in a green direction.

Transport, a Critical Sector

The governance challenge in green re-setting of the economy is not only political, but also technological. Transport illustrates the scale of the problem. In this sector, fossil dependency is closely linked to the technical advantage of fossil energies which makes it difficult to find non-fossil substitutes. Diesel and gasoline are unique when it comes to energy density per volume unit (Megajoule per litre). They are only beaten by liquid hydrogen, which scores low on energy density per litre, however.

Biofuel, while displaying similar characteristics to petroleum, has shortcomings, both ecological and with respect to providing adequate quanta. Battery technology, which is essential for powering upcoming electric mobility, has made rapid improvement, but still has some way to go before reaching commercial maturity in transport applications.

Rethinking governance for orchestrating a path out of petroleum in the transport sector therefore involves enormous technological innovation and deployment strategies to improve on alternative mobile power supplies like electric batteries or hydrogen powered fuel cells. As the transport sector contributes around one quarter of global CO_2 emissions, transport matters.

From Dilemma to Trilemma

The huge human influence on the biosphere demands that economic governance in the 21st century takes ecology into account. Solutions that could be found by balancing social against economic concerns are insufficient. Now both concerns have to be rebalanced against a third, ecological dimension.

The governance challenge is that the added concern for the environment appears to take attractive options off the table. Instead of expanding livelihoods in mining villages under the carbon economy, ecological concerns dictate shutdowns and economic and social disruption for the coal industry. Instead of expanding highways to promote the car industry and travel opportunities, with all the business, jobs, and spinoffs involved, ecological concerns motivate limitation and decline of highway construction and auto industries. For many businesses, workers and communities, ecological concerns, therefore, imply austerity imposed on their value creation and welfare. The benefits of rescuing the planet from climate change lie, at best, far ahead for future generations.

Sustainability-oriented governance initiatives, therefore, need to break out of the austerity perspective and the traditional industrial mindset. They need to seek out new opportunities that ecological considerations bring. The governance challenge is therefore to legitimate ecological transformation with a 'green growth' approach, such that the ecological concern is translated into new industrial opportunities. Renewable technologies such as wind and solar and new industrial value chains potentially offer opportunities for profitable business and good livelihoods for employees and their families. Digital technology promises a series of new 'smart' solutions for eco-management that also provide new opportunities for jobs and value creation. Last but not least, redefining the basic orientation of the economy from extractive to circular will unlock massive opportunities for business and jobs in a novel material flow that respects ecological boundaries.

From a motivational point of view, the task of green governance is therefore to show how green growth expands opportunities for value creation and social improvement, and could transform the trilemma into a triple fortuity. While some green technologies are reaching commercial maturity, others still need stimuli from the public sector. While commercial actors eventually will have to roll out the massive volumes of new green production, government must help forge transition out of ecologically unsustainable solutions, to new and attractive commercial and social alternatives that are ecologically sustainable, and potentially therefore also enhance the quality of life.

Notes

1 The word combines the root "anthropo", meaning "human" with the root "cene", the standard suffix for "epoch" in geologic time. The Anthropocene is distinguished as a new period either after or within the Holocene, the current epoch, which began approximately 10,000 years ago (about 8,000 BC) with the end of the last glacial period. 'Anthropocene' is a new term, proposed in 2000 by Nobel Prize-winning scientist Paul Crutzen.
2 Adjusted for price changes over time (inflation) and price difference between countries – it is measured in international Dollars in 2011 prices.
3 Even assuming the veracity of a 2020 study projecting the world population peaking at 9.7 billion in 2064 – more than 1 billion less than projected by the UN – the challenge will be formidable. https://www.nytimes.com/2020/07/14/world/americas/global-population-trends.html.

References

American Public Gas Association (2020) A Brief History of Natural Gas. https://www.apga.org/apgamainsite/aboutus/facts/history-of-natural-gas.

Crutzen, P. (2002) Geology of Mankind. *Nature* 415: 23.

DeLong, J.B. (2000) The Shape of Twentieth Century Economic History. National Bureau of Economic Research Working Paper No. 7569.

Dragger, C. (2001) Relying on Hard and Soft Sells, India Pushes Sterilization. *New York Times*, 22 June. https://www.nytimes.com/2001/06/22/world/relying-on-hard-and-soft-sells-india-pushes-sterilization.html Accessed November 2020.

Ehrlich, P.R. and Ehrlich, A. (1968) *The Population Bomb*. San Francisco: Sierra Club Books.

Encyclopedia of the Earth (2020) *Anthropocene*. https://editors.eol.org/eoearth/wiki/Anthropocene Accessed November 2020.

Energy Information Agency (2020) History of energy consumption in the United States. https://www.eia.gov/todayinenergy/detail.php?id=10 Accessed October 2020.

European Environmental Agency (2019) *The European Environment — State and Outlook 2020*. Luxembourg: Publications Office of the European Union. https://www.eea.europa.eu/publications/soer-2020 Accessed December 2020.

Gray, J. (2009) *False Dawn*. London: Granta Publications.

Groningen Growth and Development Centre (2018) *Maddison Project Database 2018*. Faculty of Economics and Business.

Hall, C. and Klitgaard, K. (2012) *Energy and the Wealth of Nations: Understanding the Biophysical Economy*. New York: Springer.

International Energy Agency (2019) World Energy Outlook 2019. https://www-oecd-ilibrary-org.ezproxy.library.bi.no/docserver/caf32f3ben.pdf?expires=1604079136&id=id&accname=ocid41017227&checksum=6CB2D7D0203D658FA966E8B8837421E4.

IBISWorld (2020) Global Biggest Industries by Revenue in 2020. https://www.ibisworld.com/global/industry-trends/biggest-industries-by-revenue/ Accessed October 2020.

Maddison, A. (2018) Project Database. https://www.rug.nl/ggdc/historicaldevelopment/maddison/releases/maddison-project-database-2018?lang=en.

OECD (2019) *World Energy Outlook*. https://www-oecd-ilibrary-org.ezproxy.library.bi.no/docserver/caf32f3b-en.pdf?expires=1604952093&id=id&accname=ocid41017227&checksum=0CE0ECDEBFBC011BFBC7C778B8C5BBF6.

Our World in Data (2020) Future Population Growth. https://ourworldindata.org/future-population-growth Accessed December 2020.

Our world in Data (2020) Economic Growth. https://ourworldindata.org/economic-growth Accessed December 2020.

Patzek, T.W. and Croft, G. (2010) A Global Coal Production Forecast with Multi-Hubbert Cycle Analysis. *Energy* 35(8).

Rockström, J., et al. (2009) Planetary Boundaries: Exploring the Safe Operating Space for Humanity. *Ecology & Society* 14(2). https://www.ecologyandsociety.org/vol14/iss2/art32/.

Steffen, W., et al. (2018) Trajectories of the Earth System in the Anthropocene. *Proceedings of the National Academy of Sciences* 115(33). https://www.pnas.org/content/115/33/8252.

Taylor, M. (2020) *Energy Subsidies: Evolution in the Global Energy Transformation to 2050*. Abu Dhabi: International Renewable Energy Agency. https://www.irena.org/-/media/Files/IRENA/Agency/Publication/2020/Apr/IRENA_Energy_subsidies_2020.pdf.

U.S Energy Information Administration (2011) History of Energy Consumption in the United States, 1775–2009. Accessed October 2020.

Section III

Governance Approaches

6 Neoliberal Deregulation

The Rise of Neoliberal Deregulation

Economic stagnation in the 1970s sparked a neoliberal wave that had, by the turn of the millennium, come to characterize economic policy in the West. The neoliberal shift from active state interventionism towards regulatory governance implied, once again, dis-embedding the economy from political and social ties. It involved a series of measures, including privatization of activities formerly undertaken under state ownership, the emergence of quasi-autonomous agencies with quasi-legislative powers responsible for the economic regulation of private(-ized) activities. In a 1997 essay, political scientist Giandomenico Majone sums up much of the spirit of the time by contrasting the regulatory state regime with the previous direct interventionist state which he labelled "positive" (Table 6.1). Majone pointed out how the model had shifted at the level of functions, instruments, areas of political conflict, institutions, participation of key actors, policy style, policy culture, and political accountability (Majone 1997).

Table 6.1 Comparing Two Models of Governance

	Positive State	Regulatory State
Main Functions	Redeistribution, macroeconomic stabilization	Correcting Market failures
Instruments	Taxing (or borrowing) and spending	Rulemaking
Main Arena of Political Conflict	Budgetary allocations	Review and control of rule making
Characteristic Institutions	Parliament, ministerial departments, nationalized firms, welfare services	Parliamentary committees, independent agencies, and commissions, tribunals
Key Actors	Political parties, civil servants, corporate groups	Single issue movements, regulators, experts, judges
Policy Style	Discretionary	Rule bound, legalistic
Policy Culture	Corporatist	Pluralist
Political Accountability	Direct	Indirect

Source: Majone (1997) "From the Positive to the Regulatory State: Causes and Consequences of Changes in the Mode of Governance". *Journal of Public Policy* 17(2).

DOI: 10.4324/9781315454931-6

It is easy to understand the fascination with neoliberal deregulation when one considers the massive market value growth in the 1980s and 1990s. In this period, the S&P 500 index rose from around 284 (June 1982) to 2211 (August 2000) (Figure 6.1).

However, GDP growth was not as impressive, not equalling that of the 1950s and '60s delivered under social-democratic governance regimes at their best (Figure 6.2).

De-regulation was not only pursued by the liberal right side of the political spectrum. Modernizing social-democratic governments also embraced deregulation, and successively opened up sector after sector to commercial dynamics. Core elements of the neoliberal agenda were, in other words, becoming part of the 'new Latin' of economic governance for the 21st century.

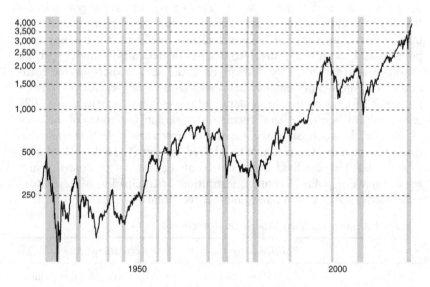

Figure 6.1 S&P 500 Index – 90 Year Historical Chart.

Source: Macrotrends (2020)Macrotrends (2020) S&P 500 Index – 90 Year Historical Chart. https://www.macrotrends.net/2324/sp-500-historical-chart-dat.

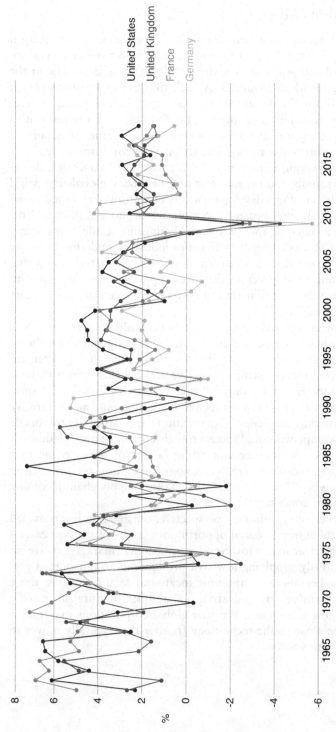

United States
United Kingdom
France
Germany

8

6

4

2

0

-2

-4

-6

%

1965   1970   1975   1980   1985   1990   1995   2000   2005   2010   2015

Figure 6.2 Growth Rrates for Selected Western Economies.

Source: Word Bank (nd) World Bank national accounts data, and OECD National Accounts data files. https://data.worldbank.org/indicator/
NY.GDP.MKTP.KD.ZG?locations=US-GB-FR-DE&name_desc=false.

A Liberal World Order

The neoliberal agenda was driven politically by the iconic 'neoliberal couple' Margaret Thatcher and Ronald Reagan, who fixed neoliberalism at the centre of the political mainstream of the US and the UK in the 1980s. Picking up ideas advanced by such thinkers as Friedrich Hayek (1960) and Milton Friedman (1970), they saw social-democratic embedding of the economy as damaging productivity and the innovative dynamics of capitalism, and championed a programme of neoliberal market reform that had a pivotal impact on Western economies.

Following pioneering initiatives in leading Western economies, deregulation spread rapidly and became part of a neoliberal globalizing world order. A core driver of this development was the outsourcing of industrial value chains, which soon became a centrepiece of modern industrial organization. In a dynamic interplay with diminishing trade barriers and standardization of market regulation, major industries undertook massive outsourcing of production to developing countries. Digital technology that simplified communication across distances supported this development. The motivation was a combination of cost-saving, concentration on core activities, and flexibility.

With location to the right countries, labour could be performed at a fraction of domestic costs, but also with strongly rebated overhead, equipment, and technology costs. Furthermore, outsourcing often involved hiring freelancers exempt from fees and benefits, which made it far more cost-efficient than using full-time employees. Besides, by spinning off the less critical operations such as back-office and administrative functions, marketing, and sales services, and IT infrastructure to outside organizations companies could focus on their core business. In addition, flexibility has become another motivating factor for outsourcing. In a rapidly changing world, where technology revolutionizes production processes, and where low-cost locations change, supply chain flexibility becomes a central concern.

From the developing countries' perspective, outsourcing has provided employment and entrepreneurial opportunities, and – in the best cases – also technology transfer. However, as consumer markets evolve in countries previously supplying low-cost production, an outsourced presence has also become an important locational factor to serve those markets. Furthermore, as industrial capabilities mature in rapidly growing emerging economies, Western global corporations may find it necessary to be close to the technology frontier that typically moves to areas with growth volume.

The Washington Consensus

Neoliberalism also had a major direct influence on the governance of developing economies. The so-called 'Washington Consensus' (Williamson 2002) promoted a set of free-market economic policies specially adapted to developing countries. It was supported by prominent financial institutions such as the International Monetary Fund and the World Bank who insisted on compliance with this governance model as a condition of financial support. Such conditionality typically involved the lifting of state restrictions on imports and exports and often included the devaluation of the currency. The final stage was to allow market forces to operate freely by removing subsidies and state controls and engaging in a programme of privatization.

A Brave New Liberal World

The neoliberal vision for the global diffusion of market-based governance rested on a broader vision of an extension of political liberalism and democratic freedom. This vision was most sharply expressed by the American political scientist Francis Fukuyama, in his book *The End of History and the Last Man* (1992). He argued that humanity had reached "not just ... the passing of a particular period of post-war history, but the end of history as such: That is, the end-point of mankind's ideological evolution and the universalization of Western liberal democracy as the final form of human government" (Fukuyama 1992).

Like many observers at the time, Fukuyama was inspired by the end of the Cold War and the dissolution of the Soviet Union in 1991. The transition of Eastern Europe into the European Union, under a liberal democratic charter, with a professed adherence to market-liberalism, was a major victory for the 'Western' model of both economic and political governance. Russia itself, under Boris Yeltsin, embarked on a liberal and market-oriented path. And even China, with Deng Xiaoping as a central mover, launched into a pro-market strategy, although the brutal crackdown by the military on a peaceful demonstration at the Tiananmen Square confirmed that the world's most populous nation would not buy into liberal politics.

Deregulation and Asymmetric Globalization

While national privatization and de-regulation stimulated globalization of markets and allowed business to develop supply chains across continents, neoliberal governance resulted in a democratic deficit. Deregulation was based on the premise that the interventionist state could be substituted by authoritative market regulation. Efficiency, productivity, and innovation was to be promoted by exposing private actors to market competition, while the public interest was supposed to be transparently enhanced by regulatory supervision under clear and democratically mandated regulatory agencies.

However, as the opening of domestic markets soon became a stepping stone to market globalization, regulation lagged behind. Limited by the territorial jurisdictions of the regulatory nation-state, governance – especially with respect to social and work-life regulation – remained largely national, although supplemented by regional extensions. The outcome of neoliberal deregulation was therefore *asymmetric globalization,* where markets expanded partly out of the reach of democratic governance, a pattern that has also been recognized global governance scholars under 'New Governace Theory' (see e.g. Ruggie 2014). This territorial expansion of the market-economy without a corresponding expansion of the polity has created a governance void at the global level where business can operate to maximize value, with few regulatory constraints.

The capacity and mandate of international institutions like the World Trade Organization, the United Nations, and the like, are nowhere near the standards of serious regulation. Their scope for action is clearly limited by consensus rules and the veto power of large actors. In this regulatory void, commercial actors themselves have joined together to build pro-industry governance mechanisms that facilitate their global operations. One such mechanism is the investor-state dispute settlement arrangement (ISDS).

The Investor-State Dispute Settlement (ISDS)

The ISDS that flourished in the burgeoning liberalization of the late 1980s and early 1990s was often included in bilateral and multilateral trade treaties. In effect, ISDS created a parallel business-friendly judicial system for transnational corporations, where decisions are made by party-appointed arbitrators who are not accountable to the public (Bilaterals 2020). The commercial sector is, in other words, re-embedding itself in a governance framework, which it largely controls itself.

While the ISDS cannot overturn local laws that violate trade agreements, it can grant monetary damages to investors adversely affected by such laws (Provost and Kennard 2015). The threat of exorbitant fines may halt regulation or legislation in the public interest and thus also impact political decisions. Much debate and criticism has therefore arisen concerning the impact of ISDS on the capacity of governments to implement reforms and legislative programmes related to public health, environmental protection, and human rights (Dupuy et al. 2010)

The controversial nature of ISDS decisions is clearly illustrated in cases such as S.D. Meyers Inc. v. Canada. Between 1995 and 1997, the Canadian government banned the export of toxic PCB waste in order to comply with its obligations under the Basel Convention, of which the United States is not a party. The US waste-treatment company, S.D. Myers, then sued the Canadian government under NAFTA Chapter 11 for $20 million in damages for putting up trade barriers to favour Canadian waste-management firms. The claim was upheld by a NAFTA Tribunal in 2000 (Global Affairs Canada (2017)

On the other hand, cases are also resolved in favour of the state, as in Philip Morris vs. Uruguay, that started in 2010, when the multinational tobacco company, Philip Morris International, filed a complaint against Uruguay seeking $25 million in damages (de Zayas 205) The company complained that Uruguay's anti-smoking legislation was devaluing its cigarette trademarks and investments in the country and based its lawsuit on the bilateral investment treaty between Switzerland and Uruguay. The International Centre for Settlement of Investment Disputes (ICSID), a part of the World Bank, decided it had jurisdiction on 2 July 2013 and three years later ruled in favour of Uruguay, ordering Philip Morris to pay Uruguay $7 million, in addition to all court costs (Castaldi and Esposito 2016).

While the ISDS plays a role in filling an obvious governance void, it does so under opaque legal premises and outside democratic control. As argued by Langford et al. (2019), the regime has been slated and criticized for the outsized role given to litigating parties in the appointment of arbiters and a lack of transparency in the appointment procedure.

Commercial De-Regulation and Social Embedding in the EU

The European Union is an example of economic integration under a common transnational free trade regime with authoritative regulatory oversight. By enforcing market rules through EU directives, and gradually expanding EU regulatory agencies to oversee them, regulatory governance has become an avenue to integration. The regulatory void that characterizes the global arena is thus partially filled in Europe. But only partially, since the unitary EU governance does not extend beyond market regulation, to the social embedding of the economy. Even within the European Union, a region where many member countries have long welfare state traditions, diversity is too large to forge a common socioeconomic compact. The common denominator has therefore been integration through markets, without common taxation social transfers and welfare services, which are mainly left to the member states.

The problem is, however, not only the lack of EU engagement in advancing the social embedding of the economy, but also that EU market liberalism overrules national prosocial policies and traditions, particularly in advanced welfare member-states, as illustrated by the Swedish-EU controversy in the Laval case: Conflict over wage settlement arose when a Latvian company, Laval un Partneri, being awarded a public tender in Sweden to renovate a school near Stockholm, posted workers from Latvia to work on the building site in Sweden. Laval invoked the freedom for services in one Member State to offer services on a temporary basis in another Member State, without having to be established there, under the so-called *posting directive* (European Commission nd). Swedish trade unions initiated a process to negotiate Swedish wage levels for the Latvian workers, when working in Sweden, but when this broke down, the Latvian company made agreements with the Latvian trade union for salaries at a Latvian level (Eurofound 2010). Estimates suggest that these posted workers earned around 40% less than their Swedish counterparts (Whittall 2008).

Concerned that the posting of cheaper labour to Sweden threatened the position of Swedish construction workers, their trade union, Byggnads, encouraged Laval to comply with the local terms and conditions of employment laid down in their collective agreement. But Laval refused to sign the existing collective agreement, and Byggnads, supported by the Swedish Electricians' Union (Svenska Elektrikerförbundet, SEF), started picketing Laval building sites in November 2004 (Whittall 2008). In response, the company took the case to the Swedish Labour Court, where the company demanded that the action be ruled unlawful. The national court sided with the workers and dismissed Laval's request that the collective action be brought to an end. The case was subsequently brought before the European Court of Justice, which took a different position, and ruled in 2007 that to force a foreign undertaking that posts workers to Sweden to abide by a Swedish collective agreement was illegal (European Court 2007). The decision undermined the right of Swedish trade unions to make collective agreements valid for foreign workers posted in Sweden.

In the Laval case, local, prosocial negotiated agreements were overrun by European market regulation, in spite of the fact that wages and strike action are explicitly excluded from the EU's competences. The Posting Directive has allowed the European Court of Justice to bring the subject of strikes in by the back door, requiring that the exercising of the right to strike comply with the neoliberal principles of the Maastricht and Lisbon Treaties (Veldman 2013).

The unions have defended the principle that cross-border business should adhere to local labour standards so as not to undermine the employment conditions of the workers already present. However, extended EU market regulation is starting to erode this in practice. The Nordic tradition of prosocial embedding of the economy on the basis of tripartite negotiated settlements is particularly vulnerable in the encounter with more formal and legalistically-oriented EU culture. Europeanization of regulation to fill the governance void thus becomes a push towards market-liberalism, as this is where the EU has the greatest leverage vis-à-vis the European nation-states.

Shifting Hegemony

Neoliberal deregulation and its stimulus of globalization have been one of the major drivers behind a massive geographic shift in industrial localization. Having enjoyed technological and commercial leadership throughout much of the 20th century, the Western economies are meeting stiffer competition in the 21st. It started with the challenge from Japan in the late 20th century, and, then by Korea, Taiwan, and Singapore – the so-called 'Asian Tigers' – towards the turn of the century. As the massive Chinese economy was commercially transformed for globalization under a socialist market economy in the first two decades of the 21st century, the challenge became more acute.

As a consequence, the past three decades have seen a geographical shift of wealth as emerging economies such as China and India have grown faster than the OECD average. Combined with these countries' large populations, such growth differences are reshaping the global macroeconomic landscape. China's transformation from a manufacturing and export-led economy to one based on services and consumption is redrawing the map of economic relations, as indicated in Figure 6.3, by the relative shift of wealth from Europe and the US to China and gradually India (Hunter nd, based on Maddison 2007).

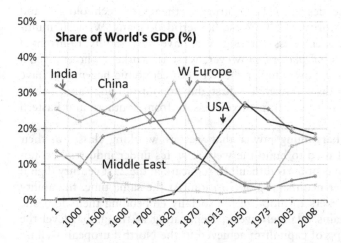

Figure 6.3 The Geographical Shift of Wealth (Share of World's GDP %).

Source: Tracy Hunter (nd), based on Maddion statistics: Angus_Maddison_statistics_of_the_ten_largest_economies_by_GDP_(PPP)#/media/File:1_AD_to_2008_AD_trends_in_%_GDP_contribution_by_major_economies_of_the_world.png.

https://www.rug.nl/ggdc/historicaldevelopment/maddison/?lang=en.

Globalized Industrial Organization

Facilitated by neoliberal deregulation, multinational corporations have been important vehicles for this development. Via their overseas subsidiaries, they have increasingly 'sliced up' their value chains at the international level, and decomposed the production process into multiple, successive, upstream-downstream stages, spread across a number of different countries. This has facilitated industrial learning, and – together with skilful entrepreneurship and industrial policies – provided opportunities for industrial expansion in new growth economies.

Rising levels of intra-industry and intra-firm trade, is in other words, creating a "Global Factory" (Elms and Low 2013), where multinationals are continuously re-evaluating their operations in order to make more effective use of the vast new pool of global labour. As a consequence, employees in the developed world are facing an unprecedented intensification of competition from low-wage economies, as manufacturing, as well as transferable services, is driven eastwards to major providers of offshore business services, such as India, China, and Malaysia. In this 'sliced up' economy across the world, the bargaining position of employees has been clearly weakened, with prosocial arrangements suffering as a result.

In the next stage, as Southern and Eastern emerging economies developed, their domestic consumer markets have become attractive targets for multinational engagement. At this point, foreign investment into production for local markets gained in importance and supplements outsourcing for production and services geared at Western consumers.

In the first decades of the 21st century, as the unique technological and economic superiority of the West has eroded, many Western multinationals are nevertheless thriving and have successfully re-invented themselves as global players. However, Western workers who enjoyed a strong bargaining power under the Western economic hegemony, have been gradually disempowered – first due to outsourcing, and, subsequently, because of the competitive pressure from Southern and Eastern multinationals.

The unique bargaining power that western working classes at their most successful used to build the welfare states under industrial economies in the 20th century is difficult to replicate in the 21st century digital economies under neoliberal globalization. At the same time, the ability for Eastern workers to mobilize for socially embedding their domestic capitalism remains relatively weak. Replicating at the global level the social embedding of capitalism achieved in the North European welfare states appears a long and uphill battle.

The pendulum that swung towards fairness in the industrial economies of the Western welfare states in the second half of the 20th century has swung back towards competitive productivity in the globalizing digital economy under neoliberal deregulation. While this has led to a fairer distribution of wealth across nations, as middle classes are growing in emerging rapid growth economies, the internal distribution of welfare within nations, especially rich ones, has largely become more unfair (Milanovic 2016). The call has therefore been for the re-engaging of a more active state also in previously hegemonic Western economies, to match strong state-led Eastern market economies, not to mention managing the multiple financial, pandemic, and climate crises that have hit the world in the early 21st century.

References

Access to European Union Law (2007) Judgment of the Court (Grand Chamber) of 18 December 2007. Laval un Partneri Ltd v Svenska Byggnadsarbetareförbundet. https://eur-lex.europa.eu/legal-content/EN/TXT/?uri=CELEX%3A62005CJ0341.

Castaldi, M. and Esposito, A. (2016) Phillip Morris loses tough-on-tobacco lawsuit in Uruguay. Reuters, July 9 https://www.reuters.com/article/us-pmi-uruguay-lawsuit-idUSKCN0ZO2LZ.

De Zayas, A-M. (2015) How can Philip Morris sue Uruguay over its tobacco laws? *The Guardian* 16, November. https://www.theguardian.com/commentisfree/2015/nov/16/philip-morris-uruguay-tobacco-isds-human-rights Accessed October 2020.

Dupuy, P-M., Petersmann E. and Francion F. (2010) *Human Rights in International Investment Law and Arbitration*. Oxford Scholarship Online. https://oxford.universitypressscholarship.com/view/10.1093/acprof:oso/97801 99578184.001.0001/acprof-9780199578184.

Elms, D.K. and Low, P. (2013) *Global Value Chains in a Changing World*. Geneva: World Trade Organization, Fung Global Institute, Temasek Foundation Centre for Trade and Negotiations.

Eurofound (2010) 'Laval Case' European Observatory of Working Life. https://www.eurofound.europa.eu/observatories/eurwork/industrial-relations-dictionary/laval-case.

European Commission (nd) *Posting Directive*. http://ec.europa.eu/social/main.jsp?catId=471 Accessed October 2017.

European Court (2007) Grand Chamber Judgment of 18.12.2007, Case c-341/05.

European Observatory of Working Life (2010) Laval Case. 29 November.

Friedman, M. (1970) The Social Responsibility of Business is to Increase its Profits. *New York Times Magazine*. 13 September.

Fukuyama, F. (1992) *The End of History and the Last Man*. New York: Free Press.

Global Affairs Canada (2017) S.D. Myers Inc. v. Government of Canada. *Global Affairs Canada*. https://www.international.gc.ca/trade-agreements-accords-commerciaux/topics-domaines/disp-diff/SDM.aspx?lang=eng.

Hayek, F. (1960) *The Constitution of Liberty*. Chicago: University of Chicago Press.

Hunter, T. (nd) 'The global contribution to world's GDP by major economies from 1 AD to 2008 AD according to Angus Maddison's estimates'. Based on Angus_Maddison_statistics_of_the_ten_largest_economies_by_GDP_(PPP)#/media/File:1_AD_to_2008_AD_trends_in_%_GDP_contribution_by_major_economies_of_the_world.png.

Langford, M., Behn, D. and Chiara Malaguti, M. (2019) The Quadrilemma: Appointing Adjudicators in Future Investor-State Dispute Settlement, Academic Forum on ISDS Concept Paper 2019/12. https://www.jus.uio.no/pluricourts/english/projects/leginvest/academic-forum/papers/papers/langford-behn-malaguti-models-trade-offs-isds-af-isds-paper-12-draft-14-october-2019.pdf.

Macrotrends (2020) S&P 500 Index – 90 Year Historical Chart. https://www.macrotrends.net/2324/sp-500-historical-chart-data.

Maddison, A. (2007) *Contours of the World Economy, 1-2030 AD: Essays in Macro-Economic History*. Oxford: Oxford University Press.

Majone, G. (1997) From the Positive to the Regulatory State: Causes and Consequences of Changes in the Mode of Governance. *Journal of Public Policy* 17(2).

Milanovic, B. (2016) *Global Inequality: A New Approach for the Age of Globalization*. Cambridge, Massachusetts: Harvard University Press.

Provost, C. and Kennard, M. (2015). The obscure legal system that lets corporations sue countries. *The Guardian*. 10 June. https://www.theguardian.com/business/2015/jun/10/obscure-legal-system-lets-corportations-sue-states-ttip-icsid.

Ruggie, J. G. (2014) Global Governance and 'New Governance Theory': Lessons from Business and Human Rights. *Global Governance* 20.

S&P 500 Index – 90 Year Historical Chart (2020) https://www.macrotrends.net/2324/sp-500-historical-chart-data Accessed October 2020.

Veldman, A. (2013) The Protection of the Fundamental Right to Strike within the Context of the European Internal Market: Implications of the Forthcoming Accession of the EU to the ECHR. *Utrecht Law Review* 9(1).

Whittall, M. (2008) Unions fear ECJ ruling in Laval case could lead to social dumping. European Foundation for the Improvement of Living and Working Conditions.

Williamson, J. (2002) What Washington Means by Policy Reform. Peterson Institute for International Economics. https://www.piie.com/commentary/speeches-papers/what-washington-means-policy-reform.

Wikipedia (nd) wikipedia.org/wiki/Gross_world_product by Tracy Hunter

World Bank (nd) World Bank national accounts data, and OECD National Accounts data files. https://data.worldbank.org/indicator/NY.GDP.MKTP.KD.ZG?locations=US-GB-FR-DE&name_desc=false Accessed December 2020.

7 Can Business Govern Itself?

Commercial Self-Regulation?

An ultra-liberalist response to the governance gap under asymmetric globalization is to let business regulate itself. In a theoretical model, Nobel Prize Winner, Ronald Coase, has argued that, under full information and no transaction costs, the negative side effects of business activity could be settled with the affected parties negotiating for compensation without government intervention (Coase 1960).[1]

In another variant of governance without government regulatory intervention, a substantive literature has emerged postulating *the business case* for Corporate Social Responsibility (CSR) or Sustainability (S); business-driven social and environmental self-regulation in other words. In Polanyian terms, the doctrine of business-driven CSR&S takes the dis-embedding of the economy full circle to its inherent contradiction: Dis-embedding the global economy from societal regulation becomes unproblematic because business-endogenous incentives will procure social and environmental responsibility. Too good to be true, one might argue, as businesses increasingly orchestrates supply chains across the globe, enveloping developing countries with weak economic, social, and environmental regulation in the maelstrom of the global economy.

The business case for CSR&S becomes somewhat more credible, however, when civic mobilization is brought into the equation. Vibrant civic communities have emerged to pressure both industry and politics to take on board social and environmental agendas. Furthermore, brand-sensitive businesses stand to lose from pursuing pure profit-centred business strategies if they lead to open conflicts with civil society. Conversely, positive engagement with civic organizations and pro-social trends may increase business opportunities, and create goodwill with public authorities. The civic pressure thus gives more credibility to the business case for CSR argument.

DOI: 10.4324/9781315454931-7

The CSR and Sustainability Boom

CSR&S, and the business case for it, is more than a new approach to business strategy. It addresses a general challenge to the neoliberal programme, which was starting to lose legitimacy towards the turn of the millennium. When the boom of the 1980s and 1990s ran into crises, and major business scandals exploded in the early 2000s, public reactions were increasingly directed beyond individual firms, and towards markets and the neoliberal setup as a whole. Submitted to public scrutiny, industry progressively had to respond and justify its role in society and its wider contribution to the public good. This need for explanation expanded as companies increased in scale, visibility, and market positions across continents. As markets expanded and the scope for commercial strategizing increased, as national regulation weakened and international regulation was found wanting, the monistic doctrine of profit seeking became too narrow. CSR, a concept that was buried under neoliberal hubris in the '80s and '90s, was thus revived to become a new central business agenda, aiming to bridge the gap between business and society. After the Enron, World Com, Tyco, Arthur Andersen, and later Lehman Brothers scandals – the iconic statement by Michael Douglas, the protagonist investor in the movie *Wall Street*: "Greed is Good" – was not acceptable any more.

From the late 1990s onwards, leading global companies and business organizations engaged with a social and environmental agenda on an unprecedented scale. Distancing themselves from the doctrine of profit maximization constrained only by public regulation, they established an influential trend whereby business adopted the doctrine of corporate social and environmental responsibility (CSR), to be followed by Sustainability and contributions to Social Development Goals. This trend is clearly reflected in rising CSR and Sustainability reporting – (Figure 7.1).

CSR, Media, and the Civic Voice

While stimulated by the consequences of the governance deficit and, to some extent, by a business case, the CSR – and later Sustainability – movements have also been driven by digitalisation and the new media. Both trends lowered the information gathering (Internet search), as well as the communication, costs for critical voices, thereby facilitating the amplification of alternative perspectives and agendas. Specialized forums, such as Norwatch, Human Rights Watch, Transparency international etc., have published critical overviews that provide information for civic campaigns and regulatory intervention in cases of social and environmental business malpractice.

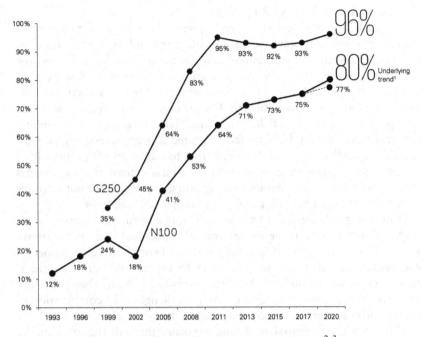

Figure 7.1 Growth in global Sustainability Reporting Rates.[2,3]

Source: KPMG Survey of Sustainability Reporting (2020) https://assets.kpmg/content/dam/kpmg/xx/pdf/2020/11/the-time-has-come.pdf.

New media also drastically reduced the mobilization and organization costs and thus increasing the strategic clout of the civic CSR challenge. In cases like Forest Stewardship Council, the Extractive Industries' Transparency Initiative (EITI)/Publish What You Pay Initiative (PWYP), and the Ethical Trading Initiative (ETI), virtual civic communities were established across geographical boundaries and helped mobilize pressure on the official regulators. Orchestrated by strategically focused Civil Society Organisations (CSOs), the new media were also used to facilitate and activate 'old' mass media in a broader marshalling of public opinion to bring pressure on established governance elites. The establishment of the ETI was inspired by a series of newspaper articles and TV programmes that exposed shocking work conditions in the supply chain of Western multinationals operating in the developing world, particularly in the garment and food industries. The PWYP campaign and FSC engagement also made extensive use of traditional mass media to engage public opinion in heaping pressure on industry and regulatory authorities. The young Swedish climate activist, Greta Thunberg's climate-protest, and the massive youth mobilization that followed around the world, has also become a media-event and a wake-up call to many industrial and political leaders, urging both to walk the talk.

Media and communicative society represent both an opportunity and a challenge to the corporate world. On the one hand, they encourage the taking of branding and market communication to a new level. This is how a new addition to the marketing curriculum – *cause-related marketing*, where CSR, Sustainability, and Purpose have been absorbed into the marketing equation – has emerged. On the other hand, critical voices like George Monbiot and Joel Bakan (Coulter 2013), have questioned whether the media and society have merely triggered a huge outpouring of CSR and Sustainability spin, with little intention to follow up with action. It all becomes an exercise in 'hyping' where business-communication experts design and package companies and reporting experts churn out selective statements and numbers that make the companies look good.

However, while the risk of greenwashing is undeniable, flagging social responsibility could, in the longer run, also promote real corporate responsibility on the ground. As companies hail social and environmental excellence, they also expose themselves to expectations and critique if these aspirations are not met. For brand-sensitive industry, bad press and negative public opinion represent serious challenges. The combination of the mobilization efficiency of the new media – orchestrated by clever CSOs – and the potential of public exposure through the mass media have, in many cases, spurred companies towards stronger CSR and 'pro-sustainability' practices. Media-backed civic engagement has also challenged the state to undertake supplementary regulatory action.

CSR for Every Business Discipline

The fact that CSR and Sustainability has penetrated into most business disciplines is an indicator of its significance. The engagement to present the business case in terms of strategy, finance, marketing, logistics etc. – and adapt it to the methods and perspectives and logic of each discipline – signifies interest and concern not only in principle but also in practice in operative business models.

Corporate Governance – From the Shareholder to the Stakeholder Perspective

The stakeholder approach has been a cornerstone of broadening business outlook. By expanding the responsibility of business leaders beyond serving their shareholders, the stakeholder perspective implicitly also extends the relevant business agenda beyond profit maximization towards larger societal welfare concerns. By making a broad set of societal interests heard in decision-making at the firm level, stakeholder theory promotes the social embedding of the economy.

In challenging the shareholder model, the stakeholder perspective reframes a traditional anchor of modern managerial theory. This is based on the premise that management are hired as the agents of the shareholders (their principals) to run the company for their benefit (Jensen and Meckling 1976). In the shareholder perspective, management is legally and morally obligated to serve shareholders' interests, restricted only by conformity to the basic rules of the society. The latter's prerogative as the ultimate authority over the firm stems from the fact that the shareholders have advanced capital which constitutes the basis for the company's operation. In return, managers are supposed to spend the firm's resources only in ways that have been authorized by the shareholders.

In contrast, the stakeholder perspective asserts that a company owes a responsibility to a wider group of *stakeholders*; not just *shareholders* (Freeman 1984; Freeman et al. 2010). The duty of managers, therefore, includes serving individuals and constituencies that contribute, either voluntarily or involuntarily, to [a company's] wealth-creating capacity and activities, and who are therefore its potential beneficiaries and/or risk bearers (Miles et al. 2006). A widely accepted interpretation takes in shareholders, customers, employees, suppliers, and the local community.

Rhetorically, numerous firms subscribe to the stakeholder perspective. To take the Danish pharmaceutical company, *Novo Nordisk* as an example (2018):

Novo Nordisk's ambition is to be a sustainable business. By this we mean:

- creating long-term value for patients, employees, partners and shareholders by developing innovative and competitive solutions to patients' unmet needs
- doing business in a financially, environmentally, and socially responsible way
- anticipating, adapting to, and creating new business opportunities from changes in our business environment.

This statement reveals that the company is conscious of the need to stay on good terms with society in a sensitive health market, where patients, public authorities, employees, and public opinion hold the keys to brand-image and economic success. Yet it also appears carefully crafted towards including stakeholders that can contribute to value creation. Hence, the premise that the social embedding of business through stakeholdership can be commercially driven rests on the type of stakeholders that are included, and their relevance for value creation.

The Novo Nordisk approach and similar practices elsewhere, suggests that although they subscribe to the stakeholder theory, it must be strongly related to economic value-creation, thereby coming close to what Michael Jensen (2002) has called *enlightened value maximization.*

Enlightened value maximization utilizes much of the content of stakeholder theory but accepts maximization of the long-run value of the firm as the criterion for making the requisite trade-offs among its stakeholders, and specifies long-term value maximization or value seeking as the firm's objective.

This does not preclude, however, that a wide variety of stakeholders may be closely involved in the preparation phase of a project to assess its social and ecological viability. Aborting socially unacceptable projects at an early stage, before large investments are made, will obviously benefit the firm economically, both by avoiding stranded assets and preventing a negative brand image from proliferating.

In addition to the extensive economic benefits that accrue from the social and ecological de-risking of projects, stakeholders may also be crucial to developing new innovative projects. They may play this role as demanding customers, as competent suppliers, as facilitators of buy-in by local communities, and/or as securers of engagement by public authorities in the stimulation of innovation. The Norwegian petroleum company, Equinor, has, for instance, attracted extensive public funding for deploying offshore petroleum technology in the production of offshore wind energy, and was warmly supported by environmental stakeholders for doing so. Stakeholdership as a key to business driven social and ecological improvement is, therefore, credible. But both the set of stakeholders and the band of activities has to tie in closely with the firm's business model, or offer a value-creating alternative which it is capable of exploiting.

It should be noted, however, that although stakeholdership appears to have emerged as a novel approach towards the end of the 20th century, the idea of including societal interests in business decision-making is much older. While the Anglo-Saxon tradition (US and UK) has cultivated a market-based shareholder model, the continental European tradition has a history of more stakeholder-oriented corporate governance arrangements. The German system, for instance, has a high degree of co-determination manifested by the strong degree of employee representation on the board of directors (Aufsichtsrat). The Scandinavian countries take a middle position.

The stakeholder model is, therefore, more of a novelty to the Anglo-American economies than to continental Europe. In fact, the concept of stakeholdership itself – usually attributed to the American business strategy thinker, Edward Freeman (1984) – originated in Scandinavia. The Swedish management theorist, Eric Rhenman, used the concept to argue for more democracy in industrial organizations (Rhenman 1964), as Freeman himself acknowledges (Strand and Freeman 2015).

Strategy – The Cluster Perspective

In business strategy, the strong engagement with CSR/Sustainability by Michael Porter – a major figure in business strategy – and his colleague Mark Kramer, has made social embedding a core driver of value creation. They have done so by extending Porter's "cluster theory" one step further, going beyond industrial relations to also include societal engagement as an avenue to business success.

Drawing on economic geography and its focus on regional industrial agglomeration,[4] Porter's cluster theory argues that the success of every company is affected by the supporting companies and infrastructure around it. Competitiveness, in this perspective, does not predominantly reside in the individual firm, but rather in its interfaces with other cluster-players. Clusters, as Porter and Kramer (2011) see it, have the potential to increase company productivity, drive innovation and stimulate new businesses.

Porter and Kramer's (2011) cluster-based argument for "Shared Value" adds a broader societal engagement to the cluster-equation. The strategic focus then becomes enhancing the competitiveness of the company while simultaneously advancing the economic and social conditions in the communities in which it operates. In other words, shared value creation focuses on identifying and expanding the connections between societal and economic progress. According to Porter and Kramer, companies should create economic value by creating societal value and in this way bring business and society together. Following decades with a narrow profit-focus, they argue that business must now reconnect company success with social progress. However, Porter and Kramer are quick to emphasize that shared value creation should not be at the margins of what companies do, but at the heart of their business focus. As they see it, social responsibility, philanthropy, and even sustainability are no longer business's "spare wheel": they are new ways to achieve economic success.

In other words, a business cluster with sufficient resources and competences to hold a key position in a given branch of economic activity can blossom even further by engaging constructively with its social and political surroundings. Clusters, such as the Silicon Valley cluster in information technology, the Hollywood cluster in film, and the North Sea cluster in offshore petroleum drilling, thrive not only as rich industrial and technological environments, but also by having well-developed public infrastructure (transport, education, research, entertainment etc.), and stimulating innovation support.

The cluster theory and the shared value perspective argue for inserting pro-sociality into the very business model itself. Embedding the firm not only in semi-collaborative/semi-competitive industrial cluster-relations, but also in a co-creative relationship to society, thus becomes a major premise both for its competitive strategy and its contribution to society.

Marketing and Branding: Embracing Values

The case for commercially driven pro-social business engagement is also made in marketing. In *Marketing 3.0*, world-leading marketing guru Philip Kotler explains why the future of marketing lies in moving beyond a product and consumer focus to a human-centric perspective where profitability is balanced with corporate responsibility (Kotler et al. 2010). In this way, he defines business's broader Purpose beyond sales targets and profitability to include wider social and environmental concerns, which become essential parts of branding and customer attraction.

Similarly, Charles Fombrun (1995) has argued for the benefits *of cause-related marketing*, maintaining that, by doing good, managers generate reputational gains that improve a company's ability to attract resources, enhance its performance, and build competitive advantage. Cause-related marketing (CRM) is thus a mutually beneficial collaboration between a corporation and a nonprofit designed to promote the former's sales and brand image and the latter's cause.

One of the earliest and most famous examples of CRM goes back to 1982. The Statue of Liberty was in need of restoration and the American Express company launched a very successful campaign, where it contributed one penny to the restoration project for every purchase a customer made with their American Express Card. The campaign raised $1.7 million, but more importantly, the transactions made by American Express cardholders rose by 28% in just the first month and the new card applications rose by 45% (Kelly 1991).

However, cause-related marketing must be skilfully applied. Unlike simple promotion, cause-related marketing, to have an effect, needs to ensure that the brand and the cause operate in the same 'territory' (Meffert and Holzberg 2009). Customers must feel that the firm's efforts to engage for the public benefit are authentic and truly supporting a cause. Businesses have to be transparent about how they are distributing funds to the cause and clearly outline the win-win solution the product or the campaign is preaching about. Under the right conditions, consumer surveys indicate that CSR & sustainability and cause-related branding remain powerful brand differentiators, with a vast majority of consumers indicating a strong inclination to shop for products and services that demonstrate social and/or environmental benefits, given similar price and quality (Sustainable Brands 2015).

Reporting/Accounting

John Elkington's coining of the phrase the "Triple Bottom Line" in 1994 (Elkington 1999) provided a normative vision for accountants to tie in with the CSR and sustainability agendas. By adding social and environmental bottom lines to the traditional financial determinant, accounting could be expanded to support the wider perspectives that were developing in other business disciplines. After all, there is much truth in the saying: 'In business, what cannot be counted does not count'. Thus, by bringing social and environmental data systematically into the picture, extended accounting can lay down a critical fundament for enhancing societal embeddedness.

The New York and London Stock Exchanges developed sustainability listings, with extensive reporting leading up to a beauty contest for sustainability leadership in each industrial sector. The Dow Jones launched their Sustainability Indices (DJSI) in 1999, gathering data and evaluating the sustainability performance of thousands of publicly traded companies. In Britain, the FTSE Group launched its FTSE4Good Index, a series of ethical investment stock market indices, in 2001. There are numerous other initiatives that place a heavy pressure on companies for sustainability accounting.

Since Elkington's innovation in the early 1990s, initiatives for extended accounting have cropped up in several settings. They have been promoted by CSOs and then gradually adopted by pioneering commercial front-runners and front-runner nations. They have then gradually been taken on board by business fora and international organizations, and subsequently subsumed into accounting practices. Typically these initiatives have responded to civic and political concerns about the negative side effects of globalizing business under weak regulatory control. However, subsequently, they have often been picked up as vehicles for brand development and commercial differentiation.

A Proliferation of Standards

The result of the abundance of accounting initiatives has been a plethora of accounting and certification standards.

With respect to social sustainability, the Social Accountability – SA 8000 standard emerged in 1997 as a central initiative, based on multistakeholder engagement to supplement under-developed work-life regulation in developing countries when their firms deliver to global supply chains. Based on the UN Declaration of Human Rights, and conventions of the ILO, it has become a basic benchmark for decent management of workers' rights, with guidelines for reporting to achieve certification from accredited verifiers.

The Global Reporting Initiative, which was to play a major role in non-financial reporting, emerged out of an environmental accounting initiative. It was launched in 1997 in Boston, USA as an environmental standard, but broadened from environmental issues to include social, economic, and governance matters. The GRI was supported and endorsed by the UN. In October 2016, GRI unveiled the first global standards for sustainability reporting.

The UN Global Compact, which was established at the turn of the millennium with the aim of promoting 'good' corporate practices, generated additional sustainability-accounting requirements. The forum, which soon became a popular arena for the global business community, committed the latter to detail compliance with nine (later ten) principles drawn from three (later four) key international texts: the 1992 Rio Declaration on Environment and Development; the 1948 Universal Declaration of Human Rights; and the International Labour Organization's 1998 Fundamental Principles on Rights at Work. The tenth principle and fourth key text (the United Nations Convention Against Corruption) were added in June 2004.

The Challenge of Consolidation and Implementation

The plethora of standards and reporting initiatives has left industry with an overload of demands for accounting, and there are calls for consolidation.

The GRI aspires to become a core platform for sustainability reporting and did at one point attempt to develop a comprehensive account of a variety of sustainability issues. But it had to retreat because of the immense complexity. The result was a stronger focus on materiality/sustainability issues that really mattered to the firm and sector in question. The variety of sustainability issues across sectors, as well as the diversity of information needs of different sustainability stakeholders, does however create challenges for standardization.

The climate issue, which after the 2015 Paris summit took pride of place on the sustainability agenda, has led to a specialized accounting demand. This is spearheaded by the Carbon Disclosure Project, which is headed by a board of advisors predominantly from sustainability oriented finance, and public service. The presence of the Financial Stability Board, representing leading central banks, behind a strong climate engagement has given further impetus to proper CO_2 accounting. The fact that the climate issue has burst onto the agenda of top-level financial institutions illustrates the unprecedented momentum behind climate-related accounting and subsequent climate action, crystallized in the Task Force on Climate-related Financial Disclosures (TCFD). This initiative has pressed for explicit accounting for climate risk, and the ways of managing it, by relevant companies.

The EU's pushing of a Directive on non-financial reporting in 2014 – with implementation by 2017 – is a sign that sustainability reporting is moving ahead (EU 2020). Even if the directive only applies to large public-interest companies with more than 500 employees it may have important normative effects on broader segments of the economy. The directive compels large companies to publish reports on the policies they implement in relation to a wide set of issues, including environmental protection, social responsibility, and treatment of employees, respect for human rights, anti-corruption and bribery, and diversity on company boards (in terms of age, gender, educational and professional background). It has also been argued that a natural next step would be to get sustainability accounting subsumed under the International Financial Reporting Standards (IFRS) regime.

To sum up, the plethora of accounting initiatives does indicate a strong pro-sustainability engagement among core industrial and financial corporations. However, integrating social and environmental factors into investment decisions, based on systematic accounting still has a long way to go. But new practices keep emerging. Demands for low CO_2 emissions are multiplying, especially among Western pension funds, but also spreading to private investors, creating a market for carbon accounting. The driver is both climate concerns, following up the 2015 Paris agenda, but also risk concerns, as investors fear being left with stranded carbon assets. When it comes to social matters, human rights issues are gaining traction as important business considerations, but systematic social accounting still lies far ahead.

Supply Chain Management

As they have massively outsourced production into developing countries, Western multinationals with CSR and sustainability ambitions have come under pressure to undertake social and environmental upgrading of their supply chains. The capacity of host countries to secure efficient regulation of the huge industrial scale-up of their supplier-industry is often limited, and the outsourcing corporations have therefore had to internalize social and environmental governance within their business model. Against this background, supply chain management has expanded its agenda from commercial logistics to encompass broader social and environmental concerns.

In traditional supply chain management logistics, outsourcing has typically been designed to maximize competitive advantage through access to valuable natural resources and/or tapping into attractive low-cost labour markets. In an extended sustainability perspective, outsourcing logistics and contracting must involve balancing profitability against social and environmental considerations.

In the overall balance, two sides have to be offset against each other. On one side, there is the attractiveness of the outsourcing of production, not only to Western corporations but also to suppliers in developing and middle-income countries such as China, India, and Bangladesh, where it has been an important source of employment generation (Barrientos et al. 2011). But the other and darker side of this development is the fact that, according to Barrientos, much of this employment is insecure and unprotected and hence associated with human and labour rights abuses. Such problems are highly likely, given that outsourcing has resulted in the devolution of legal obligations for social and environmental impacts to suppliers who are located in countries with weak or weakly enforced regulations (Sobczak 2006).

The answer, within the supply chain management discipline, has been to promote the use of codes of conduct, reporting, and monitoring systems throughout many industries – and especially for clothing, footwear, toy, and sporting goods companies. To ensure compliance with the codes, state of the art supply chain management now often includes social and environmental monitoring and auditing a firm's suppliers.

As pointed out by Blindheim et al. (2013) there has been a development towards implementation of collective and multi-stakeholder code and monitoring regimes. These regimes typically seek to harmonize the diverse firm- and sector-specific codes and develop a global social minimum standard. Such schemes may be based on NGO-business partnerships, either with public support or initiated by governments (Nadvi and Wältring 2004). The Fair Labour Association (FLA), the Ethical Trading Initiative (ETI) and Social Accountability 8000 (SA 8000) are examples of such collective and multi-stakeholder codes and monitoring regimes. Compared to corporate codes, the collectively produced codes are typically more comprehensive and make more references to internationally agreed standards such as the Universal Declaration of Human Rights and the ILO Conventions on labour rights.

Through environmentally and socially extended supply chain management, private contracting in business networks is partially filling the governance void created by asymmetric globalization, which the networks themselves benefit from. At present the business entity itself assumes direct responsibility for the social and environmental issues in its supply chains. But in the longer term such regulation is likely to be transferred to the state and evolving domestic work-life and industry associations, as countries reach maturity as industrial nations (Blindheim et al. 2013)

Human Relations

Systematic argumentation for social and environmental upgrading of business has also been present in the Human Relations literature.

Firstly, with respect to recruitment, CSR and sustainability can be viewed as new magnets for talent. Studies have shown that ambitious candidates are getting increasingly picky about who they work for, and CSR programmes and environmental strategies are taking centre stage in the list of things exceptional candidates expect from a business (Leaderonomics 2020).

Surveys have demonstrated that corporate responsibility is critical – 88% of millennials said they would choose employers with CSR&S values that reflect their own and 86% would consider leaving an employer if its CSR&S values no longer matched their expectations (Pelosi 2018). A survey amongst employees at Booking.com showed that 84% were very interested in actively participating in CSR&S activities.

In other words, brand voice and business culture matter when it comes to recruitment and retaining people. Being proud of one's workplace is important to employees, and the Sustainability brand of the employer is increasingly integral to positive image and identity-building.

Secondly, sustainability is not only important for recruitment. Studies show that when companies implement CSR&S successfully, the result is better employee morale and an improvement in retention and productivity. The HR literature points out how CSR&S activities enhance the atmosphere within an organization for every stakeholder. As argued by Bhattacharya et al. (2007), CSR&S can serve as a highly effective component of internal marketing programmes by fulfilling employee needs and encouraging workers to identify strongly with the company. Ditlev-Simonsen and Brøgger (2013) come to similar conclusions, quoting studies that show how employee involvement and motivation have positive effects on business outcomes, with CSR and sustainability engagement as major motivating factors. Taken even further, sustainability may become a stepping stone towards developing a higher purpose, which allows people involved with an organization are making a difference, gives them a sense of meaning, and draws their support (Quinn and Thakor 2018).

ESG – Finance for Sustainability

Breaking out of its traditional image of exclusive profit seeking, finance has, over the last decades, added a so-called ESG or SRI perspective, whereby environmental, social, and governance considerations – or socially responsible investment dimensions – are included in investment analyses. With this widening of the financial investment perspective comes the ability to link ESG-oriented investment to financial risk and return. The connection to risk management has served to overcome deep scepticism on the part of institutional investors. They were initially hesitant to embrace SRI and ESG, arguing that their fiduciary duty was to maximize shareholder value irrespective of environmental or social impacts, or broader governance issues such as corruption.

However, as evidence has accumulated to the effect that ESG issues have financial implications, the tide has turned. In many important markets, including the U.S. and the EU, ESG integration is increasingly seen as part of fiduciary duty (Kell 2018). The ESG approach in finance can now rely on a growing body of research showing that Environmental, Social, and Governance (ESG) factors are a material credit risk for fixed income investors and which dispels the myth that incorporating ESG means sacrificing financial returns. ESG investing is increasingly becoming part of the mainstream investment process for fixed income investors, as opposed to a specialist, segregated activity, usually confined to green bonds (Inderst and Stewart 2018).

The perception that ESG portfolios perform as well as non-ESG benchmarks is now becoming widely supported by mainstream financial milieus. The Morgan Stanley Institute for Sustainable Investing argues (MS 2019):

> There is no trade-off in the financial performance of sustainable funds compared with their traditional peers. Analyzing the total returns between 2004 and 2018, we find only sporadic and inconsistent differences in performance. Therefore, the returns of sustainable funds were in line with those of traditional funds (Morgan Stanley 2019).[5]

The statement is substantiated by a comparison of annual returns on sustainable and traditional funds (Figure 7.2).

The Morgan Stanley analysis reiterates previous investment analysis, including that of Barclays (2016) which concluded:

> Our research into the impact of ESG on the performance of US investment-grade corporate bonds in the past seven years has shown that portfolios that maximise ESG scores while controlling for other risk factors have outperformed the index, and that ESG-minimized portfolios underperformed.

The Remarkable Growth of ESG Investment

With the integration into mainstream financial investment strategies, ESG investment has enjoyed massive growth. Worldwide exchange-traded funds focused on environmental, social and governance issues had assets of more than $13.5 billion under management at the end of August 2019 and the number of ESG focused funds has grown extensively in the first two decades of the 21st century (McGrath 2019). Their proliferation is a sign that investors are taking ESG more seriously, particularly as the funds' long-term track records show similar risk-return profiles to standard market indexes from which they derive. In addition to the emerging documentation of the potential of added value from ESG screening, the prosocial reorientation of finance may in part be seen as a response to the large financial holdings of pension funds. These are funds that represent a

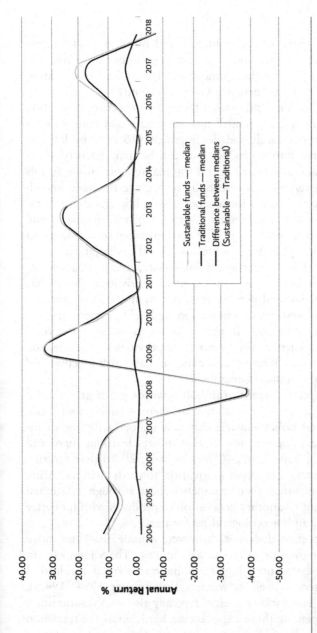

Difference in median returns (Sustainable - Traditional)	-1.50	-1.17	0.18	-0.37	-0.80	0.84	-1.37	-0.08	0.63	1.38	1.18	0.00	-0.23	3.63	-0.03
	**						**							***	
Statistical Significance	99%+ ***			95%+ **			90%+ *								

Figure 7.2 Median Total Returns of Sustainable and Traditional Funds 2004–2018.

Source: Morgan Stanley Institute for Sustainable Investing (2019) Sustainable Reality – Analyzing risk and Returns of Sustainable Funds. Morgan Stanley & Co. https://www.morganstanley.com/content/dam/msdotcom/ideas/sustainable-investing-offers-financial-performance-lowered-risk/Sustainable_Reality_Analyzing_Risk_and_Returns_of_Sustainable_Funds.pdf.

'democratic' ownership base, with strong interest in maintaining productive, socially viable and ecologically sustainable societies.

Innovation

With the increasing speed of technological and business model transformation, innovation has become an increasingly important subject in business studies. At the same time, innovation theory has, like finance, progressively taken a societal perspective into account.

From a mainly technology and market-focused perspective, innovation theory in the 'technology push model' has assumed the starting point is basic scientific applied research and development (R&D). The latter is subsequently translated into a product that can be manufactured effectively and economically and then sold on the market. According to this model, the role of government is essentially to provide the basic knowledge, typically financed through universities and public research laboratories. Commercialization is subsequently left to private industry, and related to the expected return from private consumer markets, reflecting a complementary 'market pull' model of technological development.

With the pro-social reorientation of businesses, and increasing demands for novel sustainable solutions, modern innovation theory has incorporated broader societal perspectives. A voluminous literature on national and regional systems of innovation highlights society and the public interest as major partners in the innovation process, far beyond the provision of basic science. This perspective provides a richer agenda for how public and private interests and concerns can work together and stimulate innovation to mutual benefit.

In this wider perspective, transformation towards green growth and social entrepreneurship draws on lead market theory (Jänicke and Jacob 2004), where national policy engagement is a major facilitator of innovation and private value creation. It also utilizes learning curve and niche market theory (Wene 2008; Watanabe et al. 2000) that describe how public procurement can drive innovation towards manufacturing new products that enhance their competitiveness through continued deployment. This leads to another generation of products with far better technological, social, and/or ecological performance.

The societal perspective does not, however, assume that innovative transformation – be it green or social – is without cost. The Schumpeterian insight into "creative destruction" highlights that transformative industrial dynamics creates losers as well as winners (Schumpeter 1994 [1942]). Public engagement in innovation therefore typically also involves transition management to compensate those experiencing hardship as the transition takes place.

Is There a Case for Business Self-Governance?

Returning to the question initially posed in this chapter: Can business govern itself? Or, to put it another way, what is the potential for business self-governance? The integration of CSR & Sustainability perspectives into most business disciplines indicates that there is a serious and operative agenda and a potential for considerable business self-governance, particularly if facilitated by some degree of public engagement. The meticulous revision of perspectives and operative implementation of CSR and sustainability across the board is hard to discount as a mere façade.

Furthermore, the civic and political scrutiny of industrial practices under open media display also creates pressure for real delivery. This clearly necessitates not only talking but acting as well. The preferences expressed by customers and employees, documented in multiple surveys, demonstrate that core stakeholders want to drive a sustainability transition.

Yet, the professed prosocial and sustainability engagement, together with capabilities to put it into practice in several business domains, are selective and dependent on the strategic orientation of the firm and its surrounding commercial incentives. The firm may, in other words, use prosociality and sustainability in a reactive and defensive manner, or in a proactive and strategic way (Figure 7.3).

Reactive, Defensive Modes of Prosociality and Sustainability

In conventional business, value creation from prosociality & sustainability is generally tied to its use in a reactive and defensive mode. The two are typically developed as responses to attacks from media and pressure groups for socially or environmentally unsustainable practices (Zadek 2004; van Tulder and Zwart 2005). In this model, engagement in

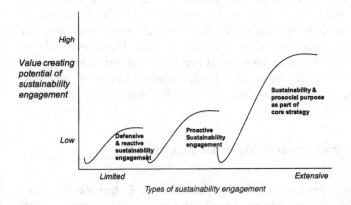

Figure 7.3 Prosociality & Sustainability Engagement and Value Creation.

Source: Author.

prosociality & sustainabiility is constructed as a risk-minimizing, safe-guarding function. It involves expunging malpractice in selected parts of the organisation to comply with new social and environmental expectations, while in essence remaining strategically focused on business as usual. The defensive and reactive nature of prosociality in this mode means it has limited business potential. It remains a defensive support function and leaves fundamental value creation to other forces.

The Proactive Mode of Prosociality and Sustainability

In more engaged accommodative and proactive modes, CSR and Sustainability have been taken further, and may become more systematically integrated into the business model. Essentially, however, they still provide a support function and lack strong and direct value-creating capacity. Potentially, CSR in a proactive mode has the ability to protect value creation at the strategic core of business – for instance preventing brand/reputation damage resulting from socially unacceptable practices. That said, it is a mere support function rather than the core of a value creation strategy.

Prosociality and Sustainability in Strategic Mode

In business models where Prosociality and Sustainability (P&S) play a strategic role, environmental and social entrepreneurship are integrated into the core business. This is where P&S, relatively speaking, have their highest value creating potential. This is also when corporate value creation is most closely aligned with the latest sustainability trends in policy and public opinion. As companies orient themselves towards the burning political issues of the day – climate change, alleviation of poverty, pollution, human rights etc. – they also build bridges between public and private goods, and potentially private and public agendas. Companies in such positions will typically find high rewards from P&S investments, and will therefore be early promoters of strong P&S agendas. These sustainability front-runners are able to develop social and environmental entrepreneurship with a strategic P&S focus, and closely integrate it into core business, thereby aligning it with new societal sustainability expectations, as well as a higher purpose for business.

Sustainability and Profitability – A Chicken and Egg Problem

The demarcation between defensive, proactive, and strategic P&S approaches can, however, shift over time. The relationship between P&S and profitability may, in many ways, come to resemble a 'chicken and egg' problem, or if you like, a dialectical interplay between the two concepts. As the expectations for sustainability increase in a society, profitability also changes. Strategies that previously were profitable may become unprofitable under the new enhanced sustainability expectations, while strategies that were unprofitable under previous conditions may now become profitable. In other words, driving up seemingly unrealistic expectations may create a different basis for profitability, which may make them reasonable in time. Conversely, previous strategies that no longer create value may be discarded.

To take an example from the transport sector: Tesla and other electric car companies have been front-runners for new sustainable transport. They have been helped by generous policy support in several countries, and emboldened by strong civic and policy engagement. As they have reached viable technologies at competitive prices that may contribute significantly towards the Paris climate goals, they create blueprints for others to follow. Eco-oriented parts of civil society have been dynamized and call for supportive political action. Politicians concerned with the climate challenge will follow suit, knowing that there are industrially-viable solutions already 'out there'. Incentives to galvanize climate laggards in the auto-industry may subsequently alter the profitability of traditional power trains and push them into complying with novel sustainability standards. The dynamic evolution of sustainability expectations, ecological entrepreneurship, political support, and technological learning may, in this way, drive sustainability-oriented change.

The vanguard companies may drive up expectations that will devalue business models based on 'unsustainable' old-fashioned profitability. By showing what can be done with new sustainability-oriented business models, the leaders pave the way for what may also become necessary for the laggards. Furthermore, P&S upgrading does not only involve individual companies. It may, at a more mature stage, also include entire industrial sectors, establishing sectoral standards that conventional actors will have to respect.

Is There a Business Case for CSR/Sustainability?
Is There a Case without Business?

Asking whether there is a business case for P&S might have sounded relevant a quarter century ago, but it appears less so today. In fact, the question of whether there is a case for P&S *without* business buy-in might be more apposite. The answer is that it takes two to tango. The business case is dependent on demanding and appreciative civic and political engagement that pushes for pro-social and ecological transformation. Society, in turn, is dependent on eliciting industrial engagement to match such transformation. The capacity to set preconditions for a dynamic interplay across these domains may lead in the direction of a more humane and ecologically balanced society. However, this does not mean that business self-governance is sufficient. While business may have important engagement in P&S, and some firms may be in a position to seriously engage, most firms often need strong pressure from demanding stakeholders, such as CSOs, consumer groups and local communities, and frequently also incentives from, and partnerships with, public authorities. The need for profitability and economic value creation, which is a prerequisite for the corporate world, establishes obvious boundaries for how far business can act on its own. Yet in tandem with civic mobilization that alters consumer choices or political acceptability, the economic calculus may change. Additionally, new incentives from governments at various levels may also shift the economic prospectus.

Notes

1 Coase developed his theorem when considering the regulation of radio frequencies. Competing radio stations could use the same frequencies and would therefore interfere with each other's broadcasts. The problem faced by regulators was how to eliminate interference and allocate frequencies to radio stations efficiently. What Coase proposed in 1959 was that as long as property rights in these frequencies were well defined, it ultimately did not matter if adjacent radio stations interfered with each other by broadcasting in the same frequency band. His reasoning was that the station able to reap the higher economic gain from broadcasting would, assuming clearly defined property rights, have an incentive to pay the other station not to interfere. (Wikipedia nd).
2 Base: 5,200 N100 companies (top 100 companies by revenue in 49 countries) and 250 G250 companies (world's largest companies by revenue based on Fortune 500 ranking).
3 The N100 underlying trend reflects the global sustainability reporting rate when analyzing reporting by the top 100 companies in the same group of countries and jurisdictions in both 2017 and 2020.
4 The importance of economic geography, or more correctly geographical economics, was also brought to attention by Paul Krugman in *Geography and Trade* (1991). Cluster development has since become a focus for many government programmes. The underlying concept, which economists have referred to as 'agglomeration economies', dates back to and the work of Alfred Marshall (2012 (1890)).
5 The study compared the return and risk-performance of ESG-focused mutual exchange-traded funds (ETFs), as defined by Morningstar, against their traditional counterparts from 2004 to 2018, using total returns and downside deviation. It used Morningstar data on exchange-traded and open-ended mutual funds active in any given year of the period. In total 10,723 were sampled using the oldest share class of each fund.

References

Barclays (2016) Sustainable investing and bond returns Research study into the impact of ESG on credit portfolio performance. *01 Impact Series*. https://www.investmentbank.barclays.com/content/dam/barclaysmicrosites/ibpublic/documents/our-insights/esg/barclays-sustainable-investing-and-bond-returns-3.6mb.pdf?pwm=31 Accessed October 2020.

Barrientos, S., Mayer, F., Pickles, J. and Posthuma A. (2011) Decent Work in Global Production Networks: Framing the Policy Debate. *International Labour Review* 150: 3–4.

Bhattacharya, C., Sen, S. and Korschun, D. (2007) Corporate Social Responsibility as an Internal Marketing Strategy. *Sloan Management Review* 49(1).

Blindheim, L., Langhelle, O. and Laudal, T. (2013) Responsible Supply Chain Management – the Economic and Political Responsibility of Companies within Global Supply Chains. In Atle Midttun (ed), *CSR and Beyond – A Nordic Perspective*. Oslo: Cappelen Damm.

Coase, R. (1960) The Problem of Social Cost. *The Journal of Law and Economics* 3.

Coulter, P. (2013) Debating CSR, Democracy and Value Creation. In Atle Midttun (ed), *CSR and Beyond – A Nordic Perspective*. Oslo: Cappelen Damm.

Desclée, A., Hyman, J., Dynkin, L. and Pollbenikov, S. (2016) *Sustainable Investing and Bond Returns*. Barclays Bank.

Ditlev-Simonsen, C. and Brøgger, B (2013) CSR and Employee Motivation. In: Atle Midttun (ed), *CSR and Beyond – A Nordic Perspective*. Oslo: Cappelen Damm.

Elkington, J. (1999) *Cannibals with Forks: The Triple Bottom Line of 21st*. Capstone

EU - European Union (2020) Directive 2014/95/EU. https://eur-lex.europa.eu/legal-content/EN/TXT/?uri=CELEX%3A32014L0095 Accessed November 2020.

Fombrun, C. (1995) *Reputation: Realizing Value from the Corporate Image*. Boston: Harvard Business School Press.

Freeman, E.R. (1984) *Strategic Management: A Stakeholder Approach*. Boston: Pitman.

Freeman, E., Harrison, J., Wicks, A. and Parmar, B. (2010) *Stakeholder Theory: The State of the Art*. Cambridge: Cambridge University Press.

Inderst, G. and Stewart, F. (2018) *Incorporating Environmental, Social and Governance (ESG) Factors into Fixed Income Investment*. Washington: World Bank Group. http://documents.worldbank.org/curated/en/913961524150628959/pdf/125442-REPL-PUBLIC-Incorporating-ESG-Factors-into-Fixed-Income-Investment-Final-April26-LowRes.pdf Accessed November 2020.

Jänicke, M. and Jacob, K. (2004) Lead Markets for Environmental Innovations: A New Role for the Nation State. *Global Environmental Politics* 1(4).

Jensen, M. C., and Meckling, W. H. (1976) Theory of the Firm: Managerial Behavior, Agency Costs and Ownership Structure. *Journal of Financial Economics* 3(4).

Jensen, M. C. (2002) Value Maximization, Stakeholder Theory, and the Corporate Objective Function. *Business Ethics Quarterly* 12(2).

Kell, G (2018) The Remarkable Rise Of ESG. *Forbes*. https://www.forbes.com/sites/georgkell/2018/07/11/the-remarkable-rise-of-esg/ Accessed November 2020.

Kelly, B. (1991) Cause related marketing: Doing well while doing good. *Sales and Marketing Management* 143.

KPMG (2020) Survey of Sustainability Reporting (2020). https://assets.kpmg/content/dam/kpmg/xx/pdf/2020/11/the-time-has-come.pdf Accessed January 2021.

Kotler, P., Kartajaya, H. and Setiawan, I. (2010) *Marketing 3.0: From Products to Customers to the Human Spirit*. Hoboken: Wiley.

Krugman, P. (1991) *Geography and Trade* (Gaston Eyskens Lectures). MIT Press: London.

Leadernomics (2020) Are CSR and Sustainability the New Magnets for Top Talents? https://www.leaderonomics.com/articles/business/are-csr-and-sustainability-the-new-magnets-for-top-talents Accessed November 2020.

Marshall, A. (2012 (1890)) *Principles of Economics*. Digireads.com Publishing.

McGrath, C. (2019) ECG ETS surge in 2019. *Pensions & Investments*. https://www.pionline.com/interactive/esg-etf-assets-surge-2019 Accessed October 2020.

Meffert, H. and Holzberg, M. (2009) Cause-related Marketing: Ein scheinheiliges Kooperationskonzept?. *Marketing Review St. Gallen 2*.

Miles, M., Munilla, L. and Darroch, J. (2006) The Role of Strategic Conversations with Stakeholders in the Formation of Corporate Social Responsibility Strategy. *Journal of Business Ethics* 69(2).

Morgan Stanley Institute for Sustainable Investing (2019) *Sustainable Reality – Analyzing risk and Returns of Sustainable Funds*. Morgan Stanley & Co. https://www.morganstanley.com/content/dam/msdotcom/ideas/sustainable-investing-offers-financial-performance-lowered-risk/Sustainable_Reality_Analyzing_Risk_and_Returns_of_Sustainable_Funds.pdf Accessed November 2020.

Nadvi, K. and Wältring. F. (2004) Making Sense of Global Standards. In: Hubert Schmitz (ed), *Local Enterprises in the Global Economy: Issues of Governance and Upgrading*. Cheltenham, UK:Edward Elgar Publishing.

Novo Nordisk (2018). *Annual Report*, 2018. https://www.novonordisk.com/content/dam/nncorp/global/en/investors/irmaterial/annual_report/2019/NN-AR18_UK_Online.pdf Accessed November 2020.

Pelosi, P. (2018) Millennials Want Workplaces With Social Purpose. How Does Your Company Measure Up?Talent Economy; Better Media Group. https://www.chieflearningofficer.com/2018/02/20/millennials-want-workplaces-social-purpose-company-measure/

Porter, M.E. and Kramer, M.R. (2011) Creating Shared Value. *Harvard Business Review* 89(1/2).

Quinn, R. E. & Thakor, A. V. (2018) Creating a Purpose-Driven Organization: How to get employees to bring their smarts and energy to work by *Harvard Business Review*, July-August.

Rhenman, E. (1964) *Företagsdemokrati och företagsorganisation*. Stockholm: Thule.

Schumpeter, J. (1994) [1942] *Capitalism, Socialism and Democracy*. London: Routledge.

Sobczak, A. (2006) Are Codes of Conduct in Global Supply Chains Really Voluntary? From Soft Law Regulation of Labour Relations to Consumer Law. *Business Ethics Quarterly* 16(2), April.

Sustainable Brands (2015) https://sustainablebrands.com/read/stakeholder-trends-and-insights/study-81-of-consumers-say-they-will-make-personal-sacrifices-to-address-social-environmental-issues Accessed October 2020.

Strand, R. and Freeman, R. (2015) Scandinavian Cooperative Advantage: The Theory and Practice of Stakeholder Engagement in Scandinavia. *Journal of Business Ethics* 127(1).

van Tulder, R and Zwart, A. (2005) *International Business-Society Management: Linking Corporate Responsibility and Globalization*. London: Routledge.

Watanabe, C., Wakabayashi, K. and Miyazawa, T. (2000) Industrial Dynamism and the Creation of a "Virtuous Cycle" between R&D, Market Growth and Price Reduction – The Case of Photovoltaic Power Generation (PV) Development in Japan. *Technovation* 20.

Wene, C. O. (2008) Energy Technology Learning Through Deployment in Competitive Markets. *Engineering Economist* 53(4).

Wikipedia (nd) Coase Theorem. https://en.wikipedia.org/wiki/Coase_theorem

Zadek, S. (2004) The Path to Corporate Responsibility. *Harvard Business Review* 82(12).

8 Re-Chartering the Firm

A Broader Palette of Governance Models

The previous discussion of the business potential for self-governance with respect to social and environmental concerns has taken the widely found shareholder corporation as a point of departure. This model, which is typical of the United States and Great Britain, is, however, complemented by many other models around the world. A study of OECD economies by La Porta et al. (1999) found that 70% of the largest traded firms in Austria, 45% in Singapore, and 40% in Israel and Italy were state-controlled, which provides a very different anchoring for social and environmental sustainability than private investor ownership. The study also found that by far the most dominant form of controlling ownership in the world is by families.

In addition to the variation in ownership highlighted by La Porta et al. the economy also consists of enterprises, such as foundations, co-operatives, social entrepreneurship, and public benefit corporations, that take social embeddedness and/or ecological sustainability into the very chartering of the firm. While the previous chapter highlighted various ways of incorporating social and environmental sustainability into conventional business models, the serious limitations to this endeavour inspire seeking a more fundamental societal embedding of business under different chartering and ownership forms.

Exploring the full plethora of alternatives would take us beyond the scope of this book. In this chapter I shall therefore concentrate on a select few: Public benefit corporations, co-operatives, and social entrepreneurship as examples of how chartering may shape business behaviour. I will return to ownership in the discussion of the role of the state in Chapter 10.

Public Benefit Corporations

The Public Benefit Corporation has emerged in the USA in response to limitations imposed on the dominant corporate model (C corporation) that locks in shareholder value as an overriding concern of the firm's

DOI: 10.4324/9781315454931-8

business model. This imperative is clearly demonstrated in a legendary 1919 decision of the Michigan Supreme Court that forced Henry Ford to operate the Ford Motor Company in the interests of its shareholders, rather than in a charitable manner for the benefit of his employees or customers:

> A business corporation is organized and carried on primarily for the profit of the stockholders. The powers of the directors are to be employed for that end. The discretion of directors is to be exercised in the choice of means to attain that end, and does not extend to a change in the end itself, to the reduction of profits, or to the non-distribution of profits among stockholders in order to devote them to other purposes...
>
> (Dodge v Ford Motor Co 1919, quoted from Wikipedia nd)

This legal 'shareholder primacy' framework clearly constrains prosocial and sustainability oriented re-embedding of business. That is, unless it can be argued – as in the previous chapter – that there is a business case for it, in the sense that the re-embedding enhances shareholder value.

The Public Benefit Corporation offers greater flexibility. It responds to the need for accommodating corporations that pursue profit, but combine accruing shareholder revenue with wider purpose for value creation and benefits to workers and other stakeholders. The Public Benefit Corporation was signed into law in July 2013 in Delaware – the leading US state for incorporation. It functions in the same way, and enjoys all the same benefits as, traditional Delaware corporations, but has three unique features, encompassing corporate purpose, accountability, and transparency. The Public Benefit Corporation is required to identify in its certificate of incorporation a specific public benefit purpose that the corporation is obliged to pursue. Directors are required to balance "the pecuniary interest of stockholders, the best interests of those materially affected by the corporation's conduct, and the identified specific public benefit purpose". Furthermore, they are required to report on their overall social and environmental performance, in addition to traditional financial reporting (Markell 2013).

Benefit corporations thereby lend themselves to social and environmental re-embedding by expanding the fiduciary duty of directors to require them to consider non-financial stakeholders as well as the interests of shareholders (Lane 2014). In other words, by chartering as a public benefit corporation, directors of mission-driven businesses acquire the legal protection and obligation to pursue an additional mission and consider additional stakeholders.

To strengthen their credibility as Public Benefit Corporations, they may register under the B corps label whereby they are subject to certification process administered by the "B Lab", a non-profit organization behind the B Corp movement, which benchmarks candidate firms against its standards.[1] As of 2020, there are over 2,500 certified B Corporations in more than 70 countries, and the B corporation has regional certification procedures in Europe, Latin America, Australia & New Zealand, East Africa, and the United Kingdom (B Corporation nd).

Although any company, regardless of its size, legal structure, or industry, can become a B Corporation, currently most B Corporations are privately-held small and medium-sized businesses (B Lab 2020). However, the case of Danone – a food and beverage company – may serve as an example of how even a sizeable multinational can adapt to a public benefit model.

Case: Danone

Danone's exceptional B corp and Entreprise à Mission chartering must be understood against the backdrop of the company's history and core products.

The company's origins are in Barcelona in 1919, where Isaac Carasso – a Jewish doctor with roots in the Balkans – started the production of yoghurt to help cure digestive and intestinal problems in children. His son Daniel took over the family business and established Danone in France and the United States as well as Spain (Grimes 2009). The company has been through several mergers and acquisitions, but has remained focused on food and beverages built on four businesses: Essential Dairy and Plant-Based Products, Water, Early Life Nutrition, and Medical Nutrition (Danone nd).

Danone has translated its founding tradition of health-based food production into the core of its mission and public benefit status.

> ...to bring health through food to as many people as possible (Our Mission – Danone nd).

This vision is especially valid for its products in specialized nutrition and early life nutrition – providing optimal nutritional solutions for infants and young children. It is also characteristic of the company's interest in advanced medical nutrition – providing nutrition to help with food allergies and faltering growth in infants.

However, the vision is also embedded in a broader ecological perspective under the heading "One Planet – One Health" vision, which reflects a strong belief that people's health and the planet's preservation are interconnected and should be at the heart of a food company's strategy.

Danone's sustainability chartering came in several phases.

Danone North America was formed as a Public Benefit Corporation in 2017 when Danone acquired WhiteWave Foods and united two companies in North America with a shared commitment to purpose, growth, and good food. The year after the company became a certified B Corporation, thereby subjecting itself to systematic scrutiny and third-party verification.

The commitment to public benefit was taken a step further in 2020 when Danone became the first listed company to adopt the French 'Entreprise à Mission' model. The concept of a "mission company", introduced by the Growth Pact law of 2019 allows a commercial enterprise to integrate social and environmental objectives into its statutes to which it must also devote resources and monitoring. As with the B corporation, the aim is to ensure that the purpose of the company is fixated on long-term objectives described in its charter (the mission).

Danone's formula for coupling purpose and profit has been to single out a portfolio of healthier products, with brands encouraging better nutritional choices and dietary habits. The public benefit is that this will have a positive impact on people's health locally. The company has also focused on supporting regenerative agriculture, protecting the water cycle, and strengthening the circular economy of packaging, thereby securing quality raw materials and compliance with climate goals.

As a major multinational – that in 2018 sold products in 120 markets generating overall sales of €24.65 billion – Danone is fairly special in formalizing its sustainability commitments through explicit chartering and demands for transparent implementation. However, the company claims that this strategic framework builds on decades of responsible business stewardship. It, therefore, sees itself as having a realistic basis to serve a dual economic and social project (Our Vision – Danone nd).

In addition, the company has received extensive external recognition for its sustainability strategy, as it has profiled itself on a number of international sustainability indexes. They include FTSE4 Good, Dow Jones Sustainability, and other Environmental, Social and Governance (ESG) ratings (MSCI, Vigeo-Eiris, Sustainalytics), which assess companies on their overall sustainability strategy and address a mainly financial audience. Furthermore, the company also claims a positive effect on employee motivation, particularly as it has placed sustainability-oriented product innovation on the agenda.

As illustrated by the Danone case, the Public Benefit Corporation or Entreprise à Mission models incorporate many elements of the business case for pro-sociality & sustainability discussed in the previous chapter. Nevertheless, for the traditional corporation any social and environmental engagement is derivative, and must be justified in terms of enhancing profit and financial value. The public benefit model, by contrast, entails giving pro-sociality and sustainability equal status with financial value as core strategic foci, and introduces a commitment that the corporation must live up to. But even in this case financial value creation is paramount. A for-profit corporation must make money for its shareholders, or if its societal mission becomes overriding it must capitalize on supplementary public support.

Cooperatives

Cooperative arrangements have been central to socio-economic organization since early hunter and gatherer societies, but declined under elitist, hierarchical, and feudal societies. Under emerging democracies and market economies in the late 19th and early 20th centuries, the cooperative movement regained momentum to strengthen the bargaining position of small producers and individual consumers (Hoogenboom et al. 2018). Some of the earliest cooperatives were producer cooperatives where farmers collaborated to establish diaries, or to improve their bargaining position vis-à-vis commercial wholesalers. Cooperatives were also developed amongst consumers to limit their exposure to monopolistic pricing and the high margins of profit-seeking retailing merchants. Other cooperatives, like the mutual insurance associations, combined both the producer and consumer roles.

Although less common than the shareholder model, the cooperative economy is far from marginal. According to the World Cooperative Monitor (2019) cooperatives hold US$20 trillion in assets and generate US $3 trillion in annual revenue. At a national level, the cooperative economy comprises over 10% of the Gross Domestic Product in four countries of the world (New Zealand (20%), Netherlands (18%), France (18%), and Finland (14%) (United Nations 2014). More than 12% of humanity is part of any of the world's three million cooperatives. Cooperatives employ 280 million people across the globe – in other words around 10% of the world's employed population. (ICA Coop nd-a)

As indicated in the definition of a cooperative by the International Cooperative Association, this business model represents a radical alternative to the privately owned for-profit corporation:

> A co-operative is an autonomous association of persons united voluntarily to meet their common economic, social, and cultural needs and aspirations through a jointly-owned and democratically-controlled enterprise (ICA Coop nd - b).

The direct need-focus of the members and the joint ownership and democratic control provides strong direct ties between business and society and potentially represents a more transparent and open governance model than the shareholder governed firm. Yet, in the cooperative construction lies a commitment to a specific group of stakeholders that benefit from the cooperative's activity. While cooperatives are all set up to cover their members' interests, their stakeholder allegiance remains particular, without – in principle – carrying any broader commitment to society at large. This is why Charity Commission, the regulator for charities in England and Wales, doesn't allow cooperatives to be charities – they pursue a 'private benefit' and charities are meant to have a 'public benefit' (Voinea 2015).

In this sense, one may argue, cooperatives become selectively socially embedded. Nevertheless, a kernel for wider social embedding lies in the fact that cooperatives are typically democratically structured. Each participant has one vote, and financial benefits from the company to the participants are scaled to the use of the cooperative's services. The fact that the membership is typically locally anchored usually makes members more concerned about their impact in the community than corporations with widely spread, and often distant, ownership. The economic and social benefits of cooperatives' activities therefore generally stay in the communities where these entities are established, and generated profits are either reinvested in the enterprise or returned to the members.

However, cooperatives are not a homogeneous group. They span a large spectrum of business models, from fairly idealistic organizations to organizations that resemble the standard shareholding company. In some cases, cooperative organization represents the historical roots of companies that have subsequently morphed into shareholder-like companies, and the membership has become a more or less passive formality with little real influence. To illustrate the co-operative model in practice, we shall briefly present OBOS – a Norwegian consumer cooperative, and Mondragon, a Spanish producer-cooperative. Both have been highly successful in commercial, as well as social, terms.

Case: OBOS

OBOS – (Oslo housing and saving society) was founded in August 1929 to build affordable housing for its house-seeking members in close collaboration with the city of Oslo that recognized OBOS as the municipality's building body. The pro-social anchoring of its business model is clear and explicit: Ever since its foundation, OBOS has been a co-operative that is owned by its members, with the profits returned to the business to fulfil the purpose of building housing for them.

The first housing complex to be completed was in 1931 and new ones followed mostly on the eastern side of the city. They were typically blocks on five floors with outer walls of brick, where most apartments were two-room and around 50 square metres in size. They were thus adapted to the expectations and means of the working class.

After World War II, OBOS expanded with a public mandate to build "As many flats as possible, as quickly as possible and as cheaply as possible", supported by loans from the newly created Housing Bank (OBOS nd). The flats were still moderate in size and were allocated according to membership seniority and family size. The expansion continued throughout the 1960s and '70s.

Under neoliberal influence during the 1980s, pro-social arrangements in the housing sector were gradually replaced by market forces. The housing market was steadily deregulated, the price regulation on plots was abolished, and the state subsidies for housing construction were reduced. And OBOS's business model changed as well. Throughout the 1990s and into the 2000s offerings and sales were driven by commercial market pricing. The pro-social allocation of housing according to family size and moderate cost was gone, and OBOS homes were eventually sold at market price, though were first offered to members.

With the commercial opportunities, OBOS has developed into a group that has branched out both geographically and functionally. It has moved into several associated business areas, including development, building, and sales of real estate and housing. It also has activities within real estate, property management, consulting, banking, rental of real estate, and renewable energy. While the largest activity is still in the Oslo region, business also takes place in other regions of Norway, Sweden, and Denmark.

From a commercial point of view, the OBOS story is thus one of success both with respect to volume and profile. It has grown to become a major enterprise in Norway. At the end of 2019 OBOS had 473,386 members, a turnover of over 14 billion Kroner and 2,632 employees, in addition to subsidiaries in Norway and Sweden.

But to what extent has the OBOS model been a success as a co-operative? Here again several success factors could be mentioned. Firstly, through its activity OBOS has had a lasting effect on Norwegian housing, and is one reason why Norway boasts one of the highest standards of housing in the world. Secondly, the OBOS cooperative business model has also served to secure a fairly sizeable share of home-ownership in the country, amply supported by municipal and national policy in the decades after 1945.

However, the neoliberal shift both in national and municipal housing policy, as well as in OBOS's business model, may be seen as more problematic from a pro-social point of view, and revealing in terms of the social limits of the cooperative model. As OBOS, in line with public policy, adjusted the cooperative model to make it market compatible, it favoured its established members who already held OBOS flats and could now sell them at market prices. And it disfavoured younger members who were entering the housing market and had to pay a higher price for their first flat.

Still, a certain element of pro-sociality remains also for new members, as the organization has continued to provide a range of new, low-price flats to cater for newcomers in the housing market. Nevertheless, reflecting the liberal market context, OBOS also provides luxury apartments, tapping into the profitable high end of the market.

What is formally left from its cooperative heritage is the need for membership in order to buy flats, and that membership seniority counts if there is more than one potential buyer for fixed-priced new flats. However, members are now free to resell at market prices, though other members have the right to enter the highest bid after the bid-contest is over. In this process, the OBOS business model has changed in line with changes in society. What remains, however, is a local ownership that anchors the organization in the cities where it operates, and that makes it a trusted partner for political authorities in urban development.

Case: Mondragon

Compared to the consumer-cooperative OBOS, the Mondragon case represents another facet of cooperative organization, a worker cooperative. Mondragon has been highly successful and since its foundation in 1956, it has grown and prospered and is today a pre-eminent exponent of the cooperative economy. As of 2019 the cooperative had a workforce of over 80,000 and total sales of more than €11,000 million.

However, Mondragon is not only a cooperative corporation (MCC), but also a cooperative community, which includes a whole cluster of enterprises, mostly located within the Basque region of Spain. The broad spectrum of industrial engagement, supplemented by education and welfare services allows Mondragon to exercise solidarity at a high level, including job security. In other words, the breadth and depth of Mondragon's social embedding of the economy in some respects comes close to that of an advanced welfare state.

Roots and History

The wide branching out of the Mondragon community has grown organically, based on the entrepreneurial spirit of a young Catholic priest, José María Arizmendiarrieta, and his ability to combine social commitment with technical and commercial skills. The project started in 1943 with the creation of a technical school in Mondragón. In 1955 five of the students bought a bankrupt firm that had produced heaters and stoves in Vitoria and moved it to Mondragón a year later. The firm eventually became *Fagor*, which was converted to a cooperative in 1958 and by the early 21st century was the largest producer of household appliances in Spain (Enc nd).

Over time the Mondragon cooperative grew both in scale and scope towards its present complexity.

In 1959, it developed both financial and welfare units within the cooperative group. The Caja Laboral Bank was formed with a dual aim: to promote savings and to channel funds into other developing cooperatives. That same year, the social welfare entity, Lagun Aro, was set up to solve the problem of pensions. Because the government considers them owners not workers, cooperative members aren't covered by Spain's social security system.

The Mondragon group continued to broaden its industrial engagement. In 1969 the supermarket chain Eroski was formed. Ikerlan, the first technological research centre of the MCC, was started in 1974.

In 1997 it also consolidated its knowledge base by establishing the University of Mondragon, combining the three industrial technical engineering schools (Mondragon, Txorieri, and Lea-Artibai), Eteo, which is dedicated to business management and administration, and the University College for Teaching. In addition to the university the MCC has formed several research centres. The objective was to foster the kind of technological knowledge that the cooperatives consider key to their success and the ability to launch new business ventures.

Organization and Values

The cooperative model implies a radical break with conventional capitalist corporate governance, which places the investor/stockholder in command. Instead it turns governance upside down and defines labour as the principal beneficiary and thereby – like Mondragon – grants labour full sovereignty in the organization of the enterprise.[2] The worker also provides the necessary investment capital. Furthermore, the organization is democratic. In the case of the Mondragon, the co-operative declares all its worker members to be equal in their rights to knowledge, property, and self-development. The model thereby erases the traditional division between labour and capital and instead establishes a local-participatory representation of all involved parties.

Mondragon has remained focused on its contribution to the local community. It is therefore set up to reinvest the majority of the net surplus obtained. A significant proportion is earmarked for funds of a community nature, in order to create new co-operative jobs, support community development initiatives, education, and co-operative promotion and ensure social security in keeping with the co-operative system, based on solidarity and responsibility.

Ever since its inception by an idealistic entrepreneurial priest, the Mondragon corporation has been held together by strong shared values. According to the corporation itself, these values include cooperation, participation, responsibility, and innovation which permeate it at various levels (Mondragon Corporation nd). Mondragon's mission thus combines the core goals of a business organization competing on international markets with worker ownership and democracy, and a pledge to look after its social environment. Its vision, as stated on its webpage, proclaims:

We would like to become committed people, with a co-operative identity who form a profitable, competitive, and enterprising business group in a global context; who apply a successful socio-business model, offering the market integrated solutions based on experience, knowledge, innovation, inter-cooperation, strategic partnerships, attracting, promoting and generating talent; and which generates sufficient resources to provide value-added employment and sustainable development for the community (Mondragon-Corporation nd).

The structure today

Building on its historic evolution, as of 2020 Mondragon is an advanced regional cooperative cluster divided into four areas: industry, retailing, finance, and knowledge. The industrial activity: (46% of turnover) includes consumer goods, capital goods, industrial components, construction, and business services. Mondragon is now Spain's leading machine tools manufacturer.

The retailing activity (49% of turnover) blends worker's cooperation with consumer membership, and is run as a hybrid worker-consumer cooperative. It boasts the Eroski brand which is a major player in the Spanish retail market.

In addition, the Mondragon group has a financial division, consisting of two units: The Laboral Kutxa, which provides banking services to support Mondragon cooperatives, including financial backing under reorganization and industrial transformation, and also the LagunAro EPSV which provides welfare for members covering retirement, widowhood and disability services. This complements Mondragon's main social security system.

The fourth division – the Knowledge section – includes research centres, the university, and cooperative promotion centres. The knowledge division is an essential basis for Mondragon's updating and industrial transformation in a dynamic business environment.

The broad scope of the Mondragon cooperative cluster is likely a pivotal factor in explaining its resilience. This diversity provides the group with a variety of options for industrial and commercial re-combination that one stand-alone unit could never do. The knowledge and financial divisions allow it to undertake systematic exploration and development for new ventures in a rapidly changing world. The combination of knowledge building and solidarity and social security allows it to internalize functions, such as 'flexicurity' (see Chapter 2) that are normally features of advanced welfare states. However, the core values and cooperative principles are obviously essential factors in providing trust and the capacity to undertake common action as well was enabling difficult downturns to be mutualized. The collective principles of decent and moderate wages, with a maximum pay differential of six times the lowest salary, also entail a higher score on fairness than is customary under shareholder-directed capitalism.

Challenges

However, its many successes do not imply that Mondragon is without challenges.

The collapse of Modragon's traditional flagship, the Fagor appliance manufacturer, in 2013, revealed some serious weaknesses in the Mondragon model. The group's strong representation in traditional areas of manufacturing has put it at risk as competitors have relocated production to low-cost countries (Bibby 2013). The organization of Fagor's international operations has also been criticized for, amongst other things, difficult work relations between core cooperative leaders and foreign employees recruited under traditional labour contracts with poor work motivation (Basterretxea et al. 2019). The global outsourcing-economy has therefore become a major threat to mature industrial segments in Mondragon's economy. However, other co-operatives within the federation were not directly affected by Fagor Electrodomésticos's collapse, and Mondragon made use of the group's diversity and research capabilities to accelerate transition into other, higher value-added areas of business.

Fagor's failure to retain profitability in the outsourcing-economy does not imply, however, that Mondragon is without internationalization. Mondragon made its first exports in early 1960s, and in 1989 it opened its first foreign manufacturing plant in Mexico. Since then, MCC has developed a strong global profile. The group now has nine international corporate offices – in Brazil, Russia, India, China, Taiwan, Vietnam, Mexico, and USA, – 125 production plants outside of Spain and a commercial presence worldwide. Of the total sales of €5,547 million, 69% are international and 31% national.

But intriguingly, internationalization also displays the limits of the cooperative model. In its international operations, Mondragon has not replicated its traditional cooperative organization but deployed the conventional shareholder model. This indicates the importance of regional solidarity and common values as underlying premises for cooperative worker-ownership. Building such relations in multiple locations across the world would be costly, risky, and time-consuming. The shareholder model provides a much easier vehicle for international expansion under Mondragon's control.

Social Enterprises

While cooperatives like OBOS and Mondragon are primarily established to serve their members, social enterprises go one step further beyond the conventional investor-driven business model and produce goods and services with a social purpose, or to promote social causes. They typically prioritize the social aim over profit-making, while practicing inclusive governance characterized by participatory and/or democratic decision-making.

Social enterprises adopt a variety of legal forms and statuses, as illustrated in the European Union (EU 2015). In France, Greece, Italy, and Poland, they charter under a separate, new legal form for social enterprise that has been created by adapting the cooperative legal form. In Croatia, the Czech Republic, Hungary, Portugal, and Spain social cooperatives (or 'social purpose cooperatives') are recognized in the existing legislation covering cooperatives. The UK has developed a legal form for use by social enterprises – the Community Interest Company (CIC). CICs are businesses with primarily social objectives whose surpluses are principally reinvested for that purpose in the business or the community.

The broad recognition of the social enterprise across nations indicates that there is a widely felt need for a pro-social alternative to the mainstream business model which provides goods and services in a charitable way. Social enterprise thereby fills a space traditionally occupied by religious communities, but also a space covered more broadly by engaged citizens. And most observers claim that social entrepreneurship is rapidly expanding. A report commissioned by the EU lists more than 180,000 social enterprises in the EU area (EU 2015).

Two cases may serve as examples to illustrate some of the variety to be found across social enterprises. The first is *Bevan Healthcare*, in Bradford, UK, which is an outreach initiative financed by the National Health Service that provides general practice health services for homeless people, people in temporary or unstable accommodation, people who have come to Bradford as refugees or seeking asylum, and others who find it hard to access the healthcare they need. This case presents the charity end of the social enterprise spectrum. The second case, also from the UK, is *HiSbe or How It Should Be*. This company champions a fair and sustainable food industry, and positions itself against the conventional supermarket. It represents the social-movement-oriented end of the spectrum.

When it comes to *Bevan,* the social enterprise format and the idealism at the core of the initiative allows the enterprise to offer more flexible health care services to some of the most deprived groups than the mainstream public health care system allows for. This flexibility and outreach is built into *Bevan Healthcare* through a modus operandi that takes it close to its clients. To achieve this they operate a street medicine team, an intermediate care service, and a 'hospital in-reach team' to help patients find accommodation after hospital treatment. These services are designed to meet patients in their own reality, and make services accessible to often multiply excluded groups (Bevan Healthcare nd).

Bevan's financial model is also key to its success. The lack of profit-seeking and the obligation to re-invest any surplus in improving patient care makes Bevan a credible partner for the British National Health Service. Bevan Healthcare's status as a social enterprise and CIC thereby gives it access to funding streams and support not available to traditional GP partnerships. In return, it is under an obligation to use any surplus it generates for the benefit of the people it serves.

HiSbe, with shops in Brighton and Worthing on England's south coast, is an idealistic enterprise that represents a clear alternative to mainstream industrial farming. It promotes seasonal farm-fresh produce, claiming that it is more nutritious and healthy, as well as cost-effective, uses less energy, and – Hisbe affirms – tastes better. In addition, the social enterprise is strongly community-oriented. Its ambition is to build a good food community in its relationships with customers, suppliers, and staff where it prioritizes the best local produce.

Furthermore, HiSbe embraces strong ecological values. It combats harmful agrochemicals, GMOs, soil-eroding, water-depleting farming methods, and big brands. HiSbe prefers to source from local farms committed to traditional farming practices where cows are put out to pasture and sheep and chickens roam free. The enterprise's ecological values also encompass waste. HiSbe takes care to avoid waste, so, wherever possible, it avoids packaged foods. Instead, it enables customers to buy the quantities they want by using their own containers or compostable alternatives.

HiSbe's explicit philosophy, and strong idealistic engagement bears resemblance to a social movement, and the enterprise aims to put these ideas into practice, leaving commercial considerations to play a secondary and facilitating role.

Embedding Through Re-Chartering

The above selection of alternative charters has illustrated some of the options available for incorporating social and environmental considerations formally into the business model. Given the limitations of the CSR & sustainability addendum to traditional for-profit corporate chartering, there is much to be said for a more explicit formal inclusion of societal concerns. To mention but a few:

Clearly, more societally oriented charters, such as benefit corporations, social enterprises, and cooperatives may play important roles in evading the negative side effects that traditional profit-only corporations easily disregard. The greater obligation to provide information that follows many alternative forms of chartering provides important transparency, often lacking in traditional C corporations. Besides information on the above-mentioned adverse effects, this transparency includes disclosure of ownership, nation-by-nation earnings, and the use of tax havens; details that are frequently held back by international corporations. Providing such information to the market, as well as to civic and political actors, is a necessary stepping stone to a fairer and more sustainable economy.

Furthermore, alternative chartering may have democratic advantages. The extended worker participation both in workers collectives and in social enterprises makes for better social anchoring than in corporations, where the ultimate movers and shakers are anonymous investors or their portfolio managers.

More 'embedded' chartering may be particularly important in the early phases of commercial evolution, where new societal and ecological visions/agendas need to be developed from idealistic movements and turned into the tangible materialization of novel products and services. In such early stages social entrepreneurship, idealistic cooperatives, and public benefit corporations may fill important roles.

Furthermore, the Bevan Healthcare case reveals an interesting interface between alternative chartering and public procurement. An NHS demand for non-profit chartering to qualify as a service provider, or indeed other relevant requirements, could be used more generally to stimulate the embedding of social and environmental concerns into the business model.

However, alternative chartering also has its limitations, and the conventional C corporation may be essential in the later stages of international standardization when technologies and business models need to be scaled up for global markets. As we have seen, the Mondragon cooperatives made use of the C corporation model in their international expansion, because of the extensive transaction costs implied in replicating their cooperative model outside of the Basque region. In the same vein, one might argue that the OBOS consumer cooperative, in its market-adapted format, is not very different in practice from a Public Benefit corporation.

It should also be noted that the picture is not black and white when it comes to the balancing of public and private benefits. In spite of Danone's public benefit orientation, it has not escaped critique. The company has been blamed for undermining breastfeeding in developing countries by over-promoting baby milk. This becomes particularly problematic as water quality is poor, and may lead to child feeding with contaminated baby milk mixture (Williams 2013).

An overarching conclusion, however, is that the fairly monolithic focus on the C corporation in US-dominated business culture, serves to overshadow important alternatives that deserve greater attention and invite a rethinking of the capitalist enterprise.

Notes

1 This process includes demands to undertake *reporting* in the form of an annual, comprehensive impact report which is transparent to the public and uses a third-party standard (GRI, BIA, Integrated Report, etc.). It encompasses a *materiality assessment* and stakeholder engagement process, conducted at a

minimum every other year which identifies relevant trends and material topics to the company, as well as assessing management strategies and performance goals. This materiality assessment must be made transparent to stakeholders. The B corp label also includes a *disclosure statement* on the company's tax philosophy/approach and government affairs (lobbying/advocacy), including the company's overall effective tax rate. In addition the company must specify its *human rights policies* either through making an explicit commitment to key human rights covenants (such as the UN Declaration of Human Rights, UN Guiding Principles on Business and Human Rights, and ILO Principles), or stating the most salient human rights issues relevant to the business and its overall operations through a human rights risk assessment (B Lab nd).

2 In Mondragon this participatory representation is formalised in an enterprise structure based on: a) The sovereignty of the General Meeting, composed of all the members, in which this sovereignty is exercised on the basis of 'one person, one vote' b) The democratic election of governing bodies, and in particular, the Board of Directors, which are accountable for its actions to the General Meeting. c) Collaboration with the management bodies designated to operate the company, by delegation of the membership as a whole (Mondragon nd).

References

Basterretxea, I., Heras-Saizarbitoria, I. and Lertxundi, A. (2019) Can employee ownership and human resource management policies clash in worker co-operatives? Lessons from a defunct cooperative. *Human Resource Management*, Special Issue Article. https://onlinelibrary.wiley.com/doi/full/10.1002/hrm.21957 Accessed October 2020.

B Corporation (nd) https://bcorporation.net/faq-item/how-many-certified-b-corps-are-there-around-world Accessed October 2020.

B Lab (nd) https://bcorporation.net/ Accessed October 2020.

Bevan Healthcare (nd) https://bevanhealthcare.co.uk/about-us/ Accessed October 2020.

Bibby, A (2013) Workers occupy plant as Spanish co-operative goes under. *The Guardian*. 15 Nov. https://www.theguardian.com/social-enterprise-network/2 013/nov/15/spanish-co-op-workers-occupy-plant Accessed October 2020.

Danone (nd) https://www.danone.com/about-danone/at-a-glance/danone-data.html

Dave Grace Associates (2014) Measuring the Size and Scope of the Cooperative Economy: Results of the 2014 Global Census on Co-operatives.

Enc (nd): Encyclopecia.com https://www.encyclopedia.com/science/encyclopedias-almanacs-transcripts-and-maps/mondragon-cooperative-corporation Accessed October 2020.

European Commission (2015). A map of social enterprises and their eco-systems in Europe. file:///C:/Users/FGL86008/Downloads/Synthesis%20report%20FINAL%20(3).pdf Accessed October 2020.

GlobeNewswire (2020). Danone to pioneer French "Entreprise à Mission" model to progress stakeholder value creation. https://www.globenewswire.com/news-release/2020/05/20/2036111/0/en/Danone-to-pioneer-French-Entreprise-%C3%A0-Mission-model-to-progress-stakeholder-value-creation.html.   Accessed October 2020.

Grimes, W. (2009). Daniel Carasso, A Pioneer of Yoghurt, Dies at 103. *New York Times*. May 20.

Hoogenboom, M., Kissane, C., Prak, M. et al. (2018) Guilds in the transition to modernity: The cases of Germany, United Kingdom, and the Netherlands. *Theory and Society* 47.

International Co-operative Alliance (2019). The World Cooperative Monitor. https://www.ica.coop/en/our-work/world-cooperative-monitor Accessed October 2020.

International Co-operative Alliance (nd - a). Facts and Figures. https://www.ica.coop/en/cooperatives/facts-and-figures Accessed October 2020.

International Co-operative Alliance (nd - b). Cooperative identity, values and principles. https://www.ica.coop/en/cooperatives/cooperative-identity Accessed October 2020.

La Porta, R., Lopez-de Silanes, F. and Shleifer, A (1999) Corporate Ownership Around the World. *Journal of Finance* 54(2), April.

La Croix (2020) Danone est devenu une "entreprise à mission", 27 June. https://www.la-croix.com/Economie/Danone-devenu-entreprise-mission-2020-06-27-1201102151 Accessed November 2020.

Lane, M. (2014) Emerging Legal Forms Allow Social Entrepreneurs to Blend Mission And Profits. *Triple Pundit*. 11 March. https://www.triplepundit.com/story/2014/emerging-legal-forms-allow-social-entrepreneurs-blend-mission-and-profits/45416 Accessed October 2020.

Markell, J. (2013) A New Kind of Corporation to Harness the Power of Private Enterprise for Public Benefit. *HuffPost*, Sept 21. https://www.huffpost.com/entry/public-benefit-corporation_b_3635752?guccounter=1&guce_referrer=aHR0cHM-6Ly9lbi53aWtpcGVkaWEub3JnJnLw&guce_referrer_sig=AQAAAGXJjz0O0MPh_jbILqp-2zzAhyaz4jU2jtrGRxYvNEVSYLNI-IucaHSHq_01TC1bJuQLujYP3v8V-7C3clSQERQ4oZNYWODIeEFpi89ucnRn623sLjXKxLdZtNrQl_efuMeuKfadA-Wsl_BJTVoe_ZzuBl4muDBDiWFd0GATXDE8l- Accessed October 2020.

Mondragon Corporation (nd) https://www.mondragon-corporation.com/en/about-us/ Accessed October 2020.

OBOS (nd) OBOS this is our history (translated by the author) https://nye.obos.no/dette-er-obos/historien-om-obos/Accessed October 2020.

Social Enterprise.org (nd) HiSbe Food. https://www.socialenterprise.org.uk/our-members/hisbe-food/ Accessed October 2020.

United Nations (2014) https://www.un.org/esa/socdev/documents/2014/coopsegm/grace.pdf Accessed October 2020.

Voinea, A. (2015) Co-ops and charities: Are they mutually exclusive? *Coop News*, 14 Aug. https://www.thenews.coop/96391/topic/legal/co-ops-charities-mutually-exclusive/ Accessed November 2020.

Wikipedia (nd) Dodge v Ford Motor Co https://en.wikipedia.org/wiki/Dodge_v._Ford_Motor_Co. Accessed October 2020.

Williams, Z. (2013) Baby health crisis in Indonesia as formula companies push products. *The Guardian*, 15 February. https://www.theguardian.com/world/2013/feb/15/babies-health-formula-indonesia-breastfeeding Accessed October 2020.

9 Civic Governance

Introduction

Numerous scholars have seen civil society as an essential element in the fabric of society. Starting in antiquity, Aristotle (1974 [330 BC]), under the term 'political community', characterized it by a shared set of norms and ethos, in which free and equal citizens lived under the rule of law. In the spirit of enlightenment, the French political thinker Alexis de Tocqueville (2000 [1835]) believed that associations operating outside the sphere of government and economic life – what we now refer to as civil society – were vital bulwarks against any incipient democratic decay and despotism.

More recently, the American political scientist, Putnam (1993), praised civil society associations for building social capital, trust and shared values, thus facilitating an understanding of the interconnectedness of society and the interests within it. In a similar vein, the 20th century American sociologist, Talcott Parsons (1970), saw modern society mostly held together not only by domination and exchange, but also by cross-cutting ties of sociability, identification, solidarity and persuasion – all essential features of civil society.

The importance of civil society, as noted by social scientists, is also reflected in its recognition within the United Nations where partnering with civil society, is seen as important because it advances the UN's ideals and helps support its work. Civil society is therefore presented along with government and business, as the 'third sector' of society.

Against this background, this chapter asks what role civil society can play in economic governance? How can it influence business and politics, and contribute towards the social and ecological embedding of the economy?

Answers to these questions are sought while exploring two cases of strong civic engagement: the shipping double hull/oil-spill prevention initiative, and the Extractive Industries' Transparency Initiative. The important role of civic engagement in both cases leads us to rethink the classic doctrine of regulatory economic governance – where social and ecological responsibility lies with public policy regulation of purely profit-

DOI: 10.4324/9781315454931-9

seeking firms. The cases indicate the need for a much wider concept of governance, where civic engagement is included alongside government and business, as indeed recognized both by the stakeholder model of business strategy (Freeman 1984) and the Policy Advocacy Coalition model of Sabatier (1998). In this wider picture, social values, implicit social contracts, and the moral bargaining rights of civil society organizations, in confrontation with commercial and political actors, must be included.

Civic Engagement in Dealing with Maritime Oil Spills

The shipwrecking of three large tankers in the 1990s and early 2000s causing massive oil spills – the *Exxon Valdez* in Alaskan waters, the *Erika* in French, and the *Prestige* off the Spanish coast – provoked massive civic outcry and mobilization for safer double hull ships.

The first case that reinforced debates and critique against the petroleum industy and its tanker-transports was the *Exxon Valdez* (History.com 2018). On March 24, 1989, the ship ran aground in Prince William Sound in the Gulf of Alaska and spilled nearly 37,000 tones of crude oil. Prince William Sound had been a pristine wilderness before the spill. The *Exxon Valdez* disaster dramatically changed all of that, taking a major toll on wildlife. Fishermen went bankrupt, and the economies of small shoreline towns, including Valdez and Cordova, suffered in the following years.

A decade later, on 12 December 1999, the Maltese tanker *ERIKA*, carrying some 31,000 tonnes of heavy fuel oil as cargo, broke in two in a severe storm in the Bay of Biscay, 60 miles from the coast of Brittany. About 20,000 tonnes of oil were spilled contaminating 400km of coastline in one of France's worst environmental disasters.

Three years later, in 2002, the *Prestige* a Greek-operated, single-hulled oil tanker, officially registered in the Bahamas, sank off the coast of Galicia, Spain (ITOPF nd). The ship was 26 years old and structurally deficient. The spill was the largest environmental disaster in both Spanish and Portuguese history and polluted thousands of kilometres of coastline and more than a thousand beaches on the Spanish, Portugese and French coasts, as well as causing great harm to the local fishing industry.

The Public and Media Engagement

The three tanker shipwrecks and the huge resulting oil spills all inspired intense civic engagement with demands for cleanup, compensation, and for guarantees that measures would be put in place to prevent them happening again. The spills also became major media events. The civic mobilization was local, regional, national, and international. Local communities were outraged at beaches full of grease with fisheries spoilt and wildlife suffering gruesome deaths, with fishermen out of work, and the tourist industry facing bankruptcy. Regions and national authorities were upset about local consequences, but also the national costs for cleanup operations. At the international level, Civil Society Organizations (CSOs) used the cases to mount a general environmental critique, with sympathy actions staged in several countries.

Case 1: The Exxon Valdez Spill

Civic engagement in the *Exxon Valdez* case started from strong reactions to the local spill, but soon expanded into a general attack on Exxon as a company, for environmental negligence. The spill in Alaska and the critique of Exxon also became a platform for a more general critique of arctic drilling and climate denial.

At the local level, the images of seabirds covered in black slicks and rescue workers power-washing boulders became iconic images for an entire generation of the dangers of oil production in general. The spill created huge media interest, many protests, and a cleanup activity that involved 10,000 people at a cost of US$ 2 billion (Perunovic and Perunovic 2011). A 1997 Pew Center study found that the Exxon Valdez spill ranked among its top 20 news stories of the decade (Sax 2019).

In April 1989, more than 2,500 demonstrators converged on the New York headquarters of the Exxon corporation as part of a series of actions planned across the nation and around the globe by environmentalists, protesting the Alaska oil spill and demanding an end to "corporate pollution of the planet". Exxon had become a symbol of petroleum's 'ecocide'. Demonstrators gathered at the Exxon Plaza in midtown Manhattan, waving balloons, chanting "Boycott Exxon!" and "Life Not Profits!" on the 19th anniversary of Earth Day. The protesters carried placards denouncing the company responsible for the worst oil spill in U.S. history (*Los Angeles Times* 1989).

The *Exxon Valdez* spill, unprecedented in its time, galvanized public opinion around oil drilling in the Arctic and environmental and safety regulations of oil transportation in general. The case became emblematic of big oil and 'ecocide' and was brought up again and again by groups mobilizing for a green agenda. In 2005, for example, a dozen environmental and liberal-advocacy groups launched a protest campaign against ExxonMobil (whose subsidiary owned the *Exxon Valdez*). They objected to the oil giant's efforts to expand drilling in Alaska and to cast doubt on the science of global warming (Friends of the Earth 2008).

In addition to its prominence in the US public debate, the Exxon Valdez spill also became a symbol for environmental critique across the world, which remained important for decades. On the 25th anniversary of the *Exxon Valdez* oil spill, Greenpeace climbers scaled an ExxonMobil rig destined to drill in the Russian Arctic calling for a ban on offshore oil drilling in the Arctic and for renewed efforts to fight climate change (Beans 2014).

Case 2: The Erika Disaster

On 12 December 1999 the *Erika*, a Maltese flagged oil tanker sank off Brittany during a transport of 30,884 tonnes of heavy fuel oil from Dunkirk to Livorno (Environmental Justice Atlas 2019).

As *Exxon Valdez* was for the US, the case of *Erika* was a wakeup call for France and Europe. The magnitude of the spill and the length of coastline affected by the disaster resulted in a large number of compensation claims. There are important coastal fisheries, mariculture (oysters and mussels), and tourism resources throughout southern Brittany and the Vendée. Salt production areas were also affected by oil pollution.

The *Erika* oil spill vastly heightened public concern about the safety of maritime transport, highlighting the risks associated with old and poorly maintained ships and the necessity of regulatory harmonization and the enforcement of maritime safety (Safety4Sea nd). About 20,000 demonstrators gathered in the northwest French city of Nantes two months after the incident to show their continued anger (Associated Press 2000a).

As in the *Exxon Valdez* case, the civic engagement about oil spills also directed itself at the petroleum company that had chartered the tanker. The chairman of the Franco-Belgian oil company, Total-Fina, was therefore a frequent target of the crowd's shouts and slogans in the Nantes demonstrations. Total-Fina was also targeted at its company meeting in the 'Pyramide du Louvre', in Paris. After demonstrations outside the French landmark, protesters including members of Greenpeace tried to break in. The demonstration turned violent as police stopped them from entering and turned them away. The protestors wanted Total-Fina to accept blame for the disaster and pay for the damage to the environment (Associated Press 2000b).

Case 3: Prestige Spill

The *Prestige* oil spill in December 2002 remains Spain and Portugal's worst ecological disaster causing significant damage to wildlife, environment, as well as to the local fishing industry. After the ship broke in two and sank, the wreck continued to leak approximately 125 tons of oil a day, polluting the seabed and contaminating the coastline, especially along the territory of Galicia. Several hundred kilometres of coastline were coated in oil sludge, and the sunken *Prestige* leaked fuel oil for years, causing long-lasting damage to the coastline of north-west Spain (*The Guardian* 2002).

The shipwreck immediately became a national concern in Spain, and a demonstration in Barcelona, calling for the resignation of the Spanish prime minister, Jose Maria Aznar, gathered 50,000 protesters. This was the biggest demonstration in a city outside the north-west Galicia region, where the disaster occurred (*The Guardian* 2002).

Occurring just three years after the *Erika* accident, the *Prestige* ship-wreck further strengthened the pressure on Spain and the EU to step up legislative measures to prevent such accidents from happening again.

Transforming Civic Pressure into Hard Law

Eventually, the civic pressure triggered legislation and new laws both in the U.S. and the EU. The mounting civic and meda pressure short-circuited the international expert negotiations in the UN-based International Maritime Organization (IMO), and pushed through unilateral legislation.

In the US strong civic mobilization and the massive media engagement in the *Exxon Valdez* case for strengthening public control of oil tankers, ra-pidly spilled over into the political arena. Under intense civic and media pressure, American politicians could not afford to wait for lengthy inter-national negotiations and woolly compromises. Unsatisfied with the existing regulations of the IMO, the US, therefore, introduced a unilateral policy to protect their economic and environmental interest from future oil spills.

The accident thus prompted an almost immediate reaction from the US regulatory bodies to draft the 1990 Oil Pollution Act, also known as OPA 90. OPA 90 required new oil tankers to be double hulled[1] and established a phase-out scheme for existing single-hulled tankers. Older single-hulled tankers were phased out starting in 1995 and the final date for the phase-out of all single-hulled tankers was set to 2015. The size of the US economy and its international political prestige allowed it to act unilaterally and bypass international negotiations like the IMO.

The phase-out of any particular single-hull tanker was based upon its year of build, its gross tonnage, and whether it had been fitted with either a double side or double bottom.

The International Maritime Organization Follow up

The United States also came to the IMO, calling for double hulls to be made a mandatory requirement of the International Convention for the Prevention of Pollution from Ships (MARPOL). As on previous occasions, there was some resistance on the part of the oil industry, due mainly to the cost of retrofitting existing tankers. Several of the IMO's member states insisted that other designs should be accepted as equivalents and that measures for existing ships should also be contemplated.

Eventually, the IMO experts agreed to make double hulls or alternative designs mandatory "provided that such methods ensure the same level of protection against pollution in the event of a collision or stranding", and that the design methods were approved by the IMO. The requirements were softened, however, by various exemptions to extend the time when a single hull tanker could carry heavy grade oil. This was in order to accom-modate various domestic and regional needs during the transition period.

Erika, Prestige, and EU Engagement

The EU's engagement with the double hull requirement was initially cautious. The first EU regulation to deal with double-hulled oil tankers and segregated ballast tanks was adopted in November 1994 and came into force at the start of 1996. The approach was non-mandatory and based on giving tankers with segregated ballast, double hulls, and alternative designs lowered fees by port, harbour, and pilotage authorities, in order to compensate for the extra installations.

However, the *Erika* catastrophe in December 1999 outraged the public and forced the French government and the EU to threaten unilateral and regional action to prevent further calamities. Futher, the *Erika* disaster forced the IMO to act in order to protect its position as the global forum for international maritime legislation (Stenman 2005).

What *The Exxon Valdez* was to the US, *The Erika* was to the EU. The EU Commission reacted in 2000 by proposing a phase-out scheme for single hull tankers similar to the OPA 90. The new regulation was approved by the European Parliament in the same year, accelerating the phase-in of double hull or equivalent design requirements for single hull tankers. Besides the pressure from public opinion, the tightened regulation was also motivated by concern that single hull tankers banned from US waters because of their age would begin to operate in EU waters.

The civic engagement and media focus on the *Prestige* accident in November 2002, brought further pressure on the EU to strengthen regulations. In December 2002, following the sinking of *The Prestige*, the European Commission proposed to accelerate the phase out scheme approved in 2001 in order to align it with the relevant phase out dates of OPA 90.

EU and IMO

The EU had been pressuring the IMO to tighten the international convention on pollution from ships in order to have a uniform regulation internationally. After political pressure from EU member states, the IMO amended Annex I of the MARPOL so that the single hull phase-out scheme would be similar to the EU's regulation. Following both the *Erika* and the *Prestige* cases, the European Commission made proposals that went far beyond the MARPOL amendments. The Commission was prompted to do so due to, among other reasons, considerable pressure from the European Parliament and French and Spanish political and civic mobilization.

The result was a shift of regimes – from the IMO industry and national interest dominated arena based on consensus, towards a parliamentary voter-dominated arena where the members of the European Parliament were under pressure to prove to voters that they could respond quickly.

The experts of the IMO did not have to prove this ability; instead they looked for a long-term solutions that could lead to a consensus across national interests and they did not have to satisfy voter demands. Given its size and economic significance, the EU was able to follow the US unilateral practice and set its own rules, thereby forcing the IMO to follow. According to this new order the EU decides what it wants before demanding the same from the IMO. The underlying threat is that if the other members of the IMO do not agree, the EU will make its own regulations. The European Commission justified this stance by quoting the example of the U.S. (Stenman 2005).

Civic Mobilization, Media Pressure, and Legislation

The oil-spill accidents illustrate a common pattern of governance innovation, where critical events trigger civic mobilization and media debates, which in turn overflow into politics and generate formal laws that establish new and improved practices. In such processes, the proximity factor is of great importance. The *Valdez* shipwreck prompted strong US legislation and only reluctant EU follow up. However, as in the case of *Erika*, the EU also had to step up. The expert channel of governance – here illustrated by the IMO and its specialist committees – that usually rules the maritime safety domain did not deliver because of its complicated decision-making structure and fragmented interests, and therefore had to be overridden.

Civic Engagement Against Corruption

The Publish What You Pay and the following Extractive Industries' Transparency Initiative cases again illustrates the critical role of civic engagement and the industrious campaigning of CSOs, this time against corruption.

The Publish What You Pay Initiative

The Publish What You Pay initiative was launched through the report "A crude awakening", released by Global Witness, a CSO focusing on corruption and accountability, in 1999 (Global Witness 1999). It presented a critical examination of corruption in the Angolan petroleum industry, placing blame on both the Angolan government and international oil companies, British Petroleum in particular. As the main generators of revenue to the government of Angola, it argued, the international oil industry and financial sector needed to acknowledge their complicity, change their business practices, and create new standards of transparency.

Following the report on corruption and accountability, Global Witness proceeded to organize stronger civic power through the Publish

What You Pay Campaign (PWYP) run by a campaign organisation with the same name, founded in June 2002. Co-founders included CAFOD, the Open Society Institute, Oxfam GB, Save the Children UK, and Transparency International UK. The founding coalition of CSOs was soon joined by others, such as Catholic Relief Services, Human Rights Watch, Partnership Africa Canada, Pax Christi Netherlands, and Secours Catholique/CARITAS France, along with an increasing number of groups from developing countries. In the wake of 'A crude awakening', PWYP was contacted by civil society and community groups from countries that faced the same challenges described in the Angolan report. As a result, PWYP assumed a co-coordinator role to facilitate its wider work. This further contributed to the global spread of the movement for transparent accounting (PWYP nd).

The early phase of the Global Witness initiative illustrates the creative flexibility of civic engagement spearheaded by active CSOs. It sought to overcome blatant regulatory failures of the multinational oil industry, in both host and home countries, by a novel combination of actors, arenas, and media attention. The initial focus on the resource curse of oil-rich countries, combined with coupling it with a new governance initiative, proved highly effective in attracting media interest. This focus also succeeded in linking the campaign to Western policy concerns about good governance, corporate accountability, and poverty reduction. In this way the campaign gained basic acceptance from Western political elites, although these ideals were not always adhered to in political and commercial practice. Through their initiatives, the entrepreneurial CSOs outlined a governance approach with a promising potential to overcome major regulatory hurdles.

Putting the Issue on Business and Policy Agendas

Having raised broad international awarness, the CSOs brought the governance challenge more directly onto business and policy agendas. The report and active CSO campaigning heaped pressure on the oil industry – in the UK in particular – to act on principles to which they were theoretically committed. Through the media the CSOs drew more attention to both corruption and voluntary sector initiatives, which compelled politicians to put their ideals into practice. As momentum increased inside western oil companies, the CSOs also lobbied for revenue transparency, in both their home countries and the oil-rich ones. They targeted the western companies in particluar, seeing them as more likely to engage in dialogue with CSOs than state-owned companies in developing countries. The latter were judged to be less compelled to by the media, brand image, and civic lobbying, to change course in corruption matters.

Human Rights Watch (HRW) added another dimension to the already complex case of transparency in countries suffering from the resource curse: the link to human rights. The theme was brought up in a report published by Stratfor Global Intelligence (2004) directly focusing on human-rights issues facing oil, gas, and mining companies. This put additional pressure on western firms operating in oil-rich countries in the developing world.

Flanked by CSO initiatives and extensive media debate, the Publish What You pay initiative provoked industry engagement, and British Petroleum (BP) – under the influence of public opinion, as well as US regulatory pressure – prepared to disclose its payment to the Angolan government. However, following strong reactions from the Angolan national petroleum company, in the form of a threat to withdraw BP's Angolan license, the company backed down. The setback for the campaign illustrates the importance of persistent learning and adaptation in scaling up and consolidating the civic pressure. Having successfully intensified pressure on industry to make the first move, the PWYP initiative faced a reversal after the Angolan government's reaction caused BP to retreat.

The PWYP initiative had successfully made an impact in public media, but it had failed to push the industry into unilateral action. The next move was to place the initiative on the public policy agenda.

Global Witness, and later the PWYP campaign, mobilized pressure on policy-makers and found considerable support in the UK Department for International Development (DFID). At the time, reports from several UK Embassies in oil-rich developing countries also expressed concern about the transparency and corruption associated with the oil industry which potentially also affected British firms.

Following BP's problematic experience with unilateral company initiatives and the expectations for strong British multi-stakeholder initiatives at the World Summit on Sustainable Development in Johannesburg in 2002, the British Government was persuaded to propose the Extractive Industries' Transparency Initiative.

The Extractive Industries' Transparency Initiative as a Champion of Transparent Business

The EITI was successfully launched at a conference in London in June 2003, with the aim of increasing payment and revenue transparency in the extractive sector. Through this move, the former civic campaign was adopted and institutionalized in the political domain, but only partly. The EITI became a novel bridging enterprise – a multistakeholder forum where the CSOs still played an essential role.

At first the EITI became a promoter of transparent accounting – much in line with the PWYP campaign. It developed 12 principles centred on the need for transparent management of natural resources, seeking to codify a workable template that was simple to undertake and use. The initiative gained promising backing from over 40 institutional investors who signed a statement of support, arguing that information disclosure would improve corporate governance and reduce risk.

Successful International Endorsement

The EITI and transparency in natural resource development was championed at a series of G8 Summits and gained tangible support. The G8 subsequently called on the International Monetary Fund and the World Bank to provide technical assistance to governments wishing to adopt transparency policies. This led to the establishment of the World Bank-administered Multi-Donor Trust Fund (MDTF) for EITI in 2004. The MDTF disbursed almost USD 60 million in technical and financial assistance to EITI programmes in over 40 countries before being replaced by the Extractives Governance Programmatic Support (EGPS) facility in 2016.

Through several stages, the EITI board and administration worked to adjust and tighten the design to ensure that it provided more intelligible, comprehensive, and reliable information. They also endeavoured to better ground the process in a national dialogue about natural resource governance. The improvements also aimed at incentivizing continuous progress beyond compliance. The process culminated with the launch in 2013 of EITI as a standard against which countries could certify their resource management regimes. This standard was subsequently revised in 2016 and 2019.

One of the elements of the standard encouraged countries to disclose "open data" online to enable users to make better use of EITI data to inform public debate about the extractive industries. This was also so that more information could be drawn from existing and emerging on-line sources rather than having to develop separate systems for collecting data for the EITI process. In addition, the standard was actively promoted by governments and international agencies as evidence of their own commitment to good governance. The EITI's tenets were reflected and exceeded in US, European, Nigerian and Liberian legislation, the World Bank's International Finance Corporation's standards for extractive projects, and an increasing set of country-level policies such as the publication of contracts (EITI nd)

Civic Participation at the Core

In spite of attracting heavy political and institutional buy-in, civil society retained a major formal role in operation and decision-making. The EITI protocol on the participation of civil society is thus an integral part of the EITI Standard, as active participation of independent civil society is seen as a prerequisite for public debate and accountability. The relationship between companies, civil society, and governments is formalized in the multi-stakeholder group (MSG,) which is central to the operation and philosophy of the EITI, and reflects how the EITI is governed and implemented. Full, free, active, and effective engagement by civil society alongside government and companies is, in fact, an essential part of the standard.

However, the inclusion of civil society in EITI has not been without its problems. EITI emerged from the political process incorporating quite a few of PWYP's original goals, but stopped short of the stronger policy measures that PWYP campaigned for. While EITI took a voluntary approach, the CSO initiative had focused on mandatory regulation. The CSOs had hoped to make mandatory transparency rules a precondition for listing on the stock exchange. They also wanted rules and accounting standards to be imposed on extractive industries in their home countries. And they demanded similar criteria be used for the World Bank, the IMF, and anyone else who lends money, such as the export credit agencies who fund infrastructure developments.

With voluntary membership, the EITI has had to strike a difficult balance between being too rigorous – and thereby undermining buy-in from countries and businesses – and being too loose to make a difference, and thereby resulting in civil society defection. The extensive resource mobilization from the IMF, the World Bank, and some mature industrial economies like the UK and Norway, is obviously a significant factor behind the EITI's relative success. Furthermore, the fact that EITI is becoming a standard reference for development finance from the same institutions contributes to making membership attractive to many African, Latin American, and some Asian countries. However, there is a telling lack of membership from the oil-rich Arab countries, and large emerging economies like India, China, and Brazil. Russia is also conspicuously absent.

The Logic of Civic Governance

The two cases discussed in this chapter share essential characteristics that lie at the core of much of civil society governance:

Firstly they appeal to a *widely shared normative basis*. The claims against industrial practice and the voicing of social and environmental concerns that were put forward in both the anti oil spill and the anti corruption cases resonated with public sentiment and appealed to widely held norms. Paradoxically, in this case, civic engagement has strong affinities with pre-democratic political theory. Already in the 18th century, Rousseau advanced the idea of a "social contract" between the sovereign and his people that obliged the sovereign to respect widely held social norms, irrespective of formal codification. Rousseau claimed that a breach of such norms gave people the right to rebel and overthrow the ruler. Civic engagement against immoral, but formally legal, business behaviour in both the Oil spill and PWYP cases thus rests on classical political theory. This has led advanced segments of industry to recognise that in addition to their duties under written law they must respect basic social norms and values. The social contract idea has, in fact, been explicitly picked up by reform-oriented business groups such as the World Business Council for Sustainable Development (WBCSD nd). Democratic governments, of course, have channels for absorbing public concenrns into formal decision-making that may be activated to override politics as usual when confronted by mounting civic pressure.

Secondly, the contestation of formal rights and established institutional practice rests on *access to communication channels*, both for information and mobilization, as indicated in both cases. The evolution of a media-society with capacity for mass-marketing also facilitates mass commu-nication of business and government malpractice. Furthermore, new media have lowered the threshold and opened global information systems to less endowed civic activists – although large disparities still remain. Against this background, the British-Australian political scientist, John Keane, has coined the term *monitory democracy* denoting a novel channel for bottom-up political engagement and adding a digital dimension to the analysis of social movements (Keane 2013). Empowered by digital com-munication, watchdog groups, CSOs, and local communities subject government and business to scrutiny.

Thirdly, in both cases, a *civic capability for strategic action* was devel-oped. In the PWYP case, Global Witness and the subsequent PWYP coa-lition could mobilize strong and persistent pressure on industry and government. Even after the EITI's institutionalization, the PWYP coalition retained seats in the governing bodies to oversee policy implementation. In the tanker-oil spill cases, strong local civic mobilization, including en-vironmentalists, businesses, workers, and local mayors instigated massive political pressure on legislators. In the *Exxon Valdez* case, this pressure led to the swift passage of the Oil Pollution Act. In the *Prestige* case, the pressure was similarly driven by local civic engagement. Galician activists founded the environmental movement Nunca Máis (Galician for 'Never Again'), to denounce the passivity of the conservative government towards the disaster. In the *Erika* case, pollution along the Brittany coast engendered strong local mobilization, spilling over into national politics as thousands of protesters from western France marched through Paris to demand tighter shipping laws in the wake of the accident (Marine Link 2000).

As I have previously argued (Midttun 2008), the emergence of strong local movements and CSOs with strategic action capability is vital for successful civic impact. Having become catalysers of public sentiment in the media, local movements and CSOs acquire 'moral bargaining rights' in formal decision-making arenas. The threat of brand damage through CSO- or local community-mobilized media exposure may hurt companies with advanced home markets that avow high social and environmental standards. Likewise, national political elites can hardly withstand compelling demands for action from local communities when faced with local disasters and strong media appeal. The participation of CSOs with global outreach may serve to generalize demands for legislative reform. Such CSOs are often capable of acting more flexibly across national jurisdictions than current national jurisprudence.

Nevertheless, both the PWYP and oil spill cases illustrate the need for pulling in formal state governance to anchor policy decisions and establish new practices that persist over time. In the PWYP case, the establishment of EITI represents an interesting hybrid-organization across government, business, and civic divides. Financial and administrative stability is anchored with governments, but civil society organizations keep up the pressure for maintaining an anti-corruption vigilance. In the oil-spill cases, new legislation on double-hull tankers represented a preliminary endpoint, with hard law engraving the outcomes of civic and local society mobilization.

Standards as an alternative to Hard Law

Ultimately, many of the normative visions may make their way into legislation at the national or regional level, and/or into some kind of international agreement. However, the endpoint of transformational governance is not necessarily only new formal regulation. In many cases – particularly when concerted action across regions is called for – arriving at implementable agreements on social and environmental upgrading under hard international law is at best a long uphill struggle, and often one that is hard to win. In this situation, CSOs often find greater progress by challenging and/or working with industry directly, and pushing to improve industrial social, environmental, and governance practices. If successful, such processes may lead to the development of industry standards that, although not legally enforceable, nevertheless may wield strong normative power and become essential requirements for selling to customers.

Such processes typically evolve along polycentric trajectories. They may emerge out of critique of industrial practices in targeted firms by CSOs and amplified by the traditional and social media. As the criticism gains traction, firms and the industry in question may be compelled to respond. If the issues are generic to a specific business sector, the process may evolve into CSO-led initiatives directed at the sector in general. In turn, this may lead to consolidation of industrial standards with buy-in from industry that may see compliance as a way of avoiding brand-damaging conflicts, or even a means of building positive brand image.

Finally, if credible third-party verification of compliance with the standard is included, it approaches the solidity of hard law, and may also attract public endorsement and even financial support.

The development of the EITI standard for good governance of petroleum and mineral resources is a case in point, and we shall further illustrate the 'governance through standards' approach relating to the forestry certification standards and the Ethical Trading Initiative. The first concerns environmental and the second concerns social upgrading of the economy.

The Forest Stewardship Case

Established in 1993 to drive forward an agenda for sustainable forestry, the CSO initiative, the Forest Stewardship Council (FSC) offered certification of sustainable and ecologically-sound forestry. The standard was based on a set of principles and criteria for forest management that addresses legal issues, indigenous rights, labour rights, and environmental impacts relating to forest management (FSC, nd).

The scheme met with critical opposition from leading forest industry groups. Although they shared some basic ecological concerns with the FSC, in their view the Council was making unrealistic demands that would impede efficient forestry practices. The forest industry therefore responded with a set of CSR&S-based regulatory initiatives to establish more 'realistic' standards for sustainable forestry, and in this way embarked on a polycentric governance process through contestation.

In North America, the 'realistic' alternative put forward by forest industry – the American Forest and Paper Association – was the Sustainable Forest Initiative (SFI) programme. A similar initiative was taken in Europe, where The European Programme for the Endorsement of Forest Certification schemes (PEFC) was established in 1999 as an umbrella organization for certification.

The rivalry between CSO-driven and industry-driven standards implied a competition for governance, with rival regulatory regimes and regulatory actors behind them.

The green movement and the FSC regarded certification as a mechanism to reward – through continued market access – only the very best forest management and to promote an ideal of forest management that mimicked natural processes and preserves so-called 'old growth'. They promoted a vision of a single, internationally harmonized system of forest certification requiring forest owners to comply with very high standards of forestry performance.

In contrast, industry and forest owner groups tended to regard certification as a mechanism to promote progressive, step-by-step improvements in forest management (Olivier 2006). These groups also believed that certification should provide an effective marketing tool to promote the environmental benefits of wood.

Leading firms in the forest and wood processing industry have generally taken a pragmatic position on extra-legal regulation. They relate to both CSO and industry standards and seek to bridge the gap between ideals and reality by flagging adherence in principle but adopting pragmatic adjustment and gradual implementation in practice. To a large extent this reflected different expectations from their customers, such as publishers and printing houses.

By promoting their own standard, the FSC managed to provoke regulatory competition and most likely raised environmental and social requirements in the forestry industry. The FSC standard, and the forest industry standards that were developed to counter it, set new norms for forestry and disciplined producer countries by exposing their compliance to customers and CSOs. The push for regulation through standards and regulatory competition with the forest industry has most likely heightened environmental and social standards in the forest industry.

The Retailing Industry and the Ethical Trading Initiative

The Retailing industry, including such branches as food supply and clothing, is another sector of the economy where polycentric regulation through standards has come to play a major role. The sector has been challenged to assume responsibility for working conditions, human rights and safety in its value chain, which often stretches back to developing countries. Negative press exposure about practices in retail supply chains has time and again had a detrimental effect in the sector's brand-sensitive consumer markets. A case in point is Nike, the footwear retailer and manufacturer, which has received intense media criticism for bad working conditions in its Asian factories. Similar criticism has been leveled at the food chain, ICA Norge, which has been forced to carry out internal investigations after the press accused it of using child labour.

The Ethical Trading Initiative (ETI) emerged as a systematic response to these challenges and is an example of 'voluntary' polycentric governance where industry joins core stakeholders in co-defining standards for commercial behaviour. It was developed collaboratively by trade unions and other CSOs, retailing businesses, and governments, building on the UN Declaration of Human Rights, ILO principles, and a convention on multinational enterprises and social policy.

The initiative has developed in response to emerging challenges, such as poor work conditions. This includes the use of child labour in China as the country became a major supplier, poor work conditions in the South African wine and agricultural industry, and poor fire and building safety in Bangladesh, to mention just a few. The initiative did not only include retailers, but also partnered with the British NHS Purchasing and

Supply Agency to help develop a policy and implementation framework for the ethical procurement of goods and services, much of which came from overseas.

The polycentric character of the ETI governance model allows governance to be orchestrated through multiple channels. These include peer pressure to conform to common standards within the ETI system, normative pressure by engaged public opinion in home markets with ties to potential consumers, and negative signals from home governments and international institutions, including financial bodies.

Several Trajectories to Sustainability

To sum up, the moral challenge by CSOs and other stakeholders has resulted in social and ecological governance along several trajectories (Figure 9.1). One trajectory involves making sustainability part of a corporate differentiation strategy where leading firms absorb ecological and social concerns successively into their strategic core. Another trajectory has been to incrementally internalize such concerns into industrial standards in an attempt to lift the social and environmental performance of whole sectors of the economy. In both cases, this contributes to embedding environmental and social concerns into industrial practice.

The differentiation strategy, as described in CSR literature, has evolved in several stages (Figure 9.1 – vertical dimension).

Many firms have started out their CSR&S engagement in a defensive and reactive, mode, responding to challenges by media and/or civil

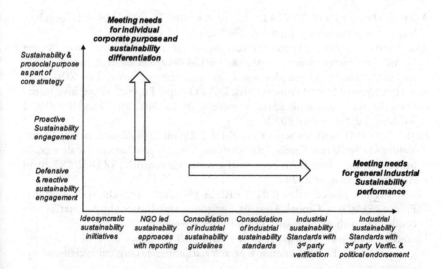

Figure 9.1 Trajectories of Governance.

Source: Author.

society. A further step towards a sustainability-differentiated business strategy has been to engage in sustainability as part of a supportive strategy. Car manufacturers developing green niche vehicles alongside their dominant combustion-driven mainstream cars are good examples. The final step is to merge CSR&S into the core business strategy in order to build a unique business model for the firm. An illustration of this is energy companies that devote themselves exclusively or dominantly to renewable technologies and link their business strategy to sustainable development and climate change.

The introduction of CSR into industrial standards has also evolved in stages (Figure 9.1, horizontal dimension). It typically also starts with ad hoc reactions to CSO challenges, often followed by CSO-led engagements in sector-specific environmental and/or social accounting. Taken further, this process leads to the consolidation of industrial guidelines and in some cases of standards. When backed by third-party verification, such standards may take on serious performance implications. Finally, standards may eventually gain political endorsement and thereby assume a quasi-legal character.

Note

1 A double hull tanker is a ship designed for carriage of oil in bulk where the cargo spaces are protected from the environment by a double side and double bottom spaces dedicated to the carriage of ballast water.

References

Aristotle (1974) [330 BCE] *The Poetics of Aristotle*. Translated by S. H. Butcher. https://www.gutenberg.org/files/1974/1974-h/1974-h.htm.
Associated Press (2000a) Demonstrators protest oil spill off French coast. Deseret News. https://www.deseret.com/2000/2/6/19489497/demonstrators-protest-oil-spill-off-french-coast Accessed November 2020.
Associated Press (2000b) France: Paris: Erika Oil Spill Protest. AP Archive http://www.aparchive.com/metadata/youtube/0208fc524b838fc0f7abd4c9b0af92 64 Accessed November 2020.
Beans, L. (2014) Activists Scale ExxonMobil Rig on 25th Anniversary of Exxon Valdez Oil Spill. EcoWatch. https://www.ecowatch.com/activists-scale-exxon-mobil-rig-on-25th-anniversary-of-exxon-valdez-oil-1881879687.html Accessed November 2020.
Environmental Justice Atlas (2019) ERIKA Shipwreck and Oil Spill, Brittany, France. EJAtlas – Global Atlas of Environmental Justice. https://ejatlas.org/conflict/erika-shipwreck-and-oil-spill-britanny-france.
Extractive Industries Transparency Initiative (nd) Guidance on civil society engagement (1.3). EITI International Secretariat. https://eiti.org/guide/civil-society-engagement.
Forest Stewardship Council (nd) https://fsc.org/en Accessed October 2020.

Freeman, E.R. (1984) *Strategic Management: A Stakeholder Approach*. Boston: Pitman.

Friends of the Earth (2008) Environmental and Public Interest Groups "Exxpose" Exxon: Landmark Campaign to Expose Exxon Mobil's Dangerous Environmental Policies. Friends of the Earth Press Release. https://foe.org/news/2008-11-environmental-and-public-interest-groups-exxpose-exx/ Accessed November 2020.

Global Witness (1999) A Crude Awakening: The Role of Oil and Banking Industries in Angola's Civil War and the Plunder of State Assets. Global Witness Ltd. https://cdn.globalwitness.org/archive/files/pdfs/a%20crude%20awakening.pdf.

The Guardian (2002) Thousands join Prestige protest https://www.theguardian.com/environment/2002/dec/16/oilspills.pollution.

History.com editors (2018) Exon Valdez Oil Spill. History.com. https://www.history.com/topics/1980s/exxon-valdez-oil-spill.

ITOPF (nd). ERIKA, West of France (1999) ITOPF. https://www.itopf.org/in-action/case-studies/case-study/erika-west-of-france-1999/.

Keane, J. (2013) Civil Society in the Era of Monitory Democracy. In Lars Trägårdh, Nina Witoszek, and Bron Taylor (eds), *Civil Society in the Age of Monitory Democracy* (Studies on Civil Society). New York & Oxford: Berghahn Books.

Los Angeles Times (1989) 2,500 Oil Spill Protesters Converge on Exxon Offices https://www.latimes.com/archives/la-xpm-1989-04-23-mn-1943-story.html Accessed November 2020.

Lubell, M. (2017) Polycentric Governance: A Concept Searching for a Theory. Center for Environment Policy and Behavior, UC Davis.

Macalister, T. (2002) 'Ethical' BP Linked to Angolan Claims. *The Guardian*. 23 February. http://www.guardian.co.uk/business/2002/feb/27/oilandpetrol.bp Accessed February 2011.

Marine Link (2000) Activists Stage Erika Protest, TotalFina Mulls Oil Treatment Contract. Marine Link. https://www.marinelink.com/news/activists-totalfina32046

Midttun, A. (2008) Partnered Governance: Aligning Corporate Responsibility and Public Policy in the Global Economy. *Corporate Governance* 8(4).

Parsons, T (1970) *The Social System*. London: Routledge & Kegan Paul.

Perunovic, Z. and Perunovic, J.V. (2011) Innovation in the Maritime Industry. POMS 22nd Annual Conference. https://www.pomsmeetings.org/confpapers/020/020–0355.pdf.

Porter, M.E. and Kramer, M.R. (2011) Creating Shared Value. *Harvard Business Review*, January-February issue.

Publish What You Pay (PWYP) (nd) https://www.pwyp.org/

Putnam, R., Leonardi, R. and Nanetti, R.Y. (1994) *Making Democracy Work: Civic Traditions in Modern Italy*. Princeton: Princeton University Press.

Putnam, R. D. (1993)The Prosperous Community: Social Capital and Public Life The American Prospect 13 (Spring), https://scholar.harvard.edu/robertputnam/publications/prosperous-community-social-capital-and-public-life.

Olivier, R. (2006) Price premiums for verified legal and sustainable timber A study for the UK Timber Trade Federation (TTF) and Department for International Development (DFID), http://agronegocios.catie.ac.cr/images/pdf/Price_premiums_for_verified_legal_and_sustainable.pdf.

Reynolds, P. (2002) Analysis: Tightening Rules on Tankers. BBC News, 19 November.

Sabatier, P. (1998). The Advocacy Coalition Framework: Revisions and Relevance for Europe. *Journal of European Public Policy* 5(1).

Safety4Sea (2018) Learn from the Past: Erika Oil Spill, Europe's Environmental Disaster. Safety4Sea.com. https://safety4sea.com/?s=Erika.

Sax, S. (2019) The 1989 Exxon Valdex oil spill, how we see climate change then and now. PBS. https://www.pbs.org/wnet/peril-and-promise/2019/03/thirty-years-exxon-valdez/.

Stenman C. (2005) The development of MARPOL and EU regulations to phase out single hulled oil tankers. Master's thesis. School of Economics and Law, Gothenburg University.

Stratfor Global Intelligence (2004) Human Rights: A New Lever for Angolan Oil Transparency?, available at: www.stratfor.com/memberships/84157/human_rights_new_lever_angolan_oil_transparency Accessed 15 September 2009.

Tocqueville A. de. (2000) Democracy in America. Translated, edited and with an introduction by Chicago and London: University of Chicago Press.

10 Bringing the State Back In

The late 20th and early 21st century has been depicted as the age of deregulation where strong state engagement in the economy has been pushed back by privatization. Dissenting voices have, however, called for 'bringing the state back in' to balance the unwanted side-effects of liberalization. These include calls for the reinforcement of the state's territorial control and capacity to forge collective action by Evans, Rueschemayer and Skocpol in 1985, and a plea for consolidating the state's contribution to innovation by Mariana Mazzucato in 2013. Most recently, the essential role of the state has again been underlined by the Covid pandemic and the urgent need for state led crisis management.

However, the neoliberal rhetoric did not reflect realities on the ground. Major OECD economies, did not scale down the state to a minimum, under the neoliberal political shift in the 1980s and 1990s but rather kept up the volume of state engagement and even increased it. In this sense, the state was never thrown out, and modern capitalist economies were characterized by massive public expenditure right through the 'neoliberal era'. This pattern is clearly documented by the statistics of public social spending throughout the 20th century (Figure 10.1).

Until the First World War, public social spending was generally under 2% of GDP, and used to finance basic functions such as maintaining order and enforcing property rights. The two world wars triggered extensive public spending as part of the war economy. However, following World War Two, spending continued to escalate dramatically, even under the neoliberal turn towards the end of the century. What took place was the build-up of a massive public economy engaged in infrastructure and welfare services, with as much as 20–30% of GDP under public management, right through the neoliberal period.

Measured by government revenues, the size of the public economy is even larger. On average in 2018, government revenues in the European Union amounted to 45% of GDP. Revenues represent more than half of GDP in advanced welfare states such as Norway (57%), France (53.4%), Finland (52.5%), Belgium (51.4%), and Denmark (51.2%) (OECD 2020).

DOI: 10.4324/9781315454931-10

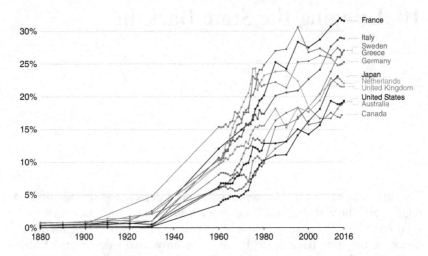

Figure 10.1 Public Social Spending as Share of GDP.

Source: Our World in Data (2020) https://ourworldindata.org/government-spending.

What needs to be brought back in, however, is novel (post-neoliberal) theorizing of the state's role in economic governance. This includes exploring the channels for the state to strengthen the public interest under asymmetric globalization, where markets have extended globally far ahead of politics.

Transcending the rhetorical battle between neoliberalism and its social-democratic and 'etatist' counterpart, this book argues that mature Western economies in the early 21st century are better characterized as *ambidextrous economies*, where both private and public elements are in a dynamic interplay. This combination, which is often seen as incompatible may, I contend, be complementary. Mature modern economies need both a private, interest-driven economy, with a strong focus on efficiency and profitability, and public interest enterprises, with financial means deployed to respond to wider societal concerns.

On the surface, this melange reiterates the 20th century concept of a 'mixed economy'. However, in the past this melange was based on stronger state control of the economy than globalization allows today. The ambidextrous economy will therefore need to promote the public interest through different institutional mechanisms, while making use of novel developments in organization theory that today presents a plethora of hybrid solutions allowing for exiting the traditional market versus plan straightjacket.

Purpose and Agency

Under the modern theory of economic organization, the critical distinction between public and private economies is not necessarily tied to ownership, but refers to purpose and agency.

With respect to purpose, the private economy most often has private investor interests at its core. This typically implies a preference for relatively short investment horizons, and at best only secondary attention to social ramifications that are not essential to the firm's or the project's financial bottom line. This does not preclude engagement in products, services, and projects with great value to society, but they need to be relatively close to commercial maturity with quite low risk, or alternatively very high profitability. As shown in previous chapters, the private business model may be modified by explicit charter, which allows for inclusion of some specific public interest. However, the need for financial liquidity sets boundaries as to how far this can go.

The public economy can take a broader view where the public interest is at stake. While public agencies have budgetary constraints, and public corporations are under pressure to deliver on the financial bottom line, they may have mandates and resources that allow longer investment horizons, and a wider scope to include broader social and environmental concerns.

As a consequence of differences in purpose, private and public interest driven economies differ with respect to agency, who is mandated to make strategic choices, and who occupies subordinate roles to implement them. Under a public interest economy, where public resources are mobilized, representatives of the public interest must be the principals at the helm. In the private interest-driven economy, where private means are invested, representatives of private investors must be in charge. Admittedly, cooperative chartering may include a wider set of private principals – workers or consumers – but even so, their decisions could not be said to represent the broader interests of society.

Recent theory of economic organization allows more flexibility than before in mixing purpose and agency. While the traditional view has been that public interest, supervised by government, presupposes a planned economy, modern theory of economic organization – in part inspired by neoliberal thought – allows for flexibility and both public and private agency (see e.g. Milgrom and Roberts 1992). Thus, while the general direction in the public economy must be set by a public-interest-focused principal, lower-level agency may be left to private market actors, for instance on a tender basis; alternatively, publicly-owned entities may be exposed to market competition.

It follows that economic efficiency, traditionally ascribed to private interests, can indeed be achieved also in the public interest economy, even under public ownership. Yet it also follows that public interest dictated goals, beyond the business case, can be pursued through considerable private agency.

That said, for the ambidextrous economy to be both fair and productive, multilevel selection must also apply. Collaborative pro-social organization at one level must be competitively challenged at another to retain efficiency and productivity. Yet sufficient collaborative capacity must be built in as counterpoints to competition at various levels to promote fairness.

As a consistent re-theorizing of the state's role in post-neoliberal economic governance by far exceeds the scope of this book, we can just single out elements reflecting the need for state engagement in core domains. They include:

- Crisis management – the need for the state in economic and epidemiological crises;
- Distributive fairness – requiring a stronger state in establishing fairness in the economy;
- Transition to eco-modernity – with the state supporting innovation dynamic and societal transformation;
- Inclusive work-life – where the state facilitates societal accommodation of massive AI opportunities.

The two first elements are discussed below, while the two latter will be the subject of the subsequent chapter.

Ambidexterity for Crisis Management

The limits of the private interest-driven economy and the need for massive support from the public economy when crises arise have been amply demonstrated by the 2008 financial crisis and the 2019–2021 Covid-19 pandemic. The diverse crisis-resistance of the private and public economies stems from differences in the very construction of private and public entities.

Enterprises operating under private capitalist principles are concerned with trimming their investments to optimize returns. In the conditions of crises and instability, this approach easily triggers a 'race to the bottom': crises elicit, understandably, a strong tendency for private investors to undertake a flight to safe assets and a rush to liquidity. This again increases the risk of widespread defaults, with ensuing unemployment.

The public interest economy is generally more resilient, and is typically more purpose-driven than attuned to reflect immediate market signals. Furthermore, in well-managed advanced economies, it is typically more financially robust, backed up by public budgetary commitments. Admittedly, such budgets will be hurt when crises severely affect public tax revenue. However, this effect is usually delayed, giving more leeway to bringing in added resources. Moreover, public authorities have recourse to various financial reserves and instruments that may keep public enterprises, or enterprises contracting with the public sector, going for a good while. Additionally, countries with their own currency may de facto 'print money' until they eventually run into serious inflation.

In both the 2008 financial crisis, with the subsequent 'Great Recession', and the Covid-19 pandemic, followed by massive economic losses, much of the private economy moved into lockdown and a downward spiral. Only strong public policy intervention and huge mobilization of the public economy managed to stop it and gradually return the economy back to some kind of normality.

The Scale of the Crises

The 21st-century financial crises were enormous. Among the 19 OECD countries which experienced a banking crisis over the period 2007–11 the median loss in output as much as six years later – in 2014 – was estimated to be about 5½ percent, compared with a loss in aggregate potential output across all OECD countries of about 3½ percent. The loss, however, varied widely across countries, amounting to more than 10% for several smaller European nations (Ollivaud and Turner 2014).

With respect to the Covid pandemic, the International Monetary Fund (IMF) expected that the global economy in 2020 would experience its worst recession since the Great Depression of the 1930s, surpassing that seen during the global financial crisis. The advanced economies, the IMF forecast, were in line to experience a 6.1% contraction in 2020. With a projected downturn of –7.5%, the Euro area is even more exposed.

The reactions from the private interest-driven economy included – predictably – shutdowns, layoffs, and a scramble for liquidity, as its marginalist efficiency orientation dictates it to do. Airlines went bust or were kept afloat by public economic support. Hotel and restaurant sectors were also massively hit with huge layoffs of employees, and large parts of the culture-economy stagnated.

Failing growth triggered unemployment. In the USA, already in March 2020, over 20 million Americans had applied for unemployment benefit (World Economic Forum 2020) and a research study from Cornell Law School (Alpert et al. 2019) assessed that more than 37 million (mostly lower-wage) jobs might be vulnerable to short-term retrenchment due to the COVID-19 crisis and the response to it (Richter 2020).

In Europe, a McKinsey study estimated that up to nearly 59 million jobs (26% of total employment) across Europe were potentially at risk of reductions within hours, or pay temporary furloughs, or permanent layoffs (Chin et al. 2020).

The Public Economy Saving Operation

The scale and scope of the public interventions, over a decade apart, were equally massive. In the United States the Economic Stimulus Act of 2008 provided $152 billion stimulus designed to help stave off a recession following the financial crisis (CW Politics 2008). The 2008 Troubled Asset Relief Program allowed the federal government to deploy $700 billion to stabilize the struggling financial system (TARP nd). Much of the first half of that money was spent injecting cash into troubled banks during the final months of 2008, ensuring that the financial system did not collapse (Fratianni and Marchionne 2010).

In the EU, most Euro area governments responded to the financial crisis by providing economic assistance to ailing financial institutions with the aim of safeguarding financial stability and preventing a credit crunch. Over the period 2008-14 accumulated gross financial sector assistance amounted to 8% of Eurozone GDP. These measures contributed to a massive increase in Eurozone general government debt, which rose by 27 percentage points between 2008 and the end of 2014, when it stood at 92% of GDP (European Central Bank 2015).

With the COVID-19 crisis, the public economy had to step in once again with towering resources, setting new records both in the US and the EU. Firstly, massive rescue packages were unleashed to secure financial liquidity and to keep the private economy alive. Together with unemployment benefits to laid-off workers, this has served not only to prevent human tragedies but also to maintain the necessary level of consumption in society.

In addition, there has been long term intervention, for recovery and economic growth. In March 2020 the US launched the single largest relief package in American history – a $2 trillion formula to help unemployed workers and industries hurt by the COVID-19 crisis (World Economic Forum 2020, Pramuk 2020). In April 2020, European Union finance ministers agreed on half-a-trillion Euros worth of support for their coronavirus-battered economies but left open the question of how to finance recovery in the bloc which was headed for a steep recession (Strupczewski 2020).[1] The stronger role of the states in the European Union implies that more of the public economic engagement takes place at the national level.

The Public Economy's Role as a Tool of Crisis Management

Both the financial and COVID-19 economic crises illustrate the fragility of the deregulated, privatized neoliberal economy. In both cases, private markets went into a tailspin which was only arrested by massive public intervention. As private investors in crisis-struck sectors shut down, or moved into gold and safe havens as best they could, the public economy to a large extent prevailed. Furthermore, enormous public investment was brought in to save leading market economies. All across the capitalist economies, irrespective of their political orientation, public money was pumped into the private economy on a scale never seen before.

Reinventing a monetarist 'super-Keynesianism' made the neoliberal aversion to active state intervention in the economy evaporate, as long as it was channelled through the central bank and pumped into the banking system. This new central bank activism was scaled up dramatically under the financial crisis, to set an entirely new standard. As this book is written, a massive intervention under the financial crisis is being complemented by new central bank activism to counteract the economic downturn precipitated by the COVID-19 crisis.

What is striking is that, as the pandemic unfolded, vast institutions of the ordinary public economy – administration, schools, universities, transport, health care system etc. – have kept on operating throughout the crises. They have acted as economic and social stabilizers, without which societies might not survive in a 'civilized' form. Admittedly, a few private sectors that thrive on the crisis – such as ICT communication under Covid – are part of this pull in the right direction, but they are clearly insufficient to carry society and the economy through to economic and social recovery. For that to happen, we are dependent on mobilizing the full force of the public economy alongside the private sector, in an ambidextrous effort to pull us out of the mire.

The Erosion of Fairness

While the second half of the 20th century saw the extensive rise in equality in most Western economies, the late 20th and early 21st century witnessed the start of a reversal towards inequality. This shifting trend has come in parallel with the political wave of deregulation and economic liberalization and weakening of the bargaining position of the working class. As de-regulation and globalization have translated international inequalities into competitive pressure on Western wages, the bargaining power of Western workers weakened. Minimum wage differentials of up to 1 to 9 (Figure 10.2) between Western, and Eastern, and Southern economies proved to be irresistible stimuli to outsourcing as trade barriers declined.

The current pressure against Western industrial jobs stands in stark contrast to its heyday in the previous century, when the Western worker enjoyed a unique bargaining position. Under Western industrial hegemony, S/he operated unique technologies only available to western workers, and produced for a mass-consumption society that became steadily richer. This was an economy where the consumption power of industrial workers was a necessary component for the economic wheels to go around.

Raymond Vernon's (1966) classic work on the international product cycle captures the essential traits of the US and Western industrial hegemony in its halcyon days:

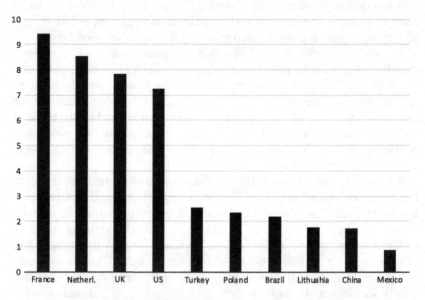

Figure 10.2 Minimum Wagers Selected Countries (2012/2013 Values).

Source: Naitionmaster (nd) https://www.nationmaster.com/country-info/stats/Labor/
Salaries-and-benefits/Hourly-minimum-wage.

- Technologically advanced products made their breakthrough in America. They exploited advanced skilled labour and production capabilities production serving high-income consumers in the home market.
- As the product matured and became more of a commodity, and demand from consumers in other markets rose, production increasingly shifted abroad to other advanced industrial nations, enabling the firm to maximize economies of scale and bypass trade barriers.
- As the production process became increasingly standardized, this enabled further economies of scale and increased the mobility of manufacturing operations. To counter price competition and trade barriers or simply to meet local demand, production facilities often relocated to lower-income countries.

With deregulation, globalization, and diffusion of technological parity, or even sometimes leadership, to emerging Asiatic economies, the Western hegemony, described by Vernon in the 1960s, has been declining. Western private interest-driven enterprises have realized this and globalized, thereby capitalizing on the competitive advantages of Asiatic production, while serving Western consumers with a high willingness to pay.

The Western worker, on the other hand, was forced to compete with products made in Japan, made in Korea, and made in China. Intriguingly, the state and the public economy has followed suit. Under pressure to increase productivity and efficiency in public service delivery, public procurement has enthusiastically engaged in global outsourcing, also thereby undermining wages in public sector employment. As former secretary of Labor, Robert Reich remarked: "For three decades after World War II, America created the largest middle class the world had ever seen. During those years the earnings of the typical American worker doubled, just as the size of the American economy doubled. Over the last thirty years, by contrast, the size of the economy doubled again but the earnings of the typical American went nowhere" (Reich 2015).

Nevertheless, large parts of the public economy, in Western countries have enhanced distributive fairness through its redistributive service functions. As illustrated in Figure 10.3, the predominantly private interest-directed economy (first columns) is therefore far more unfair than the ambidextrous combination, where the public interest economy is also involved (see second columns). Without public services and transfers being factored in, even the supposedly egalitarian Nordic countries have inequalities closer to countries like the USA and the UK, known for their liberalist orientations. In other words, the public economy is still essential for promoting fairness, even if public sector neoliberal efficiency and procurement policies point the other way.

Monetarist Super-Keynesianism

One of the major debates between welfare-state-oriented, Keynesian economists on the one hand, and neoliberalists on the other, has been that they offer supposedly different policy prescriptions to promote economic growth. Neoliberal doctrine has traditionally involved imposing fiscal restraint, if not austerity, on the state. A common argument has been that public cushioning of the troubled industries to save jobs and withstand downturns in business cycles should be avoided. Instead, one should allow transformation towards new competitive business, and prevent public debt piling up. This position stands in explicit contrast to Keynesian fiscal activism, traditionally advocated by social-democratic economists.

This difference in outlook on economic stimulus translates into distributive consequences in so far as state, or public interest-financed growth-investments may have distributive policies attached to them, while pure private interest-driven investments seldom do.

However, in response to the financial crisis, liberalist governments started up what turned out to be massive public investments in the economy, channelled through central banks. This new central bank activism was scaled up dramatically when the financial crisis erupted, thus setting an entirely new standard, only to be vastly expanded under the Corona pandemic little more than decade later. Under monetarist 'super-Keynesianism', the neoliberal allergy towards active state engagement in

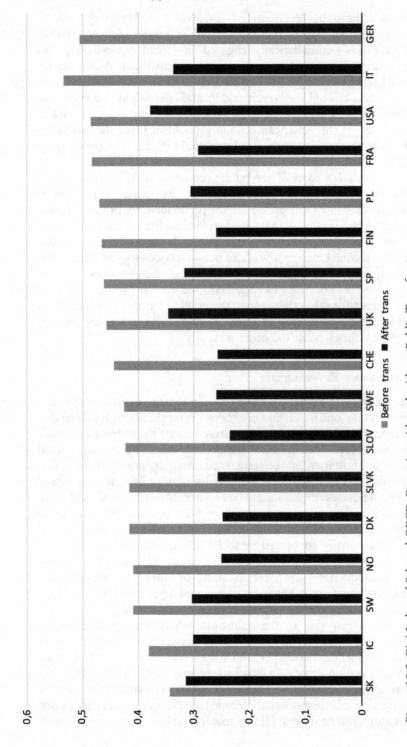

Figure 10.3 Gini Index of Selected OECD Countries with and without Public Transfers.

Source: World Bank (2020) and OECD (2015) https://www.oecd.org/social/income-distribution-database.htm, https://datacatalog.worldbank.org/dataset/all-ginis-dataset.

the economy vanished, as long as it was channelled through the central bank, and pumped into the banking system, a process known as 'Quantitative Easing' (QE).[2]

While it is easy to understand the need for state engagement to save the economy under deep crises, the QE way of doing it has several weaknesses. The effects on the 'real economy' are fairly indirect and weak. The broader effects on output and employment are only secondary, after banks and other asset holders have increased their wealth. Typically, however, they will invest in the 'financial economy' in property and financial holdings, and thereby continue to drive up asset prices. Only after this has occurred will investors seeking a higher return venture into riskier 'real economy' investments in services and industrial production. In short, while the QE injects massive amounts of cheap money into the banking sector, only a fraction trickles down to non-financial sectors (Bank for International Settlements 2018).

Inequality and Unfairness

The direct impact of QE on asset prices, especially equities, has predominantly benefited rich investors who save more than the poor. While keeping borrowing costs down, low-interest rates and QE drive up asset prices, heightening inequality and exacerbating social injustice. Such inequalities hit young people in particular. They typically have few assets, and face rising house prices, sluggish real wages, and job insecurity.

A study by the French Bank, Société Générale, (Huynh and De Boissezon in Watts 2020) has estimated that the Federal Reserve's extraordinary monetary policy actions, particularly Quantitative Easing, have hugely lifted the S&P 500 and Nasdaq 100 (Figure 10.4). Without QE, the Nasdaq-100 NDX should be closer to 5,000 than its 11,000 level at the end of October 2020, while the S&P 500 SPX should be closer to 1,800 rather than 3,300.

Monetarist 'Super-Keynesianism' without Political Control

The result of large-scale continuous Quantitative easing entails enormous expansion of the financial sector, with little social or sustainability policy direction. Before the Covid-19 crisis and following the financial crisis, public investment in the private economy through monetary policy stood at over $5,000 billion in the US, and €2,700 billion in the EU. This is likely to more than double in the early 2020s, transferring huge assets from the private to the public economy through central bank investments (Figure 10.5). Given the severity of the crisis and the expected duration of recovery, this only represents a dramatic start of what is likely to be a gigantic financial bloating of the public economy to supplement and stimulate the private interest economy.

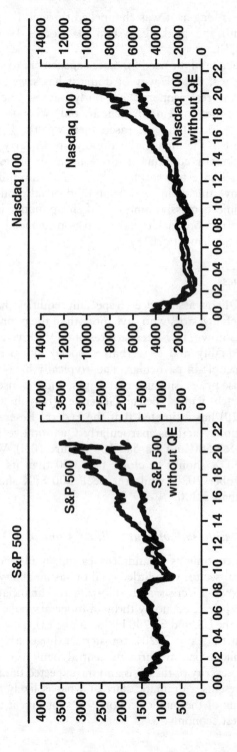

Figure 10.4 Effects of Extraordinary Monetary Policy on S&P 500 and Nasdaq 100.

Source: Huynh, S. & De Boissezon, C. (2020) 'US Equity Strategy' Societe Generale, Cross Asset Research.

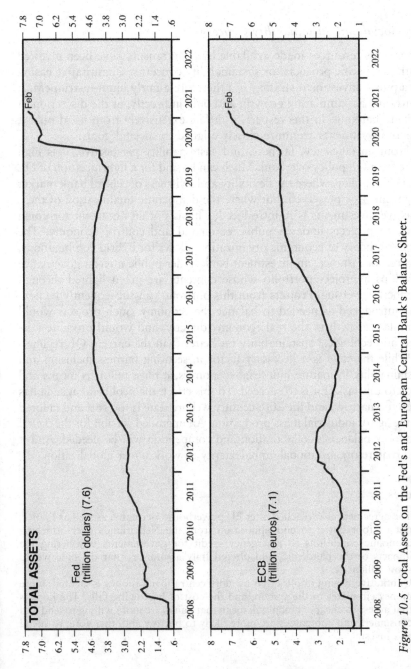

Figure 10.5 Total Assets on the Fed's and European Central Bank's Balance Sheet.

Source: Yardeni Research (2020) Central Banks: Monthly Balance Sheets. https://www.yardeni.com/.

Much of the extra money 'printed' by the central bank has gone to swell the cash reserves of private banks and businesses, while when it comes to how these investments relate to ecological sustainability and social inclusion the general public remains sidelined.

Pro-Social and Sustainability Concerns

Enormous resources made available by governments have been invested without specific prosocial or sustainability concerns. Quantitative easing as a public investment strategy is a therefore a fairly blunt instrument. It aims only at stimulating growth, and only indirectly, at the discretion of private banking. In this respect, it differs extensively from fiscal policy, where investments are more closely aligned to societal goals.

From an efficiency, fairness, and sustainability perspective, it is high time for a QE policy overhaul. Much can be said for a hybridization of QE and fiscal policy, where the flexibility and swiftness of central bank market engagement is preserved, but where the democratic qualification of these massive investments is re-introduced. This is not an argument for going back to projects under a public command and control economy. The modern theory of economic organization allows for hybrid combinations, where, for instance, an investment bank under public interest governance develops a project portfolio whose contents are green lighted through democratic vetting. Projects from this portfolio can subsequently be flexibly introduced as needed to balance the economy. Such projects would stimulate growth in the real economy directly, and would promote fairness and ecological sustainability far better than the current QE regime.

While the state is a necessary factor in securing fairness inclusion and sustainability in mature industrial economies, it must tailor its means and ends to this task if it is to succeed. To this effect, the neoliberal agenda has been too narrow, and the 20th-century welfare state is too stiff and tailored to the age of industrial mass production. An upgraded version for the digital economy balancing collaboration and competition will be needed. And it will require organizational ambidexterity to work under globalization.

Notes

1 The agreement was reached after EU powerhouse Germany, as well as France, put its foot down to end opposition from the Netherlands over attaching economic conditions to emergency credit for governments weathering the impacts of the pandemic, and offered Italy assurances that the bloc would show solidarity.
2 Qantitative Easing implies that as more central bank money is created, more money circulates in the system, and the cost of borrowing falls. The hope is that access to cheaper credit will mean that banks are more willing to lend and consumers and companies are more likely to borrow and, therefore, to spend and invest.

References

Alpert, D., Ferry, J. and Hockett, R.C. (2019) The U.S. Private Sector Job Quality Index. Cornell Law School. https://www.jobqualityindex.com/ Accessed October 2020.

Bank for International Settlements (2018) Structural changes in banking after the crisis. CGFS Papers No 60. Basel: BIS.

Chinn, D., Klier, J., Stern, S. and Tesfu, S. (2020) 'Safeguarding Europe's livelihoods: Mitigating the employment impact of COVID-19' Mc Kinsey Article 19 April https://www.mckinsey.com/industries/public-and-social-sector/our-insights/safeguarding-europes-livelihoods-mitigating-the-employment-impact-of-covid-19

CW Politics (2008) https://edition.cnn.com/2008/POLITICS/02/13/bush.stimulus/ Accessed October 2020.

European Central Bank. (2015) The fiscal impact of financial sector support during the crisis. ECB Economic Bulletin, Issue 6, 2015. https://www.ecb.europa.eu/pub/pdf/other/eb201506_article02.en.pdf Accessed October 2020.

European Central Bank. (2020) Asset Purchase Programmes. European Central Bank, Eurosystem.

Evans, P, Rueschemeyer, D. and Skocpol, T. (2008 [1985]) *Bringing the State Back In*. Cambridge: Cambridge University Press.

Fratianni, M. and Marchionne, F. (2009) Rescuing Banks from the Effects of the Financial Crisis. SSRN Working Paper. SSRN 1476786.

Fratianni, M. and Marchionne, M. (2010) Banks' Great Bailout of 2008-2009. *Banks and Bank Systems* 5(2).

Huynh, S. and De Boissezon, C. (2020) 'US Equity Strategy' *Societe Generale*. Paris: Cross Asset Research.

Mazzucato, M (2013) *The Entrepreneurial State – Debunking Public vs Private Sector Myths*. New York: Anthem Press.

Milgrom, P. and Roberts, J. (1992)*Economics, Organization and Management*, 1st Edition. New Jersey: Prentice Hall.

NationMaster (nd) https://www.nationmaster.com/country-info/stats/Labor/Salaries-and-benefits/Hourly-minimum-wage Accessed December2020.

NationMaster tracks thousands of statistics as and when they are released. The database is composed of data from trustworthy sources such as national statistic agencies, governments, international organizations... (UNDP, UNESCO Institute for Statistics, UNCTAD, WTO, World Bank, World Health Organization, OECD and many others).

OECD (2015) *Income Distribution and Poverty: By Country*. Paris: OECD https://web.archive.org/web/20150402093506/http://stats.oecd.org/index.-aspx?queryid=46189

Ollivaud, P. and Turner, D. (2014) The Effect of the Global Financial Crisis on OECD Potential Output. *OECD Journal: Economic Studies* 2014. OECD. https://www.oecd.org/economy/growth/the-effect-of-the-global-financial-crisis-on-oecd-potential-output-oecd-journal-economic-studies-2014.pdf

Our World in Data (nd) https://ourworldindata.org/government-spending Accessed October 2020.

Reich, R. (2015) *Saving Capitalism: For the Many, Not the Few*. New York: Knopf Doubleday Publishing Group.

Richter, F. (2020) Coronavirus Outbreak Puts 37 Million U.S. Jobs at Risk. 23 March. https://www.statista.com/chart/21204/american-jobs-at-risk-due-to-coronavirus-outbreak/ Accessed October 2020.

Strupczewski, J., and Baczynska, G. (2020). EU ministers agree half a trillion euro coronavirus rescue plan. Reuters. https://www.reuters.com/article/us-health-coronavirus-eu-economy-idUSKCN21R0S4 Accessed October 2020.

Troubled Asset Relief Program (TARP) (nd) https://www.history.com/topics/21st-century/troubled-asset-relief-program Accessed October 2020.

Vernon, R. (1966) International Investment and International Trade in the Product Cycle. *Quarterly Journal of Economics* 80(2).

Watts, W. (2020) How much of the stock market's rise over the last 11 Years is due to QE? https://www.marketwatch.com/story/without-qe-the-s-p-500-would-be-trading-closer-to-1–800-than-3–300-says-societe-generale-11604688442 Accessed November 2020.

World bank (nd) https://www.oecd.org/social/income-distribution-database.htm Accessed May 2021.

World bank (nd) https://datacatalog.worldbank.org/dataset/all-ginis-dataset Accessed May 2021.

World Economic Forum (nd) https://www.weforum.org/agenda/2020/04/united-states-unemployment-claimants-coronavirus-covid19 Accessed October 2020.

World Economic Forum (nd) https://www.weforum.org/agenda/2020/03/u-s-senate-passes-2-trillion-bill-for-strange-and-evil-coronavirus-crisis Accessed October 2020.

World Inequality Database. (nd). Top 10% national income share. Wid.World. https://wid.world/world/#sptinc_p90p100_z/US;FR;DE;CN;ZA;GB;WO/last/eu/k/p/yearly/s/false/23.626/80/curve/false/country Accessed October 2020.

Yardeni Research (2020) *Central Banks: Monthly Balance Sheets*. https://www.yardeni.com/

11 Governing Transitions

As pointed out in the introduction, some major challenges to modern economies appear only solvable through major transitions. These are transitions of such scale and scope that they demand broad ambidextrous mobilization of both the public and private economies, as well as extensive civic engagement. The 'green transition' discussed in Chapter 5 is obviously a societal shift in this category. I also argue that the development of capitalist economies into fair and inclusive societies demands transitional change.

Governance of transitional change in democratic societies will necessarily involve broad mobilization of both the public and private economy, but also civil society. As multiple societal actors and arenas become involved, each of them operating with some degree of autonomy, we are often talking about polycentric government processes. As argued by transition management scholars, this distributed power enables the process of mutual adaptation and the evolving of self-organized socio-technical "trajectories towards emergent collective goals" (Kemp et al. 2007).

Transition necessarily takes time, and new actors and arenas become engaged as it evolves. As we have previously argued in *Perspectives on Ecomodernity* (Midttun and Witoszek 2015) the dynamics of transition can be likened to product innovation, where emergent technologies are gradually commercialized and matured into new mainstream products, through the stages of a *product cycle*. However, while technological and economic factors characterizing the *product cycle* may be central, a holistic governance analysis must add two other 'cycles': the *visionary cycle* – where a new societal vision develops and matures – and the *institutional cycle* which codifies and formalizes supportive organizational development. Transition-governance may thus be fruitfully analyzed as a parallel evolution of novel visions, new technologies, and business models, as well as emerging institutional approaches, where the interplay between the three cycles is also essential (Figure 11.1).

By highlighting the broad polycentric mobilization that takes place under major transitions, the triple cycle model widens the governance analysis to include the wide-ranging set of factors that make possible an

DOI: 10.4324/9781315454931-11

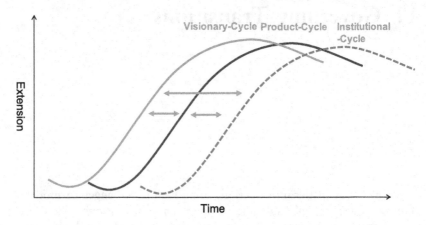

Figure 11.1 The Visionary, Product and Institutional Cycles.

Source: *Energy and Transport in Green Transition: Perspectives on Ecomodernity*, 1 Ed. by Atle Midttun and Nina Witoszek, Copyright © 2016 by Routledge. Reproduced by permission of Taylor & Francis Group.

extensive transitional re-embedding of the economy. While interplay between private and public interests remain central, and the state remains an important institutional governance anchor, major transitions imply that basic perceptions, technologies, and state institutions may undergo change.

Governing Green Transition

The industrial transition from fossil-driven industry to eco-modernity to mitigate the climate crisis is a daunting task that demands ambidextrous mobilization of both the public and private economies. Industrial transition of this scale and scope also necessarily entails societal transformation, which again involves public policy and the public economy. The scale and scope of this transition transcends the capacity of any single governance model and clearly demands a broader polycentric approach, where civil society, government, and industry engage in redefining visions, reshaping institutions, and developing novel technologies and business models.

The novel vision of green transition evolved in several stages – from early focus on environmental values and critique of industrial society for exceeding limits to growth, to green growth and eco-modernity. Diverse movements as the Sierra Club, Deep Ecology, or the anti-nuclear mobilization were early movers behind ecological visions that later crystallized into strong demands for policies against climate change.

As in the case of disruptive product innovation, cultural innovation towards ecomodernity began from inspiring but unrealistic ideas. The pioneering 'prototypes' have ranged from "small is beautiful", deep and shallow ecology, sustainability and ecological villages and cities, to massive public mobilizations for the Earth manifest in the success of the social mobilization platforms such as 350.org, Avaaz, and climate change campaigns by the Friends of the Earth.

The growth of Green parties brought demands for stronger climate policy into mainstream politics. Their success in the 2019 EU elections signals that the Green parties are reaping the benefits of widespread climate activism and global social-media phenomena such as the student protest movement popularised by Greta Thunberg.

These visions were initially dismissed as mere chimeras by mainstream industrial actors. But as they matured into a broader agenda of Ecomodernity – running parallel to incremental green innovation in the power industry – they became part of what I have termed in a different context a "battle for modernities" (Midttun and Witoszek 2015). "Carbon modernity", as the traditional mainstream, had the advantage of incumbency and could for many years present itself as the only credible guarantor of safe energy supply, efficient transport, and economic success. This was in spite of its failure to reinvent itself as "nuclear modernity" due to protests against the risks involved.

On the other side, ecomodernity combined a critique against carbon- and nuclear modernity's side effects with a vision of sustainable development. This was a vision which proclaimed new agendas such as "natural capitalism" (Hawken et al. 1998), and the "Factor Five" economy (Von Weizsäcker et al. 2009). And it was based on technologies compatible with ecological balances, including saving humanity from global warming, and combining this reconstructed world with well-being and quality of life, also known as "green modernity".

A critical step in the development towards winning the battle for ecomodernity has been the redefinition of climate strategy away from austerity and in favour of green growth. This entailed exchanging restrictions for opportunities and was a major incentive in bringing industry on board.

The proponents of carbon modernity have traditionally held hegemony in the field by combining energy, growth, and employment. The cognitive formula that buttressed their position has involved a trajectory where a carbon-based energy supply delivers cheap power, which in turn produces industrial competitiveness and growth, and hence generates employment (Figure 11.2). Adopting a green growth perspective, proponents of ecomodernity could call on a competing economic vision. In this view, ecomodernity, due to its combination of rapid technological learning, declining costs, and ecological sustainability, will stimulate growth in a green direction and thereby create jobs.

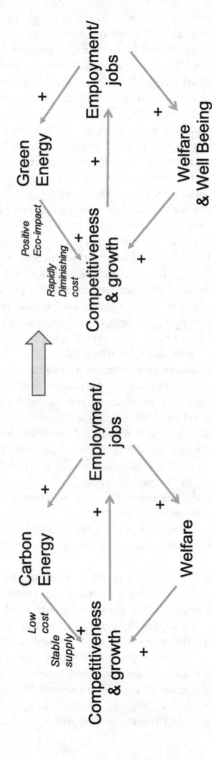

Figure 11.2 The Shift from Carbon- to Eco-Modernity.

Source: Energy and Transport in Green Transition: Perspectives on Ecomodernity, 1 Ed. by Atle Midttun and Nina Witoszek, Copyright © 2016 by Routledge. Reproduced by permission of Taylor & Francis Group.

Stimulated by the visionary development towards ecomodernity, a **techno-economic transition** has been emerging, with new technologies and business models, particularly in the field of green energy. Starting their journey with serious cost and quality handicaps, and in need of public and niche market stimuli, many of them have managed through industrial learning to reach competitive parity with incumbent fossil technologies.

Learning-curve theory provides an effective framework for technological transition under major societal change – such as the transition to eco-modernity – and demonstrates clearly the need for economic shift across the public-private divide. The core of this theory is that technology evolves through technological, organizational, and commercial learning as it is deployed in practical use over time. Typically, the learning curve experience is that technology performance improves by 10–20% every time volumes double (Wene 2008).

Both wind power and photovoltaics have followed learning curve trajectories and have grown into major green energy alternatives thanks to public deployment and technological learning. They are now taking over substantive market shares from the mainstream carbon-based energy supply. To take Photovoltaics as an example, in a previous study (Midttun and Toporowska 2014) we have followed PVs from the technology's early stages in the US space industry, through later phases in Japan and Germany, and finally mass production in China, from where PV is now spreading on a purely commercial basis. This global innovation journey has taken PVs down the learning curve from over USD 500/watt in the 1960s to less than 1 EUR /watt in 2020, with the prospect of further price drops. Each lead market has taken its share of development costs, but gradually experienced limitations which halted further development. Termination or slowdown has occurred because of the limited scope of niche markets, waning political support, and institutional weaknesses. At the same time, however, new lead markets have emerged as a result of technological learning and a journey of innovations.

The technological breakthrough in the green energy sector would not have been possible without a parallel mobilization of eco-friendly policy and institutions. This involved the engagement of national innovation systems, the establishment of favourable support schemes and regulatory arrangements, as well as massive public deployment, supplemented with the construction of green niche markets. These were all set up to drive industrial learning towards commercial equality with fossil technologies.

The institutional backing of green technologies has been part of an international rivalry for technological leadership. This has provided an industrial policy incentive in addition to the ecological motivation. Pioneering countries have therefore introduced strong state policies to ready lead markets for technology development and gradually raised the quality and decreased the costs of 'green' technologies such as wind and solar power. But technology and institutions typically go together. Lead markets will therefore generally foster both advanced technological and commercial conditions as well as innovate supportive policies and advanced regulation.

In a previous work (Midttun and Gautesen 2007) we have pointed out how various policy tools and institutional arrangements can be used to further technologies at various stages of technical maturity. These tools include novel green market construction – the most prominent being the European Emission Trading System which was developed to stimulate further CO_2 reduction. In earlier work we have shown how these developments in turn stimulated new business models, which brought CO_2 reduction into the centre of business strategy (Midttun and Piccini 2017).

Ambidextrous interplay between state-led public and private investor-led commercial economies in several countries gradually produced a seminal technology for transition to eco-modernity at competitive cost.

In line with lead market theory (Jänicke and Jacob 2004), PV's 'relay journey' is a story that illustrates environmental energy technology's intimate dependence on public economies. Public incubation can foster technological competence, financial investment, entrepreneurial engagement, and policy support, to move the technology forward to commercial success. But this is also a story of how the private interest economy needs to be triggered to generate the mass-market volumes to change the world.

To sum up, the current shift towards eco-modernity has been dependent on an intimate interplay between civic and political visions, techno-economic development, and policies and institutional facilitation, and not least a dynamic reciprocation between these factors over time. An essential characteristic of this process has been the polycentric interaction between actors and arenas, where processes in one domain, such as the evolution of green growth idea, trigger supportive policies and deployment strategies. This, in turn, has stimulated commercial investment and technology development in many parts of the world.

Green Transition at the City Level

Green transition does not only involve interplay across multiple arenas, it also takes place on many levels, not the least through an extended role for cities. As an increasing share of the population leaves the countryside, urban planning – including such sectors as energy supply, transport, and housing – reflects the expanding importance of cities. As has been argued, for example by Benjamin Barber (Barber 2014), many cities have initiated innovative major climate policy initiatives, sometimes way ahead of national policies.

Urban collaboration across national boundaries is often easier than collaboration between nation-states. For instance, the mobilization of the massive public procurement behind the green policy turn of large cities in global procurement-collaboration has extensive industrial implications, and creates room for new green product development. Forging governance for green transition at the city level is therefore often as important as engagement at the national level, and may be equally important for industrial development. When cities form consortia to deploy new technologies in order to facilitate their green transition, they become attractive partners for leading industrial players.

Furthermore, in pursuing green transition, cities may differ considerably from their national authorities, and may press on with green transition in spite of conflicting national policy and signals. A striking example is the contrast between Oslo's urban greening and Norway's national petro-economy. Or between President Trump's withdrawal of the United States from the Paris Agreement, and New York City's commitment to climate obligations.

Governing Transition to Fairness and an Inclusive Digital Economy

Like eco-modernity, the quest for fairness and inclusion is a major challenge of our time, symptomatically displayed by the massive populist mobilization behind fascistoid leadership under Donald Trump in the world's largest capitalist economy.

The formula for fairness and inclusion under 20th-century industrial mass production in advanced Western economies used to be massive upscaling of the public economy and building welfare states on top of productive capitalist economies. Chapter 2 illustrated the basic features of this model in the Nordic countries.

However, as shown in subsequent chapters, neoliberal globalization has challenged the welfare state model on several fronts. Firstly, by delegitimating the active state. Secondly by dismantling trade barriers in an increasingly open economy, thereby weakening national policy-making. This in turn has created acute collective action problems when it comes to upholding social standards.

Consequently, the 21st century has opened on a downward path of social inequality for western industrial nations, countries that for much of the 20th century were evolving into fairer middle-class societies. Measured by wealth distribution, this development is most pronounced in the core neoliberal economy – the United States – where the 1% richest in 2019 controlled 18.7% of income, up from 10,3 in 1980 (Figure 11.3).

In other words, the dominant capitalist economy is moving towards a new 'class society' where elites take disproportionate shares of the cake. And other western economies are following in the same direction. As Milanovic has observed, one of the consequences of the rise in inequality

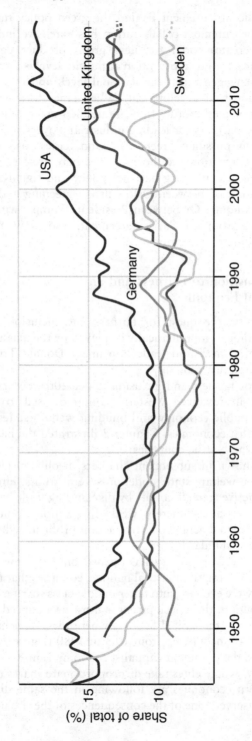

Figure 11.3 Top 1% National Income.

Source: World Inequality Database (nd) https://wid.world/world/#sptinc_p99p100_z/US;FR;DE;GB;SE/last/eu/k/p/yearly/s/false/4.2129999999999999/45/curve/false/country.

in the rich countries has been the hollowing out of the middle class and the rising political importance of the rich (Milanovic 2016).

Even in terms of economic growth, the picture is mixed. While the neoliberal turn in the late 20th century may be said to have delivered a boost of stock prices in the 1980s and 1990s and, intermittently, in the first decades of the 21st century, it has not outshone the economic growth-rates of the social democratically managed 1950s, '60s and '70s. Rather, as shown in Chapter 6, it has consolidated growth rates on a downward path in leading OECD economies.

In one sense, reimagining fairness for the 21st century should not be difficult. As with the breakthrough for mass production in the 20th century, the digital revolution in the 21st entails great productivity increases, and hence abundant wealth to be shared.

Yet other aspects of digitalization pull the opposite way: Firstly, the logic of the digital network- or platform economies (the Googles, Facebooks, and the like) is such that they tend towards oligopoly, or winner takes all solutions. The classical doctrine of free trade benefits from simple competitive market exposure is less and less relevant, and competition authorities are struggling to cope with the ramifications. As a consequence, the network and platform economies, by their basic logic, generate huge wealth but distribute it unfairly.

Secondly, in addition to the oligopoly effect, there is the potential challenge of artificial intelligence and robotization to employment. As shown in Chapter 3, influential technologists and economists like Brynjolfsson and McAfee (2014), echoing Hans Moravec (1995) and Paul Krugman (2013), contend that if left to liberally governed market dynamics, AI and robotization could potentially replace human labour and precipitate widespread unemployment. Recapitulating Moravec's three-stage predictions from Chapter 3:

A first generation of universal robots, around 2010, will have enough general competence to do relatively intricate mechanical tasks.

By adding more memory and computing power and enhancing the software, he foresaw that by 2020 we would have a second generation that can learn from its own performance. This means that it can learn and adapt.

By 2030 robots will become more competent, efficiency and productivity will keep going up, and the amount of work for humans will keep going down.

By around 2040, Moravec argues, "there will be no job that people can do better than robots". AI/robots will be preferred to humans and replace workers over time.

The novel platform-based digital business models are already creating low-paid and insecure jobs in the gig economy. Without a major re-orientation of economic governance, this would drive large parts of the population into unemployment and relegate provision for human livelihood to other sources and domains, such as citizens' wages or basic income. In other words, governance initiatives to re-embed the economy according to wholly new principles are needed.

Towards an Agora Economy?

The critique of distributive unfairness and poor work conditions under the gig economy warrants the need for a new paradigm, much like under the early stages of the green transition. The new visions of corrective action include increasing transfers – basically building on elements of the welfare state – such as the 'flexicurity' model described in Chapter 2, entitling workers to benefits whilst re-training for new participation in the regular labour market. Stronger collective action by trade unions to enhance the labour share of value creation is also part of the recipe for enhancing fairness in society.

More radical solutions talk of citizens' wages, where citizenship presupposes an entitlement to permanent income (Van Parijs and Vanderborght 2017). If robotization and AI can massively substitute for work, then provision for livelihood will have to come from other sources, such as entitlements from citizens' shares in the AI economy. In other words, one can imagine the emergence of an increasingly robotized economy, with humans engaging more and more in civic, social, and cultural activities, as the upper classes have done for millennia.

Indeed, the much-praised classical Athenian polis or city-state might serve as a model. In antiquity this polis was largely based on slave- and female labour, with male citizens participating in cultural and civic life in the central forum: the Agora. In a modern version, a more extensive deployment of robot-labour would allow both men and women and to join the free citizenry in a novel Agora.

The vision of an 'Agora economy', with trivialities undertaken by robotized 'slavery', breaks with the idea of work as the dominant source of livelihood, and liberates mankind to explore a new state of freedom. However, the scale and scope of such transition dictates a cautious, gradual implementation, calibrated to the evolution of AI and robotization in society. Borrowing a well-tested mechanism from academic institutions, citizens' wages could be introduced through *sabbaticals*. Rights to civic engagement and knowledge acquisition during leave-periods could be given for a period of up to a year, every so often. Such rights could be widened in line with productivity increases, and distributed fairly across the population in order to gain broad political support.

It is frequently held against such arrangements that people need work, and should not remain idle. However, the elites, the gentry, landed aristocracy, and heirs with fortunes have done so for ages, so it is more a question of acculturation than anything else. With a proper educational system for arts, crafts, civic engagement, philosophy, poetry, motorcycle repair, sailing, and the like – alongside incentives to stimulate engagement in innovation and entrepreneurship – there should not be any problem of finding meaningful life projects and innovative and rich pastimes.

Moving towards a modern version of the classical Athenian Agora society does not have to imply a sweeping revolution, but might take place through incremental add-ons to existing welfare state arrangements. As a point of departure, such states already undertake massive public service-transfers to their populations throughout their lifetime. In return, the public cedes huge contributions back to government. In other words, we live in an ambidextrous mix of private and public economies over our lifetimes.

Taking a modern welfare state as an example, for the first 20 + years, every citizen is a net beneficiary of public support. The latter includes such elements as child allowances, free health care, free teaching through the primary, secondary, and university levels. The citizens then turn into net contributors and transfer money to public authorities until they are in their mid-60s. From this point and on, they can again become net receivers of public transfers, including pensions and health and social care. The public transfers over the average person's lifecycle from 0 to 80+ years are illustrated as in Figure 11.4 (solid line).

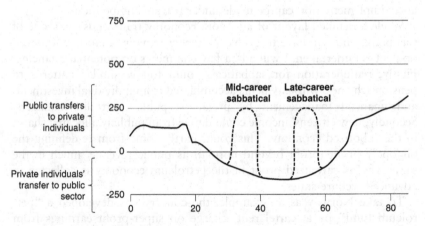

Figure 11.4 Public Transfers through an Individual's Life with and without Sabbaticals.

Numeric values 2010. In NOK.

Source: Author, building on Norwegian Government White Paper (2017) "On Socio-Economic Scenarios".

In addition to the transfers in youth and old age, the welfare state model – as outlined in Chapter 2 – already contains a 'flexicurity' mechanism that provides social security and re-training for the unemployed. With strong AI-based productivity growth there would be room for expanding this to include a right to a sabbatical to upgrade old, and acquire new, knowledge. This could be modelled on current university practice, and inserted into the transfer balance model as shown in Figure 11.4, (stapled lines).

Sabbaticals should, as in academia, be knowledge and productivity-enhancing, and include a personal plan for development in the sabbatical period. However, in line with the 'Athenian Agora' vision, part of the sabbatical could also be devoted to civic training and engagement, and would provide people with meaningful roles when they were unemployed, redirecting them to sectors with the need for staff, thus strengthening civic training.

The ideal scenario would be to gradually see a migration towards a broader appropriation of robotic productivity as advanced industrial societies evolve towards hyper-productive welfare societies with more and more time for civic and creative lives. Such a scenario is infinitely preferable to 'gigification' under the oligopolistic propensity of digitalization.

There are elements in this model that point to the concept of the citizens' wage (Van Parijs and Vanderborght 2017). However, my proposal is more limited and gradualistic, thereby avoiding many of the dilemmas inherent in the citizens' wage idea. Nor is the Agora economy a formula for socialization. While novel institutional arrangements for transfers and ownership will need to be made under democratically mandated governance, implementation can be made under private competition.

While a detailed layout of an Agora economy transcends the scope of this book, and will have to evolve as further experimentation and development is undertaken, I will add a few comments on potential financing. Firstly, remuneration for sabbaticals could follow similar patterns to pension schemes, with payments accumulated from individual investment, and financial management by private/or public portfolio managers. Secondly, new citizens' income could derive from publicly allocated shares in the robotized economy. This could partly come from re-defining the oligopoly profit (profit beyond normal) as public revenue, much in the same way as cartelized profit in the petroleum economy is collected in advanced welfare states.

To take Norway as an example, the country has developed a "petroleum fund" by a 'cartel rent' charge on super-profit earnings from offshore petroleum exploration of the Norwegian continental shelf. In March 2020, the fund had a market value of more than 11 trillion Norwegian Kroner, or more than 1.2 trillion USD, and is one of the largest fund in the world. The oligopoly rent from network and platform economies like Google, Microsoft, and Facebook could likely amount to massive public revenue, while normal profit, as in North Sea petroleum extraction, could be left to the companies. Furthermore, as Nobel Prize Winner Joseph Stiglitz has argued, reduction of super-profits could also enhance efficiency: "Policymakers should zero in on any market in which there are excessive rents because they are a sign that the economy could perform more efficiently" (Stiglitz 2019).

While a transition from a fossil to a low carbon economy is well on its way, a shift towards an Agora economy still has a long way to travel. The moral imperative to work to earn one's living has been deeply ingrained in Western culture ever since Adam and Eve's expulsion from paradise. Exemptions are made only in the case of persons who for legitimate reasons cannot work, as well as for wealthy 'privilegencia' (gentlemen and ladies of leisure). Major cognitive and institutional transformations may therefore have to be made before mankind can thoroughly enjoy the fruits of AI and robotization. Re-distribution of wealth from the super-productivity of robotization is not only central to secure fairness, but also to stimulate demand. The lack of jobs, lost to AI, will give rise to a lack of demand and economic stagnation.

References

Barber, B.R. (2014) *If Mayors Ruled the World. Dysfunctional Nations, Rising Cities.* New Haven: Yale University Press.

Brynjolfsson, E. and McAfee, A. (2014) *The Second Machine Age: Work, Progress and Prosperity in a Time of Brilliant Technologies.* New York: W.W. Norton.

Hawken, P., Lovins, A. and Lovins, H. (1998; 2008) *Natural Capitalism: Creating the Next Industrial Revolution.* New York: Back Bay Books.

Jänicke, M. and Jacob, K. (2004) Lead Markets for Environmental Innovations: A New Role for the Nation State. *Global Environmental Politics* 4(1). Feb 2004.

Kemp, R., Loorbach, D. and Rotmans, J. (2007) Transition Management as a Model for Managing Processes of Co-evolution towards Sustainable Development. *The International Journal of Sustainable Development and World Ecology* 14(1).

Krugman, P. (2013) Sympathy for the Luddites. *New York Times*, 14 June. https://www.nytimes.com/2013/06/14/opinion/krugman-sympathy-for-the-luddites.html Accessed November 2020.

Midttun, A. and Gautesen, K. (2007) Feed in or Certificates, Competition or Complementarity? Combining a Static Efficiency and a Dynamic Innovation Perspective on the Greening of the Energy Industry. *Energy Policy* 35(3).

Midttun, A. and Piccini, P.B. (2017) Facing the Climate and Digital Challenge: European Energy Industry from Boom to Crisis and Transformation. *Energy Policy* 108.

Midttun, A. and Toporowska, E. (2014) Sequencing Lead Markets for Photovoltaics. In Achim Brunnengräber and Maria Rosaria Di Nucci (eds), *Hürdenlauf zur Energiewende.* Wiesbaden: Springer Verlag.

Midttun, A. and Witoszek, N. (2015) *Energy and Transport in Green Transition: Perspectives on Ecomodernity*. London: Routledge.

Milanovic, B. (2016) *Global Inequality*. Cambridge, Massachusetts: Harvard University Press.

Moravec, H. (1995) 'Superhumanism' Interview in *Wired* https://www.wired.com/1 995/10/moravec/ Accessed November 2020.

Norwegian Government White Paper on Socio-Economic Scenarios (Perspektivmeldingen) (2017) https://www.regjeringen.no/no/tema/okonomi-og-budsjett/ norsk_okonomi/perspektivmeldingen-2017/id2484715/

Stiglitz, J.E. (2019) *People, Power, and Profits: Progressive Capitalism for an Age of Discontent*. W. W. New York: Norton & Company.

Van Parijs, P. and Vanderborght, Y. (2017) *Basic Income. A Radical Proposal for a Free Society and a Sane Economy*. Cambridge Massachusetts: Harvard University Press.

Von Weizsäcker, E.U., Hargroves, C., Smith, M., Desha, S. and Statinopolous, P. (2009) *Factor Five*. London: Earthscan.

Wene, C.O. (2008) Energy Technology Learning Through Deployment in Competitive Markets. *Engineering Economist* 53(4).

World Inequality Database (2020 nd) https://wid.world/world/#sptinc_p99p1 00_z/US;FR;DE;GB;SE/last/eu/k/p/yearly/s/false/4.212999999999999/45/ curve/false/country

12 Polycentric Governance in a Bipolar World

Polycentric Governance as a Remedy for Asymmetric Globalization?

As argued in previous chapters, neoliberal globalization has been asymmetric in terms of market and governance outreach. It unleashed global market dynamics, not least through outsourced multinationalization, massively supported by digitalization. Global governance, on the other hand, was lagging far behind. This has left the global space fundamentally undergoverned, although a regional federation like the EU represents an intermediary position, with considerable economic and political collaboration among member states, but also with extensive integration challenges.

The answer to this governance deficit has been to supplement the state with auxiliary governance tools and approaches, such as CSR, civic governance, and other 'softer' forms of regulation. They may be less constrained by territorial boundaries and can therefore allow governance outreach into the wider global arena. This alter-governance 'toolkit' includes novel business models that may incorporate social and environmental considerations.

In some cases business leaders have embraced prosociality or sustainability at the core of their strategy. Tesla, with its marketing of the electric car, is a well-known example. Furthermore, there is a spectrum of alternatively chartered businesses with different potential for prosociality/sustainability. The Spanish cooperative, Mondragon, and the French public benefit dairy company, Danone, are good examples.

That said, we cannot ignore the governance potential of civil society, where social values, implicit social contracts, and the moral bargaining rights of civil society organizations (CSOs) – in confrontation with commercial and political actors – are crucial agents in the process of re-embedding capitalism. There are also many examples of social mobilization combined with CSOs exerting pressure on industry to adopt wider social and environmental practices that discipline whole sectors. These developments have yielded a flourishing array of novel governance initiatives intertwining with parliamentary democracy and court rulings in a mix of soft and hard power.

DOI: 10.4324/9781315454931-12

Figuratively speaking, this new governance mosaic can be seen as a large, polycentric patchwork of partly complementary, partly competitive elements (Figure 12.1).

At a global level, a new normative context has emerged across national, regional, and global realms, some of it in the form of new norms and principles – witness the Sustainable Development Goals – with little implementation power behind them, but with a normative power articulated through civic mobilization, communication, and monitory democracy. When allied with classical regulatory supervision, the promoters of these norms have increased their implementation capacity. In addition, there are initiatives backed by active CSO monitoring, or by investor groups and other consortia with influential leverage on business outcomes, sometimes through court action. Last, but not least, consumers also play a role through implicit sustainability impulses in their product choices and businesses see this as an opportunity to pioneer frontrunner sustainability strategies.

Our examples have shown how initiatives in one arena may spill over into others, and global measures may trickle down to national and local follow-ups, or vice versa. This is one reason why the UN's normative agendas, such as the Sustainable Development Goals, can be translated into a set of actions. When the Task Force on Climate-Related Financial

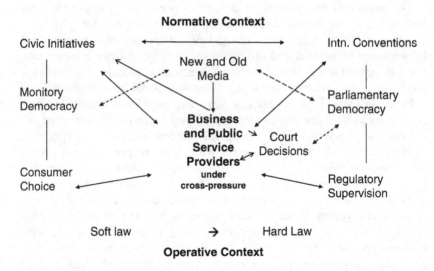

Figure 12.1 Novel Governance Horizons.

Source: Author.

Disclosure (TCFD) converts sustainability norms into financial disclosures they make them relevant for market actors and investors, lenders, and insurance underwriters can subsequently incorporate sustainability into commercial practice. Similarly, civic initiatives like Transparency International which reveal secret money flows from extractive industries into the pockets of rulers, trigger both commercial and political reactions. Civic initiatives have also triggered legal action, such as the climate cases against Shell in the Dutch court, and against the German state in the constitutional court. These initiatives point to yet another channel of transforming soft power into hard governance.

While pluralist governance evolves 'naturally' in a context of polycentric decision-making, I have also argued that it can also be put systematically into operation through "partnered governance". In cases such as the Extractive Industries' Transparency Initiative, coalitions between the state, civil society, and industry have been formed to combat commercial and political malpractice.

Promoting corporate social responsibility and civic social and ecological idealism through partnered governance may be particularly attractive for advanced welfare states with higher humanitarian and sustainability aspirations than bare political and economic power. Through CSR and monitory democratic paths, partnered governance may allow advanced states and pioneering companies to work together to raise the social and environmental bar. While CSOs thereby satisfy their moral communities, the state is able to raise domestic approval as well as international influence. Businesses operating under advanced domestic social and environmental regulation in their home countries may see the partnership as a basis for setting international standards to enhance their competitive advantage and compel rivals to raise their social and ecological ambitions and standards.

The serious and multiple challenges facing western liberal capitalism and democracy in the 21st century, as I see it, confirm the necessity of mobilizing broadly across a broad range of governance models. 'Redemption', for economic as well as politically liberal societies, involves strengthening checks and balances in a pluralist polycentric world. One way of conceiving such broad governance for sustainable and inclusive capitalist societies might be to reframe governance as an act of balancing the power of the state, business, and civil society. What I argue for is re-imagining Montesquieu's 18th-century argument for balancing the three state powers: the legislative, the executive, and the judiciary. In the current context – a Montesquieu "version 2.1" is needed – one which addresses the needs of the 21st century. It would involve a transfer of his insights in state theory to a broader theory of societal governance that encompasses the state, markets, and civil society in a rivalled interplay. The rivalry between the state, market, and civil society creates new roles for each. The role of the state in this model combines its formal prerogatives with adaptation to civic society exposure of unsustainable practices that are deemed illegitimate in the eyes of the public. Business may also have to transcend formal legal rules and adjust to public sentiment and political realities, as well as being prepared to legitimize commercial practice in broad public debate. Civil society, in turn, must demonstrate credible moral authority. As CSOs rely on indirect bargaining power derived from their standing in public debate, they must engage with clear and credible interventions which hold the other actors to account. This balancing would enhance diversity while at the same time institutionalizing checks and balances.

Governance in a Bipolar World

Civilizing capitalism in the 21st century – if indeed it can be civilized – encounters one more pivotal challenge. While governance in the late 20th and first years of the 21st centuries struggled with neoliberal globalization, the subsequent decades have seen the global economy becoming increasingly marked by a new, bipolar rivalry between authoritarian and liberal spheres. This has been most prominently displayed in the much-publicized US-China trade war, but this is not the only case, and many countries have increased their use of restrictive trade measures. This again makes for complex and fragmented trading environments, with more use of unilateral, non-tariff trade restrictions. The fragmentation of neoliberal globalization has come as the West and Western-oriented economies are losing their hegemony to a rising Chinese economic powerhouse alongside Russia.

The Western supremacy in world trade and world politics for over half a century was based on a formula of double liberalism: liberal free trade markets and liberal (free election) politics. This vision was famously expressed by the American political scientist Francis Fukuyama, in his book *The End of History and the Last Man* (1992). He argued that humanity had reached "not just... the passing of a particular period of post-war history, but the end of history as such: That is, the end-point of mankind's ideological evolution and the universalization of Western liberal democracy as the final form of human government" (Fukuyama 1992).

This was the 20th century's optimistic an erroneous prediction. The 21st century has witnessed impressive Chinese industrial modernization, based on authoritarian one-party leadership. China proved that capitalism was not only reconcilable with authoritarian rule, but that the combination of both offered competitive advantage. With this hybrid formula of authoritarian politics and strategic use of market competition, the country found a solution that could compete with the Western model and vie for influence in a bipolar global economy.

In contrast to the Cold War between the West and the Soviet Union, the rivalry with China is not about the economic system. Modern China embraces capitalism, as part of a globalized market economy, while its socialist market economy is a cornerstone of its rapid growth model. The current confrontation of capitalist models is therefore a confrontation of interests which go beyond politics and touch upon norms, values, and the principles of both democratic and authoritarian rule. For the West, respect for human rights, including protecting civil liberties, individual rights, and democratic institutions have been at the forefront of their value-hierarchy, alongside competitive markets. Authoritarian powers, on the other hand, led by China and Russia, emphasize values such as law and order, patriotic nationalism, and obedience to the ruler, and push back on norms they view as Western-centric, such as liberal democracy, a free press, and interference in internal affairs under the pretext of defending human rights.

Governance Challenges

All in all, post-liberal competitive globalization offers a whole set of challenges to economic governance and business strategy across the various elements outlined in Figure 12.1. In the formal governance channel, parliamentary or electoral democracy vies with authoritarian rule. In the informal civic channel, monitory democracy vies with government-led civic mobilization. At the global level, they both vie for influence over the normative agenda of international institutions and the global public debate. Figure 12.2 displays the extended bipolar governance agenda.

Businesses that operate globally may thereby come under difficult cross-pressure from contradictory legislation and civic expectations that makes it difficult to operate across the democratic-authoritarian divide.

The Chinese technology giant Huawei, for instance, experienced massive hindrances as it aspired to deliver technology at the heart of Western communication infrastructure, while operating what Westerners see as a

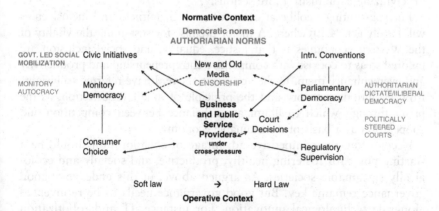

Figure 12.2 Democratic and Authoritarian Governance Horizons.
Source: Author.

repressive Chinese information system. A system which employs massive internet censorship, blocks access to selected foreign websites, and bars foreign internet tools (e.g., Google search Facebook, Twitter, Wikipedia, and others as well as mobile apps).

The Swedish multinational Hennes and Mauritz, likewise got caught in the normative crossfire as Western CSOs like Human Rights Watch and Amnesty pressed the company for action against Chinese cotton suppliers in Xinjiang on account of human rights abuses against the Uighur population. The company's withdrawal from Xinjiang was met by staunch critique by the youth league of the communist party that mobilized critique by patriotic consumers who regard allegations of human rights abuses in Xinjiang as forays in a Western-led smear campaign. The pressure from such reactions increases as China matures into a major consumer economy and abandons its role as a mere producer of industrial goods for sales abroad.

Liberal Society at Stake

With the impressive industrial modernization of China, the Western role as the vanguard of the modern economy will not so much hinge on its technological lead as its ability to integrate technological excellence in democratically free, just, and fair societies. The book has shown how the reign of neoliberalism has neglected these dimensions and argues that only by reversing increasing social discrepancies, tuning the economy to ecological realities, and cultivating and stimulating its freedom of expression and liberal democracy, will the West be able to maintain its soft power and attraction as an alternative to the authoritarian world. And paradoxically, the increasing challenge from authoritarian competitors in the new bipolar world may provoke Western elites into taking the task of 'civilizing capitalism' more seriously.

But substituting neoliberal competition with fairness and inclusiveness will hardly get us anywhere. A major premise for sustaining the vitality of the Western economies is that justice, equality, and social inclusion are tailored so as to coexist with competitive entrepreneurship and productivity and even enhance them. In the argument above, I have referred to insights from evolutionary theory and the principle of multilevel selection, as the prism through which to illuminate a balance between competition and cooperation as a basis of a sustainable economy.

Recognizing the competitive advantage of collaboration should be a starting point for fostering healthy, productive, and socially and ecologically sustainable societies. As argued above, in this endeavour good governance remains key. But good governance needs to be re-invented alongside technological innovation. For instance, IT and robotization need to go together with social and institutional innovation – so as facilitate inclusive solutions, in line with the 'Agora economy' outlined in the previous chapter. There is a world of difference between robotization that puts people into gig-jobs and harvests super–profits for rich oligarchs, and robotization that allows productivity gains to be used for civic and competence building sabbaticals. Ambrogio Lorenzetti's fresco paintings on good and bad governance on the walls of the Siena city council have not lost their relevance for reimagining capitalism in the 21st century.

Index

Locators in **bold** refer to tables and those in *italics* to figures.

Printed in the United States
by Baker & Taylor Publisher Services